Fatal Ascent

HMS Seal, 1940

FATAL ASCENT

ASCENT

HMS *SEAL*, 1940

by

Melanie Wiggins

SPELLMOUNT

To Taff Harper, Happy Eckersall and Ernie Truman

The author acknowledges permission by Robert M Buckham
to quote material from:

Forced March to Freedom: An illustrated diary of two forced marches and the
interval between, January to May, 1945, by Robert M Buckham, published by
Canada's Wings, Inc., 1984.

British Library Cataloguing in Publication Data:
A catalogue record for this book is available
from the British Library

ISBN 1-86227-318-9

First published in the UK in 2006 by
Spellmount Limited
The Mill, Brimscombe Port
Stroud, Gloucestershire
GL5 2QG

Tel: 01453 883300
Fax: 01453 883233
Website: www.spellmount.com

1 3 5 7 9 8 6 4 2

Printed in Great Britain by
Oaklands Book Services
Stonehouse, Gloucestershire GL10 3RQ

Contents

List of Abbreviations

ADM   Admiralty Series, National Archives – previously the Public Record Office (NA)

AIR   Air Ministry, National Archives

FO   Foreign Office, National Archives

HO   Home Office, National Archives

HW   Government Communications Headquarters, National Archives

KV   Security Service, National Archives

NARA   National Archives and Records Administration, Washington, D.C.

NA   The National Archives (previously the Public Record Office)

RG   Record Group

RNSM   Royal Navy Submarine Museum, Gosport

WO   War Office, National Archives

Preface

The *Seal* crew reported for duty at the end of January 1939, met disaster in May 1940, and spent the rest of the war years incarcerated in Germany. Miraculously, all the men made it home to the British Isles except Able Seaman Smith and Petty Officer Barnes. The crew's physical and mental strength, along with a great deal of perseverance and sense of humour saved their lives during five interminable years of loneliness, boredom, hunger, and privation. None of the three that I interviewed expressed regret for having served on submarines; they recounted their memories candidly and without rancour.

In the German POW system men were assigned to different camps according to their service and nationality; thus, many of *Seal's* crew spent the majority of the war years in a navy prison called Marlag-Milag, near Bremen. Navy men from the world over traditionally had regarded each other with respect; and the German officers at Marlag-Milag provided a fairly comfortable existence for their prisoners until near the war's end in 1945. The other *Seal* crewmen did not fare so well, ending up in different Silesian work camps, where army guards sometimes meted out brutal treatment. When the going got rough, the Brits would occasionally get a good laugh by playing tricks on the German guards.

As the war grew more intense in Europe, life became increasingly hard for POWs: food supplies diminished, prison camps grew horrifyingly overcrowded, and life became unbearable. From the moment new prisoners marched into the compounds after being captured, they dreamed of escaping; they spent a great deal of time studying layouts, thinking of ways to outfox guards, possibilities for tunnel digging, places to hide, and thousands of schemes that could lead to freedom. On rare occasions one or more prisoners broke out and succeeded in making it back to their homeland; and as time went by, Hitler responded with harsher treatment for prisoners of war. In this account of the *Seal* crew's war experiences, I have included some of the more daring and meaningful escapes, as well as the events of the war that affected the prisoners.

Swiss Legation and Red Cross reports in the National Archives (formerly the Public Record Office) revealed intimate details of prison camp life, describing conditions in the camps and treatment of prisoners, as well as other details. Comparing these reports with the stories by survivors, I concluded that the neutral camp inspectors either did not see everything or looked at the compounds through rose-coloured glasses – possibly to appease the Germans and prevent them from marching into Switzerland. The German camp officials may have occasionally hidden certain things when inspection times came around, as well.

Air Force documents brought out a true picture of the British planes that were involved with *Seal* in the battle for Norway; they also described bombing problems in Germany; and they revealed experiences of pilots who had parachuted into Hitler's realm. Those RAF pilots who had been captured and who contrived to break out then reported their experiences to Military Intelligence in England, who compiled the cogent facts and sent information back to prisoners of war to use for their own escapes. The RAF pilots had the reputation for being the most skilled getaway artists, and as the war progressed, escape techniques became more and more refined and suggestions somewhat humorous. A document entitled "Lessons Learned from Escapees of British Personnel after Capture during Recent Operations" concluded that as for appearance, the escaper should find civilian clothes as soon as possible; get rid of army boots; wear a beard among peasants; obtain extra socks; and should not wear grey flannel trousers or use a walking stick (it looked too British).

Air reports from 1944 and 1945 tell of one of the tragic aspects of the massive Allied raids on Germany that involved the accidental bombing of prisoner of war camps. Documents say that the British pilots made enormous efforts to unleash their deadly loads away from the camps, but bombing in World War II was not a precise art, and a few POW barracks and factories where prisoners were working did get destroyed or damaged, resulting in needless deaths. With fearsome chaos gripping Germany at the war's end, the POWs were faced with slim chances for survival.

The three *Seal* veterans in England, Herbert ("Taff") Harper, Ernie Truman, and Albert ("Happy") Eckersall, together with written accounts contributed by Mickey Reynolds' son Lawrence, provided the most telling evidence of the *Seal*'s wartime drama. Their candour, humour, and colourful language enlivened the narrative, and I thank them wholeheartedly for their patience and cooperation.

Many others took time to look up materials, answer questions, copy photographs, and to do a myriad of other chores for this book: Peter Petersen; Mrs Rupert Lonsdale; Pauline Bennett; Denise Hull; Margery Palmer; Irene Rice Johnson; Donna Malcolmson, Portsmouth City Museum and Records Office; Cdr John Holt, U.S. Navy, Ret.; Tim Mulligan, National Archives and Records Administration, Washington, D.C.; Debbie Corner, Royal Navy Submarine Museum, Gosport, England; John Augelli,

Rosenberg Library, Galveston, Texas; the staff at the National Archives (formerly Public Record Office), Kew, England; Photography Department, Imperial War Museum, London; Prof Dr Ralph Uhlig, Kiel University; Hauptstaatsarchiv Stuttgart; Frau Lippmann, Museum der Stadt Colditz; Thomas Weis, Bibliothek für Zeitgeschichte, Stuttgart, Germany; Horst Bredow, U-Boot Archiv, Cuxhaven, Germany; and Herr Döringhoff, Bundesarchiv-Militärarchiv, Freiburg, Germany. For making my research trips to England comfortable and extremely pleasant, I salute the friendly staff of the Petersham Hotel in Richmond, England.

Robert Buckham, former Canadian Air Force officer, has my profound gratitude for allowing me to include portions of his colourful wartime diary about the prisoners' forced marches at the end of the war.

Lastly, my editor David Grant expertly polished up my manuscript and helped me to transform my "American English" into "English English." Jolly good!

CHAPTER I

Chasing the Altmark

At dusk on 14 December 1939 the German pocket battleship *Graf Spee* limped into the neutral harbour of Montevideo, Uruguay. Recently attacked by three British cruisers nine miles offshore, the shell-holed war-ship made it to temporary safety with intentions of making hasty repairs. A few wounded German sailors were immediately taken off, and then sixty-two jubilant British merchant seaman trotted down the gangplank: the raggedy group included crew members and five masters of vessels that the *Graf Spee* had demolished. The men climbed into a launch provided by British consular authorities and headed for the docks. However, before freeing the prisoners, the Germans had forced them to sign statements swearing not to reveal anything they had seen aboard the *Graf Spee*.

In a ceremony at the headquarters of the Uruguayan naval prefecture, *Graf Spee*'s captain, Hans Langsdorf, and the German naval attaché, both wearing formal white navy uniforms, surrendered the men to Uruguayan officials. Then the Uruguayans turned the sixty-two former prisoners over to British consular and legation representatives, and apparently it was then that Captain William Stubbs of the *Doric Star* disclosed to them the startling news that three hundred more British merchant seamen were being held captive on the *Altmark*, fuel ship for the *Graf Spee*.[1]

At 2:25 the next morning the naval attaché sent a secret message to the Admiralty in London; Commander in Chief South Atlantic; Commodore South America Division; Assistant Naval Attaché, Rio de Janeiro; and N.C.S.O. Buenos Aires, as follows:

> Ascertained from Captain of British Ship *Doric Star* that German armoured ship *Admiral Spee* ... oiled from German ship *Altmark* at 023° South 026° West 6 December. ... *Altmark* painted black, white deckhouse, yellow funnel with *Norge* painted on bridge deckhouse and flying Norwegian flag. It is understood she is prepared to paint U.S.S.R. and fly that flag. She has concealed guns behind deck house.[2]

1

First Lord of the Admiralty Winston Churchill, greatly cheered by victory over the *Graf Spee*, now set out to rescue his captured merchant sailors. "It was believed that she had on board the crews of the nine ships which had been sunk by the raider," he wrote. "It would be very good if all the returning forces could scrub and search the South Atlantic on their way home for the *Altmark*."[3]

In 1939, spotting a small merchant ship in the vast Atlantic would have taken a miracle: planes of that day could carry just enough fuel to patrol several hundred miles from shore, leaving the main search to navy vessels. The oiler, having heard nothing from *Graf Spee*, lingered in mid-ocean until 24 January, but rumours of the battleship's defeat were reaching the ears of *Altmark*'s officers and prisoners. The tanker's captain, Heinrich Dau, concerned about fuel and provisions, set course for Germany, steering the ship northward through the mid-Atlantic, then close to Iceland, staying well away from Great Britain.[4]

As naval intelligence frantically worked to locate the *Altmark*, news arrived at the Admiralty at 4:00 P.M. on 14 February that an RAF plane had sighted the prison ship after she passed between Iceland and the Faroes. They next spotted her as she sailed southward of Bergen at noon on the 15th. Churchill, already expecting the tanker's arrival in northern waters, sent a message on the 16th to First Sea Lord Sir Dudley Pound saying, "It would seem that the cruiser and destroyers should sweep northward during the day up the coast of Norway, not hesitating to arrest *Altmark* in territorial waters should she be found. This ship is violating neutrality in carrying British prisoners of war to Germany. ... The *Altmark* must be regarded as an invaluable trophy." A few minutes after midnight on the 17th, five cruisers set out to reinforce the six destroyers already searching the waters off Jøssing Fjord – all with boarding parties. Commander in Chief Rosyth ordered an air search at dawn to the south and east of the warships.[5]

That same day three submarines joined the war party: HMS *Seal*, Polish sub *Orzel*, and HMS *Triad*. *Seal* had sailed from Rosyth (Scotland) on 5 February, and although Commander Rupert Lonsdale's war diary reads as though the *Seal* was patrolling for ships carrying contraband, her mission was to locate the *Altmark*. A "Most Secret" message on 5 February sent by the Admiralty to *Seal* read: "*Seal* is to try and seize a German merchant vessel or to detain a neutral vessel carrying iron ore and to send any ship thus seized ... into Kirkwall, accompanying her if possible and reporting particulars ..." Further, the orders stated that an escort for any ship seized or detained would be sent to relieve *Seal*, if possible. "In this event *Seal* is to return and complete her patrol. A boarding officer and boarding party of petty officers and eight other ratings will proceed to sea in *Seal* as a prize crew or armed guard." On the last page of his report, Lonsdale explained that "eight ordinary seamen and two spare crew stokers from H.M.S.

Forth were taken to act as prize crew for any ship captured." Not one of the young men had ever set foot on a ship, and the entire group grew seasick as the submarine ploughed and wallowed through rough winter waves.[6]

Three days out of Rosyth, Lonsdale reached his designated area off the southern tip of Norway, where he sighted a merchant ship. He ordered her to stop, and the vessel signalled her name as *Storm*, bound for Esbjerg (Denmark) with a cargo of coal. "Her markings and size agreed with information in Lloyd's Shipping Index," noted the commander. After studying the situation for a bit, Lonsdale decided to let the coal ship proceed. "We exchanged courtesies and *Seal* dived to continue patrol."

Capturing the *Altmark* meant keeping a close watch on every merchant ship approaching southern Norway and the Kattegat. In the first four years of the war Germany deployed merchant ships equipped with hidden heavy guns and torpedoes and decked them out as Allied or neutral vessels. "German ships are not allowed to enter Norwegian ports if they are wearing false names or colours," wrote the Admiralty staff. "For this reason it is believed that if false names are used, they are painted on at sea, and if false colours are displayed they are also painted on ships' sides ... or on canvas boards." Submarine commanders had an almost impossible task finding and inspecting the many merchant ships plying northern waters, but Lonsdale succeeded in stopping a number of them.[7]

Again on the 10th Lonsdale spotted a freighter, ordered her to halt, and once more ascertained that everything looked legitimate. "I came to the conclusion that she could in no way be regarded with suspicion and she was told to proceed." During the night of the 11th, snow and ice built up on the bridge and mine casing "in larger quantities than previously; the gun was completely coated in ice, voice pipe cocks and the upper lid froze up solid, visibility was very poor at times."[8]

The next night, near Lister Fjord, Lonsdale came upon two ships and approached them to investigate. "Their silhouettes could not be made out owing to the bright lights which they were showing." Using signal lights, Lonsdale questioned the rear ship, who replied that she was Norwegian, the SS *Bergsten*, bound from Antwerp to Oslo. "This agreed with information shown in Lloyd Index, and together with their early arrival and the direction from which they came brought me to the conclusion that they could in no way be regarded with suspicion." Following an incoming order from Vice Admiral Submarines, Lonsdale then speedily headed towards Hansthome, on the west coast of Denmark.

After sighting no ships, *Seal* set off towards Lister Fjord, just south of Jøssing Fjord, arriving on 14 February. "Merchant ships seen proceeding down the coast inside territorial waters," Lonsdale reported. On the morning of the 15th an order flashed in from the Admiralty for *Seal* to patrol near Stavanger, off the south-western tip of Norway; and with that, Lonsdale began a submerged patrol to keep a close eye on the exit from Karm Sound and the passage between Utsire Island (near Stavanger) and the mainland. Lonsdale saw two Danish merchant ships entering territorial waters and a three-masted steamer leaving Skudesnes Fjord. Just before dark *Seal* surfaced, chugged along "with bridge awash" until just after sunset, then listened to another message from the Admiralty. Here was vital news about *Altmark*. It was now known that she had passed Bergen on the 15th. "It was hoped that this tanker would be met this evening."

Another message from the Admiralty indicated that the *Seal* should cover the channel between Utsire Island and the mainland, as they thought a ship the size of *Altmark* would not use Karm Sound. Lonsdale broke radio silence on 16 February, transmitting a message that he had patrolled the indicated area and had seen nothing of the *Altmark*. After sighting a Danish ship and a seaplane, Lonsdale heard from Vice Admiral Submarines that he was to proceed at full speed to Jøssing Fjord. Excitement must have been high at that point, with the crew expecting to see some action.[9]

At 10:30 P.M. on 16 February, as *Seal* was nearing her destination, she met two British destroyers, the *Intrepid* and the *Ivanhoe*, and exchanged light signals. The *Arethusa*, a third destroyer, had spied *Altmark* off the fjord, about a mile from shore, and signalled the *Intrepid* and *Ivanhoe*: "Go in and board *Altmark* and I will cover you." A Norwegian torpedo boat and an aircraft accompanied the prison ship, which was then proceeding at six knots towards the fjord entrance. Apparently, naval higher-ups decided that two destroyers rather than a submarine should give chase, as the warships were much larger and had greater stopping power. *Seal* stayed in the area awaiting orders, then at seven the next evening started her homeward passage – with a crew that probably felt keenly disappointed.[10]

Events that followed the sighting of Churchill's "trophy ship" escalated to full speed. *Ivanhoe* and *Intrepid* charged ahead in pursuit of the *Altmark*, now accompanied by two torpedo boats. Both destroyers hoisted signals to "Stop your vessel instantly" and "Steer to Westward." Seeing that these orders were not being followed, *Ivanhoe* gained a position inshore of the fleeing ship, trying to make her give way to seaward, while *Intrepid* fired a salvo from her 4.7-inch guns. At that instant *Altmark* seemed to be stopping, so *Intrepid* lowered her whaler and sent away a boarding party. "The Norwegian torpedo boat got in the way as much as possible and on one occasion came alongside and protested," said *Intrepid*'s captain. As the whaler neared *Altmark*, with *Ivanhoe* astern, Captain Gordon of *Intrepid* ordered *Ivanhoe* to follow her in and to machine-gun the bridge if she refused to stop, and at that point the *Ivanhoe* recalled her whaler.[11]

Ivanhoe's captain, P. H. Hadow, had attempted to get alongside the *Altmark* as she headed toward Jøssing Fjord. "I therefore manoeuvred accordingly, and a satisfactory position had just been reached, and the boarding party was about to go on, when *Altmark* increased speed and

4

altered course to port, causing *Ivanhoe* to sheer off." Hadow refrained from machine-gunning the bridge, even though he had orders to do it, because he knew there was a Norwegian pilot aboard. By the time Hadow could change course for a second attempt, the prison ship had entered the inner fjord, and two Norwegian torpedo boats rushed to block *Ivanhoe*'s passage. "These torpedo boats were protesting vehemently both verbally and by flags," said Hadow.[12]

Now the destroyer *Cossack* appeared on the scene. Captain Philip Vian signalled Admiralty, described the situation, and awaited further orders. *Intrepid* then told *Ivanhoe* to investigate a darkened merchant ship to seaward, which proved to be the German *Baldur*. Hadow fired two shots across her bow, ordering her to stop, and sent over a boarding party, but "The boat had not got alongside before *Baldur* was observed to be on fire and the crew taking to the boats." Hadow then recalled his whaler, being fearful of an explosion. *Baldur*, set afire by her captain, quickly settled into the sea. "It was apparent that she had been scuttled." Soon after the encounter, *Ivanhoe* and *Intrepid* picked up the *Baldur*'s crew.[13]

Cossack now had the honour of stopping the notorious *Altmark* before she reached port. Churchill, when he heard that Norwegian gunboat officers had told Vian that the *Altmark* was unarmed, had been examined in Bergen, and had received permission to proceed to Germany through Norwegian territorial waters, hit the ceiling. "When this information reached the Admiralty, I intervened, and with the concurrence of the Foreign Secretary, ordered our ships to enter the fjord," he said. "I did not often act so directly; but I now sent Captain Vian the following order":

> Unless Norwegian torpedo-boat undertakes to convoy *Altmark* to Bergen with a joint escort, you should board *Altmark*, liberate the prisoners, and take possession of the ship, pending further instructions. If Norwegian torpedo-boat interferes, you should warn her to stand off. If she fires upon you, you should not reply unless attack is serious, in which case you should defend yourself, using no more force than is necessary and ceasing fire when she desists.[14]

As Churchill wrote in *The Gathering Storm*, "Vian did the rest." Using powerful searchlights, the captain entered the frozen, dark fjord, making his way between ice floes, then coming alongside torpedo boat *Kjell*. To Churchill he reported: "I delivered your message to the Commanding Officer. His refusal was, he said, based on instructions of his Government. I informed him that at whatever cost I must substantiate his assurance that there could be no British prisoners on board *Altmark*, as vessel had been twice examined in Norwegian ports." Vian then invited the Norwegian officer to embark with his boarding party and accompany them during the search of the ship.[15]

Kjell's captain declined the invitation, due to the "ice conditions." Vian, seeing *Altmark* temporarily stuck in an ice pack at the inner end of the fjord, signalled the ship to stop the engines, that he was coming aboard. "Order was disregarded, and he freed himself," wrote Vian. "Directing a powerful searchlight on my bridge and working his engines at full power ahead and astern, he attempted to ram me as I came alongside, and secondly to drive me ashore when boarding was taking place."[16]

Both ships were now manoeuvring under high power, with varying space between the two. "Under these conditions the act of boarding offered an uninviting aspect ..." Lieutenant Commander Turner, leader of the commando party of forty-five officers, leaped about six feet onto the *Altmark* and pulled in the petty officer, who had fallen short and was hanging by his hands. Only thirty-three commandos managed to jump across, and these were divided into four parties. Turner secured the hawser and led his loudly cheering band of followers to the bridge, running. "It was an inspiring demonstration," declared Vian, "and induced in the Germans, evidently of two minds regarding a policy of active resistance, a tendency to let things be." In truth, the British sailors met no opposition.[17]

When Turner arrived at the bridge, he and his group disarmed the German officers, who were carrying revolvers; pushed aside the starboard engine telegraph man, who had "Full Speed Ahead" showing; and changed the arrow to "Stop." With that, the telegraph man dashed to the port telegraph and cranked it over to "Full Speed Ahead" again, after which Turner grabbed the indicator and once more put it on "Stop." He held the German officers with hands up until the *Altmark*, going about four knots sternway, ran aground with a loud crunching noise. "Rudder and screws were probably damaged and put out of action," reported Turner.[18]

At the moment *Altmark* stopped, *Cossack* changed course to avoid the same fate, and Vian's crew heard cries for help. Hans Berendsen, one of the German sailors, had leapt from the ship in an attempt to make it to shore, and had fallen into an ice hole. Seeing his plight, two sailors from *Cossack* jumped from the stern into the frigid sea. "They were in the water for a considerable time, since it was not possible to send a boat to the German whilst the position of the ice hole was awkwardly situated as regards the ship," wrote Vian. Unfortunately, in spite of every effort to save him, the escaping sailor died from exposure.[19]

While the German officers were being held on the bridge and the ice rescue was going on, one of the squads of commandos, advancing up a narrow passage on the ship, was shot at, and a sailor was hit in the arm. Others were ducking more bullets, apparently coming from shore. Vian said that some of the German seamen had jumped from *Altmark* and were firing from shore at the boarding party on the stern. The commandos now fired back, as their orders had been not to shoot unless fired upon, with the result that four Germans died and five were wounded.[20]

Turner, having left two guards with the German officers on the bridge, demanded that he be shown to the prison quarters. "I went away with a sentry and the two German officers to arrange the release of the prisoners." He soon found out that the British merchantmen were being held in four groups: two captains in a cabin amidships; about 150 white officers and ratings forward; Lascars (Indians) in a separate compartment; and the rest of the white ratings aft, on three separate levels.[21]

About 11:00 P.M that night, as the prisoners were keeping watch through a spyhole, they observed a great deal of activity on deck. "I was on duty," explained George King, "and the next thing I heard was an Englishman shouting down our hatch, 'Are you British prisoners?' I answered 'Yes.'" With that the officer informed them: "You are safe, we have come to rescue you." Deafening cheers went up, and King quickly climbed on deck so that he could supervise the prisoners' orderly emergence from all three levels. "This was very well done indeed," he noted. Captain Dau and Lt Schmidt of the *Altmark* shook hands with King, who observed, "Apparently the Captain had flatly denied we were on board, and persisted in this, but at last the young Lieutenant at his side, threw down his hand and admitted we were down there."

Immediately after taking the prisoners aboard, Dau had ordered an extremely heavy iron tank lid to be placed over the main exit hatch. During the rescue, six of the heftiest prisoners clambered out a smaller hole so that they could remove the unwieldy cover. One of the German guards, still armed, saw the sailors starting to hoist the impediment and jumped in their way, telling them: "It will take fifty men to lift this lid." King told the guard it might take fifty Germans, but not fifty merchantmen. "He still got in our way so I knocked him out, as I have done a little amateur boxing."

King and two other British officers, Creer and Peterson, searched all prison quarters to be sure no one was left on the tanker. "The men were in fairly good health; everyone was able to walk off the ship, there being no stretcher cases. Then Creer and I left, being the last 2 British prisoners to step off the *Altmark*."[22]

Upon hearing the news that 299 Allied prisoners had been rescued, Winston Churchill sent ambulances, doctors, press, and photographers to the port of Leith, Scotland, to greet them. "As, however, it appeared that they were in good health, had been well looked after on the destroyers, and came ashore in hearty condition, no publicity was given to this aspect. Their rescue and Captain Vian's apparently decent conduct aroused a wave of enthusiasm in Britain almost equal to that which followed the sinking of the *Graf Spee*."[23]

The day after the dramatic rescue, First Sea Lord Sir Dudley Pound issued a message to all submarines on patrol: "German ship *Altmark* is to be torpedoed at sight outside, repetition outside, neutral territorial waters if her identity is clearly established. One submarine is to be stationed in the vicinity of Josing [sic] Fiord." In a pencilled note at the bottom of the page Winston Churchill replied, "But not I hope tied down too closely." In response to that, Pound scribbled: "No – he has considerable freedom." The submarine they had chosen for the task was the *Seal*.[24]

Notes

1. *New York Times*, 15 December 1939, 1.
2. NA, ADM 199/128, 35.
3. Churchill, *The Gathering Storm*, 526, 527.
4. Frischauer, *The Altmark Affair*, frontispiece; ADM 223/146, Map of Altmark's wanderings.
5. Churchill, *The Gathering Storm*, 561.
6. NA, ADM 223/27, Message 17 February 1940; NA, ADM 199/1840; RNSM, Patrol Report HMS *Seal*, 5 February–23 February, 1940.
7. NA, ADM 199/1830, 12.
8. RNSM, Patrol Report HMS *Seal*, 5 February–23 February, 1940.
9. Ibid.; NA, ADM 199/1940, 28.
10. NA, ADM 199/940, 46.
11. Ibid., 47.
12. Ibid., 44.
13. Ibid., 44, 45.
14. Churchill, *The Gathering Storm*, 562.
15. Ibid.; NA, ADM 199/281, 33.
16. NA, ADM 199/281, 33.
17. Ibid., 48.
18. Ibid., 49.
19. Ibid., 35.
20. Ibid., 48; NA, ADM 199/1940, Appendix to Daily Operations Report, No. 166; NA, ADM 1/25843.
21. NA, ADM 199/281, 49.
22. NA, ADM 199/281, Report of an Interview with Mr. G. A. King, 129–141.
23. Churchill, *The Gathering Storm*, 563.
24. NA, ADM 1/25843, Secret Message from Admiralty, 18 February 1940.

CHAPTER II

Germany Invades Norway

Just after the *Altmark* capture, *Seal* and her boarding party received instructions to proceed to a new position south of Jøssing Fjord and there to keep a lookout for any "suspicious" ships, in other words, the fleeing prison tanker. For the second time, the Admiralty ordered the big minelayer to pursue the elusive German tanker. From 18 to 21 February Lonsdale scanned the sea but saw no vessels entering the Skagerrak, where the *Altmark* would be likely to sail on her way back to Germany.

In Lonsdale's log he described several problems he had earlier experienced: "At the end of the day's diving on the 8th and 7th the Battery was exhausted. ... Depth keeping at periscope depth was difficult owing to weather condition and high speed had to be used on all occasions. ... It is submitted that *Porpoise* class submarines [minelayers] are under-batteried compared with all other classes. ..."

Lonsdale further commented that on 9 February at the 6:00 A.M. routine message-receiving hour – when submarines went near the surface to communicate with headquarters – he heard nothing until 6:13; then came the words, "Have nothing to communicate." Expressing his impatience, Lonsdale wrote in his log: "During this time *Seal* has been in a dangerous position at thirty feet, when it was too dark to see, and speed and water noises were handicapping the reception. ... It is submitted that it is most important for Rugby to make this operating signal at once if they have no signal to make." He stressed that messages be sent on schedule "to reduce the time that a submarine has to remain in a possibly dangerous position while reading messages which are not of any immediate importance." ("Rugby" referred to the town in central England from which low frequency radio transmissions were being sent and received.)

Regarding enemy shipping, Lonsdale summed up his observations, saying that "ore ships are either using the passage via the Sound or else that they have no definite starting place for leaving the Norwegian coast; for, by leaving territorial water at dark between Jaederene Point and the Naze they can reach Danish Territorial water by daylight the following day." As crew member Ernie Truman explained the situation, "The reason we were up there was to keep an eye on the Germans, because they were taking iron ore from the northern end of Sweden down through these fjords, carrying iron ore back to Germany for their munitions. That was why we were up there, and we knew jolly well that they were using [neutral] Norwegian waters; so we were trying to spot them and, if we could, to apprehend them."[1]

Ending his war diary, Lonsdale described the behaviour of his thirteen-man boarding party, taken along in case of encountering the *Altmark* or capturing a prize vessel. "None of the ordinary seamen had ever been to sea before; most of them were under twenty-one, and all were seasick at the beginning of the Patrol. The behaviour of these men ... was splendid: they got down to all manner of dirty work cheerfully and were employed cleaning out Heads and Bath Room, drying up the deck [mopping spills inside compartments] and as a permanent 'gashing' party. Such was their keenness that on one occasion gash [leftovers] was brought along to the Control Room while *Seal* was at seventy foot: it is considered that credit is due to these young and wholly untrained men." Such was their enthusiasm with the *Altmark* adventure that two or three of the greenhorn "gashers" joined the submarine service after they returned.[2]

On the 23rd Lonsdale and his disappointed crew safely returned to Rosyth. The Admiralty wrote in at the end of the commander's war diary: "This was an arduous patrol and *Seal* was unfortunate not to capture a prize."[3]

Churchill's efforts to sink the *Altmark* proved fruitless: the notorious oiler apparently remained in Jøssing Fjord for about a month undergoing repairs, then moved over to Sandefjord, south of Oslo Fjord, and by 21 March was ready to depart. Dau's war diary explains that Oberleutnant zur See Petersen and Captain Eckhoff came on board for a meeting, where they decided to move the *Altmark* with the tugboat *Atlantic* to the outer harbour in early evening; they planned to set sail at break of dawn and approach Oslo Fjord in the daytime. Next they contacted the German naval attaché in Oslo to get permission for the *Altmark* to remain briefly at Oskarborg Fortress. To reach the citadel, a ship had to sail to the northern end of the immense Oslo Fjord, proceed around a sharp bend to the right, then continue to the end of the fjord, where the obsolete garrison stood with its three 28-cm. guns (made by Krupp in 1892), a few other 15-cm. guns, and some torpedo tubes. From there Dau would sail the short distance to the Skagerrak and there meet German escort boats. It was a brilliant idea, for a safer and more secretive place could scarcely have been found. But the Norwegians said no. Perhaps they felt that as a neutral country they had already given sufficient aid to the Germans.[4]

Altmark hauled anchor from Sandefjord on 21 March, and was towed by the tug *Atlantic* until she met the Norwegian destroyer *Odin* and a Norwegian minesweeper, which then accompanied her out to sea. Later that day the two escorts departed, and on 27 March at 11:30 in the morning a German escort boat, two blockade-runners and a minesweeper sailed up to welcome the escaping prison ship. At 12:53 *Altmark* anchored outside Kiel, and Admiral Güse, Vice Admiral Hormel, and Captain Niemand came aboard to welcome the celebrated tanker. With great ceremony the officers presented each *Altmark* crewmember with an Iron Cross, and the ship then steamed into the harbour at Kiel.[5]

The *Altmark* incident had already stirred up a storm of controversy when the news hit the front page of newspapers worldwide. Enraged, Hitler told reporters that the British navy had flagrantly violated Norwegian neutrality by carrying out "a most swinish, most bestial attack on unarmed German seamen." The Norwegian government blasted the British by lodging "a serious protest against this grave violation of Norwegian territorial waters, which has caused strong indignation, as it took place in the interior of a Norwegian Fjord. ... The Norwegian Government must demand that the British Navy be instructed ... to respect Norwegian Sovereignty." In conclusion they added, "The Norwegian Government expect of the British Government that they will hand the prisoners over to the Norwegian Government and make due compensation and reparation."[6]

In a private message to naval bigwigs, Churchill, then First Lord of the Admiralty, expressed his opinion: "The territorial waters of Norway have been and are being used as a kind of communication trench along which not only are supplies of all kinds passed ... into Germany, but in which German military operations have been conducted. German U-boats have sunk British, Danish, and Dutch ships in Norwegian territorial waters. ... Finally, in the case of the *Altmark* ... it has been allowed to proceed in its attempt to carry 300 British prisoners ... into confinement in Germany."

Churchill directly expressed his sympathy with the Royal Norwegian Government in "the outrages to which they have been subjected by the German Government." He continued by saying that His Majesty's Government had been forced to conclude that the Norwegian Government was acting under duress, "and is not capable of maintaining ... impartial neutrality. ..." Furthermore, he announced that the British were determined to close and keep closed the passage through Norwegian territorial waters "which has been abused in so flagrant a manner." To accomplish this he stated that His Majesty's Government proposed to "lay and maintain three minefields, starting inside Norwegian territorial waters ..."[7]

Prior to the *Altmark* affair Germany had been shipping vast quantities of iron ore – six million tons annually – from Sweden, by traversing the three-mile wide Norwegian waters, then called the "leads." Churchill, angered by the enemy flagrantly defying international law in transporting contraband through neutral seas, had come to the end of his rope. On 14 March he conceived one of his bizarre ideas, which he presented in a

"Most Secret" memo to the Admiralty: "Now that we are not allowed to interfere with the Norwegian Corridor, would it not be possible to have one or two merchant ships of sufficient speed specially strengthened in the bows, and if possible equipped with a ram. These vessels would carry merchandise and travel up the leads looking for German ore ships or any other German merchant vessels, and then ram them by accident." In response to Churchill's wacky idea, Vice Admiral Gordon Campbell replied on 30 March, "Although it is quite practicable to fit a ship for ramming purposes, so many complications would arise if this proposal was proceeded with, that I cannot recommend it." His was an easy decision, for two days earlier the Supreme War Council (France and Great Britain) had approved Churchill's proposal to lay minefields in Norwegian waters.[8]

On 28 March the Council designated 5 April to set out the mines, then changed the date to 8 April. "I called the actual mining operation 'Wilfred'," explained Churchill, "because by itself it seemed so small and innocent. As our mining of Norwegian waters might provoke a German retort, it was also agreed that a British brigade and a French contingent should be sent to Narvik to clear the port and advance to the Swedish frontier. Other forces should be dispatched to Stavanger, Bergen, and Trondheim, in order to deny these bases to the enemy." As the Allies discussed the possible repercussions of mining during the month of March, Lonsdale set out on patrol, leaving Rosyth on 12 March and heading for an unspecified position. Two days later German B-Dienst (Beobachtungs-Dienst, the German radio monitoring and cryptographic service) reported: "The following positions of enemy submarines have been received." Fifth down on their list of thirteen British subs appeared "*Seal* ... under way to position 58° 50' N, 9° 50' E." The Germans, of course, were correct: Lonsdale's boat was headed towards Larvik, on the southern coast of Norway near Oslo Fjord, where he was to search for merchant ships carrying contraband.[9]

From Vice Admiral Submarines Horton a message came in on 21 March saying that "*Seal* is to proceed towards Arendal so as to intercept ... *Johann Blumenthal*. No repeat no bombing restrictions arranged. If ship not intercepted by 2200 23rd March *Seal* to proceed as desired by you."[10]

In October 1939 British Naval Intelligence had ascertained that some "powerful potential raiders are still in German waters and any disguised raiders which have been fitting out since the outbreak of war must be nearing completion." It could be said that the Germans were masters of disguising ships, as seen in the constantly changing "costumes" of the *Altmark* and *Graf Spee*, one a merchant ship, the other a battleship. For example, late in 1939 work began for converting the large vessel *Goldenfeld* into an armed merchant ship with the new name *Atlantis*. On her they installed four torpedo tubes, ninety-two mines, twelve guns, large quantities of supplies, and two seaplanes with spare parts. Large cargo crates covered the deck armament, and there were fake smoke stacks, ventilators, and masts, plus a crewmember dressed in a dress and wig, to look like the captain's wife. With such an array of disguised German ships running around, it is small wonder that Churchill became frustrated and wanted to ram them with his own clandestine vessels.[11]

By March of 1940 Intelligence knew of a disguised German cruiser sailing under the name *Johann Blumenthal* and assigned *Seal* to try to attack and destroy her – hence the instructions to freely attack.

On the 22nd Lonsdale patrolled west of the Skaw, waters near the northern tip of Denmark, in the Skagerrak. "Many merchant ships were sighted," he noted. Later that day he proceeded towards Arendal, reporting weather and visibility very good. At 2:34 A.M. he sighted a darkened ship and closed in on her, flashing light signals to stop. "Ship switched on Navigation light and stopped instantly. She gave her name as the Estonian ship *Otto*, bound from Copenhagen to Bergen in ballast. *Seal* passed within 100 feet twice and a close inspection was made." Lonsdale could see that the colour, name, nationality and Estonian port of registry were displayed prominently, decided that she was a bona fide neutral, and allowed her to proceed. He had no inkling that two weeks later he would again have a close encounter with *Otto*.

Patrolling off Arendal near the edge of territorial waters, Lonsdale sighted a ship "exactly resembling *Johann Blumenthal*, which was expected to leave on this Saturday afternoon." With engines at full speed *Seal* chased the suspect vessel for thirty minutes, attempting to cut her off or get a closer look. "She, however, kept close inshore and a better view was not obtained. *Seal* encroached half a mile inside territorial water." Again no luck. Later that afternoon the commander spied the mast and funnel of a questionable ship, but she entered Kristiansand Fjord, and so he turned off once more. After waiting a while, he noticed the same vessel exiting the fjord, so he dived and closed in on her, observing through his periscope that "she resembled *Johann Blumenthal*." After surfacing, he signalled the ship to stop, then investigated. "She was the Danish SS *Cyril*, and had Danish colours painted in three places on her side, as well as name and nationality. She resembled the *Johann Blumenthal* in all respects, except for the fact that she did not have a cruiser stern." Lonsdale remarked that the *Cyril* crew were noticeably terrified; therefore, he exchanged courtesies before allowing her to proceed.

At eleven o'clock that night Lonsdale stopped and examined one more ship he thought might be the *Blumenthal*, without catching his quarry.

Ending this frustrating patrol, Lonsdale headed the *Seal* back to Rosyth. Possibly her entire mission had been monitored by B-Dienst: since 1935 they had been able to decode Royal Navy messages set in Naval Code or Naval Cypher – World War I systems that were still being used at the beginning of World War II. At the same time, cryptographers at Bletchley Park, near London, struggled to crack the Germans' complex Enigma code and would not succeed until 1941.[12]

At the bottom of the Germans' 14 March list of British submarine locations, two short paragraphs had been added, including the statement: "Apparently all available submarines have been assigned to the sealing off of the Heligoland Bight and the exits of the Baltic Sea. It is presumed that the English intend to carry out an attack on Norway."[13]

As *Seal* continued her missions, the Admiralty received intelligence reports that Hitler intended to invade Norway, and the Admiralty then justified their actions accordingly. Reports came in to London that "They [the Germans] decided in the last week of March to use the Norwegian corridor to send empty ore ships northward, filled with military stores and German soldiers, concealed below decks ... in order to seize various ports on the Norwegian seaboard."[14]

Events that spring of 1940 had a direct bearing on *Seal*'s activities. A long, bulky Porpoise-class minelayer, she was commissioned in September of 1936 and was ideal for expediting the Allies' plan for forcing German ore ships out of Norwegian waters. She was 289 feet long, had six torpedo tubes and one 10.2-cm. deck gun, as well as fifty mines. The fifty-nine-man crew, fully aware of the hazards of their next mission, felt confident of success: Stoker Herbert ("Taff") Harper had supplied *Seal* with a good luck charm.

Just after *Seal* was completed in 1936, the time came for deep diving trials out of Oban, Scotland. One day Taff had some time off and went into the small town, "a nice fishing village," and after enjoying a couple of pints in the local pub, he noticed a fairground on an adjacent street and wandered over. When he spied a shooting gallery, he said to himself, "I'll have a go. In those days I was considered a good shot with a rifle, and I shot down seven ducks. They gave me this statuette of a naked lady, about fourteen inches tall, nice looking and well-proportioned."

Taff took her aboard the submarine and placed her atop his toolbox in the engine room. "Tubby Lister, who was in charge of our watch, said to me one day, 'Taff, if we have a crash dive, you're going to lose that thing.'" In Tubby's view, the sexy doll should be rigged up with a sling and attached to the port diesel engine, which was under Taff's care. "The little lady was with us from the very start: she went on every mission, patrol and convoy duties, so she was a professional submariner."

As Taff described her, "she was a nice, lovely white lady with a very black bottom. It was the crew's practice when going to diving stations to pat her bottom for luck. I've often wondered afterwards what the Germans thought of it."

When it was time for inspections on Sundays the crew covered their girlfriend with a rag so that Lonsdale would not see her, "but we all seen him at times when he was passing have a sly pat himself." In the months to come, the pretty maiden sometimes bestowed her blessing on *Seal* but could not save her from ultimate disaster.[15]

Seal's next adventures came about as a direct result of "The Phoney War," that interval after Britain declared war on Germany and neither side did much. British naval historians tell us that on 14 December 1939 Hitler ordered his Supreme Command to prepare plans for the invasion of Norway and Denmark, and their organising continued until March 1940, when Hitler decided that his operation "Weserübung" should take place about a month before his projected invasion of France and the Low Countries. He fixed 9 April as invasion day. Already aware that their mine-laying was likely to provoke Germany into invading Norway, the British decided to keep troops ready to land at Stavanger, Bergen, Trondheim, and Narvik and to start laying mines on 8 April. "Thus it came about that each of the belligerents independently was initiating operations scheduled to take place in neutral Norway within the same twenty-four hours, a sufficiently intriguing situation, though the scope and method of their plans were very different," wrote historians.[16]

British ships for Stavanger and Bergen assembled in the Firth of Forth under Vice Admiral John Cunningham, and four vessels departed with supplies and troops. Various destroyers and minelayers went to sea to begin mine-laying operations off Stadtlandet and to patrol the area. Germany had begun to embark troops on the 6th, and the first of these groups was destined for Narvik and Trondheim. On 7 April a British reconnaissance aircraft reported a German cruiser and two destroyers to the west of southern Denmark, steering northward. Shortly thereafter, the Commander in Chief, Home Fleet, received a message from Commander in Chief, Rosyth, stating that the cruiser was probably the Nürnberg class, that there were six destroyers, and that twenty-three British Wellingtons and twelve Blenheims were leaving at 11:15 and 11:50 to bomb the enemy. A second signal from Rosyth said that aircraft had reported three enemy destroyers "homeward bound." The Admiralty responded to these ominous words twenty minutes later:

> Recent reports suggest a German expedition is being prepared. Hitler is reported … to have ordered unostentatious movement of one division in ten ships by night to land at Narvik, with simultaneous occupation of Jutland [Denmark]. Sweden to be left alone. Moderates said to be opposing this plan. Date given for arrival at Narvik was 8th April.
>
> All these reports are of doubtful value and may well be only a further move in the war of nerves. Great Belt [narrow passage between the islands of Denmark, south of the Kattegat] opened for traffic 5th April.[17]

Many additional intelligence reports arrived at naval headquarters, but their implications were wrongly assessed. "In the light of later events," remarked the Commander in Chief, Home Fleet, Admiral Sir Charles Forbes, "it was unfortunate that the last paragraph was included." Indeed, Germany's invasion of Norway went into full swing in the early hours of 9 April, and British warships could not stop them. The British destroyer *Glowworm* became separated from her group, was attacked by German destroyers and sunk on 8 April. In an ironic event on 17 April, two British destroyers blew U-49 to the surface; while rescuing the crew they discovered secret documents showing total U-boat dispositions for the Norwegian invasion.[18]

Near Stavanger on 8 April Lonsdale picked up "hydrophone effect of two ships passing at high speed in a Westerly direction at range of 2 ½' [probably 2 ½ miles] from *Seal*." Hoping for a successful attack, he brought all torpedo tubes to ready position, turned onto a firing course, and waited for louder hydrophone noises of the heavy ships that should be approaching. He reported the two ships' positions; and Lonsdale's message, along with another from the submarine *Truant*, proved that the Germans were in fact invading Norway. It appears that the two submarines were acting as observers, as the lightning attack on defenceless Norway went into high gear.[19]

On 8 April, eighteen minutes after Lonsdale reported hearing two enemy ships, *Seal* experienced a terrifying incident. As authors Warren and Benson described it in their excellent book, *Will Not We Fear*, *Seal* was patrolling on the surface after nightfall in a dense fog; and Lonsdale decided to remain on the bridge until daybreak. With engines running dead slow, the captain and four men on watch strained their eyes and ears for engine sounds. Gradually they began to hear a ship's foghorn, then the starboard lookout yelled, "Light dead ahead, sir." There it was, a white light high above them, coming rapidly closer. Without wasting a second, Lonsdale ordered his vessel full ahead and hard to starboard; as the boat lurched to the side he saw that the "white" light was green, indicating the ship's right side. Instead of veering away from the ship, the *Seal* was now crossing in front of it. Lonsdale yelled instructions: "Midships, hard-a-port," causing his boat to shudder and slow down as the enormous freighter loomed up on them. *Seal*'s engines burst into full power and swung her around, causing her to rub along the side of the ship. "There was a frightening scrape and a thud and a bang and a sound of tearing metal as the bows of the merchantman struck the after hydroplane guard of the submarine." At that moment Lonsdale glanced up and saw the name SS *Otto* on the bridge – the identical freighter he had inspected about two weeks before. Taff's white plaster lady had saved *Seal* from tragedy; and after the boat's terrifyingly close call, she no doubt enjoyed many a grateful pat on her derrière.[20]

The next morning Lonsdale noted that visibility varied throughout the day: a gale was blowing, with heavy seas, snow, and at times fog.

"Whenever the Periscope was raised to three and generally more, aeroplanes were in sight proceeding to and coming from the Norwegian coast." He then advanced to a new patrol position in accordance with 9 April instructions from Vice Admiral Submarines Max Horton. It may be noted that on that day, Admiral Horton, convinced that a German invasion of Norway was imminent, signalled all submarines to deal with German merchant ships in the Skagerrak east of 8° as warships and to sink them with no warning, probably because they could be carrying troops. Indeed, two days later, several messages flashed to England from citizens in Norway saying, "This is Egersund S.O.S. Two German cargo ships discharging troops. We ask British warships to come to our aid." Another message pleaded: "Please send British warships at once, as there are three boatloads of Germans landing at Aalesund." At the time, Norwegian naval forces consisted of about ten torpedo boats, two minesweepers, six escort ships, and a small destroyer. No help ever came.[21]

On 10 April Lonsdale sighted a floating German mine, and his actions regarding it are unexplained, but one assumes he blew it up. By that day the German blitzkrieg invasion of Norway and Denmark had begun, with no opposition. Then on the 11th the *Seal* arrived off Skudesnes Fjord, the entryway to Stavanger. While patrolling on the 12th he described conditions as "too bad from 0800 to Noon for depth keeping at periscope depth. Continual air activity." When the 13th rolled around, Commander Lonsdale wrote that in view of his orders and "with the object of keeping up morale of crew as high as possible, decided to dive as close to Stavanger as possible." Perhaps in the harbour he could find some German warships to torpedo.

Nothing in *Seal*'s war diary reveals what happened next, but we know from *Will Not We Fear* that in a dead calm sea, submerged at ninety feet, the submarine proceeded during daylight into the dogleg fjord. Slowly they inched their way along, occasionally rising to take a peek through the periscope; and by using navigational skills and the new Asdic equipment, they made it into Stavanger harbour. As Happy Eckersall explained it, "We went in using the Asdic sounding from port, then starboard, all the way through and stayed in the middle." After this nerve-wracking effort Lonsdale reported, "No warships in sight … and the only Merchant ships identified were painted with Norwegian colours; accordingly gave up object to fire torpedoes into harbour: proceeded out by Fjord." Again no rewards for *Seal*.[22]

At this point the German invasion of Norway was in full swing: they had captured Oslo, Bergen and Trondheim; vital airfields at Aalborg (Denmark); Sola Airfield, eight miles south of Stavanger; and another air base at Trondheim, while the British diddled around. The German navy had sent no warships into Stavanger, but on 9 April six Messerschmitt 110s had bombed the only two Norwegian aircraft on the ground and two machine-gun posts at Sola (there were no anti-aircraft guns at the field); then ten German transport planes flew in carrying 120 paratroopers, who floated down and, after a quick skirmish, took command of Sola. Capturing by paratroopers was a new idea at the time and worked splendidly: the entire seizure of Sola Field took place in a single day. Next arrived the main German force of 180 bombers and fighters, which landed at Sola and the nearby seaplane harbour and went directly into operation, thwarting British access to southern Norway.[23]

On the way out of Stavanger, Lonsdale sighted a German torpedo boat patrolling in Haasteen Fjord. "An attack could have been carried out, but as target only drew six feet, this was not done. [Torpedoes travelled too low in the water to hit the vessel.] Waited at entrance to Kvidso Fjord in case [troop] transports might be going to arrive." He watched the torpedo boat as it headed into Stavanger, then made his way out to sea.

Instructions arrived for *Seal* to carry out "a reconnaissance on Sunday 14th April to determine the extent to which the [Sola] aerodrome is visible from seaward, the result of which will be signalled." The message said there was one large hangar, a wireless transmission station, and a meteorological office. "If you cannot distinguish objects through periscope … try landing a man on Kjoro Island after dark, subsequently withdrawing well clear before reporting."[24]

Lonsdale began his cruise along the Norwegian coast and, without having to send a sailor ashore, made his periscope observations and reported that air activity off Skudesnes Fjord (outside Stavanger) was "continuous by day, except during recognised meal hours, and British Air Raids by day and by night were observed …" By now the Admiralty was sending over groups of Blenheims, Hampdens, Hudsons, and Whitleys in unsuccessful attempts to destroy Sola Airfield and German planes. Too many admirals, commanders in chief, and Sea Lords were trying to run the show, wasting a great deal of time, and causing the situation to go from bad to worse.[25]

Notes

1. RNSM, Patrol Report HMS *Seal*, 5 February–23 February 1940.
2. Ibid.
3. Ibid.
4. Derry, *The Campaign in Norway*, 36.
5. Militärarchiv, Freiburg, Kriegstagebuch des Trossschiffes "Altmark"; Schnellkurzbrief, Geheime Kommandofache, 2 April 1940.

6. *New York Times*, 18 February 1940, 1; NA, ADM 1/25843, Message from Royal Norwegian Legation to Viscount Halifax.

7. NA, ADM 1/25843, Statement by Winston Churchill, N.D.

8. NA, ADM 1/10795.

9. Churchill, *The Gathering Storm*, 579; Happy Eckersall, Translation of German Naval Document, March 1940.

10. NA, ADM 199/1840, 56.

11. Muggenthaler, *German Raiders of World War I*, 15–17; NA, ADM 199/227.

12. RNSM, Patrol report HMS *Seal*, 12 March–24 March 1940; Kahn, *Seizing the Enigma*, 211, 212.

13. Eckersall, Translation of German Naval Document, March 1940.

14. Churchill, *Blood, Sweat, and Tears*, 252.

15. Taff Harper to author, 7 March, 2 April, 24 April, 2001; Taff Harper, interview with author, Newcastle, England, 3 February 2002.

16. NA, ADM 234/333, *Naval Staff History*, 3

17. NA, ADM 199/362, Despatch of the Commander-in-Chief, Home Fleet, covering the period 1st March 1940 to 15th June 1940, 12.

18. NA, ADM 199/362, 12.

19. RNSM, Patrol Report HMS *Seal* 6 April–19 April 1940; NA, ADM 234/333, *Naval Staff History*, 17.

20. Warren and Benson, *Will Not We Fear*, 35, 36.

21. NA, ADM 234/333, *Naval Staff History*, 45,46; NA, AIR 22/8, Summary No. 268, 13 April 1940.

22. Happy Eckersall, telephone interview with author, 9 July 2000.

23. Roskill, *Churchill and the Admirals*, 103.

24. NA, ADM 199/1840, 85.

25. Previous sections from Lonsdale's Patrol Report 6 April–19 April 1940; Derry, *The Campaign in Norway*, 39, 40, 268.

CHAPTER III

Air-Sea Debacle

Max Horton and the Admiralty were already planning *Seal*'s next mission – the "Bombardment of Stavanger Aerodrome," otherwise known as "Operation Duck." A few days earlier, the Germans had quickly and easily captured every major Norwegian air base, the five largest ports in the country, and all radio and telephone networks. "We have been completely outwitted," Churchill said to First Sea Lord Dudley Pound.[1]

Trying to make up for lost time, the Admiralty formulated a group attack on Stavanger airfield at Sola, to secure a foothold on the southern coast. They included *Seal* in the operation, along with the heavy cruiser HMS *Suffolk*, four destroyers, fighter aircraft and spotting aircraft – intending to inflict "the greatest possible damage to the aerodrome so as to restrict the operation of aircraft therefrom." *Seal* had conducted her reconnaissance mission on the 14th, and preparations now went into high gear. Navy planners noted that civilian airways pilots who knew the location of the air base had told them that it should be visible from seaward between the bearings of 290° and 250°. "The control tower is conspicuous," they reported.[2]

Other events created a secondary objective for Operation Duck, but the navy did not mention it in their plan: British invasion forces were due to land at Andalsnes, and the bombardment of Sola airfield would be a supportive action.[3]

First, *Seal* was to take up position at 58° 57' North, 5° 10' East by 3:30 A.M. on Wednesday 17 April and would then flash "LL" every thirty seconds in a certain direction. "A box lamp with full aperture and white light is to be used." Then the *Suffolk* would approach, turning to a southerly course when at the desired range; she would detail a destroyer for identification purposes with the *Seal*. When the destroyer reached a position twenty miles short of Position A, she was to transmit by Asdic "LL" every thirty seconds in a certain range of bearings and continue to do so until *Seal* had been identified by her flashing signal, up until 4:45. This destroyer would be the leader of the group of four. "If for any reason contact between surface forces and *Seal* is not made, *Seal* will dive at 0415."

21

When *Seal* spotted the "LL" signals from the destroyer, she was to identify herself by firing yellow smoke candles. Supporting aircraft were to rendezvous in "Position A" at 3:55 on 17 April, as well.[4]

Next, the *Suffolk* would catapult one Walrus aircraft "in time for it to give aerial observation and prepare her second aircraft for catapulting." Launching aircraft from a cruiser in those days was difficult and risky: a carriage with the attached plane whizzed down a track – accelerated by an explosion from a big blank shell – and hurled the plane into the air at what was hoped to be flying speed. The second Walrus, a standby spotter, would be sent up if need be, then a Hudson from a Scottish base would go in and drop a flare in the centre of the field to enable *Suffolk* to obtain the correct line and check the range. At that point "a bombardment is to be carried out … the particular objective being the junction of the runways." In the plan *Suffolk* would use H.E. (illumination) shells for salvos needed to establish the target, then fire broadsides of concrete-piercing shells "to cause the maximum effect on concrete runways." Admiralty gave the *Suffolk* captain, J. W. Durnsford, permission to modify the execution of the plan as he desired and to cancel the operation if necessary.

For air protection, three Blenheim fighter escorts were due to arrive at Position A before daylight (4:30), and then at 6:39 three Hudsons would come in to take over. Two more Hudsons were to arrive: one for second standby spotting duties and dropping a parachute flair, the second for protection. *Suffolk* was to signal one of the Hudsons to release a parachute flare over the centre of Sola Airfield at a certain time, indicating the target.

After completing the mission, *Suffolk* and the four destroyers were to withdraw "at best speed" and return to Scapa Flow; and the Walrus aircraft would fly back immediately, being unable to land again on the ship. At 4:15 or after the five ships had passed, *Seal* was to act independently, keeping clear to the north. In sum, she was to act as a rendezvous beacon.[5]

The plan sounded terrific, but it did not work out exactly as scheduled. *Seal*, on 17 April at 2:20, proceeded to Position A, sighted the *Suffolk* and four destroyers as they approached four miles to the south, then made the arranged light signal contact. At 4:35 *Seal* dived as some surface ships passed, then Lonsdale kept patrol in the entrance to Skudesnes Fjord. All was going well from *Seal*'s point of view.[6]

Then the trouble started. Stormy weather at Lossiemouth, Scotland, delayed the three Blenheims' departure an hour and forty-five minutes, and they at last managed to take off in formation. "This escort did not find HMS *Suffolk*," wrote air force officers. "It joined two Hudsons and searched coastwise to the North of Bergen and some distance back, looking for HMS *Suffolk* and our four destroyers. … Visibility was very poor near the coast where they were searching." (Later it was ascertained that the *Suffolk* was forty miles to seaward.) One Blenheim, whose pilot became sick, flew back to base, then the others followed.

The three Hudsons that were to be the second escort for *Suffolk* took off from Wick on time at 4:40, overlapping the time for the Blenheims. One of the Hudsons developed engine trouble and had to turn back; the other two could not locate the *Suffolk* due to heavy clouds and returned to base at 10:15. As the air force explained, "At this time there was no indication as to the whereabouts, course or speed of HMS *Suffolk*." We can see by their reports that the Royal Air Force specifically upheld their innocence in the Stavanger affair and blamed the Royal Navy.[7]

In any event, the two Hudsons meant for spotting and flare-dropping managed to take off at 1:15 A.M., and they landed twenty miles north of Stavanger. Then they flew south for fifteen miles, passing over the *Suffolk* and reaching the point of rendezvous at the proper time, 3:53. One aircraft signalled the cruiser, "Am ready to observe," but received no answer. The pilot then turned west and circled over the mouth of the fjord until he received the expected signal from *Suffolk* at 4:30. At that point he took off and at 4:35 dropped bombs and a flare, then flew west to take up a spotting position. A Junkers 88 now roared in and attacked him, and after the two briefly fought, the Hudson flew back to the *Suffolk* and attempted to make a spotting report. The pilot saw two Walrus planes in flight and was about to report them to the cruiser when the *Suffolk* opened fire at him with anti-aircraft guns. "*Suffolk* appeared to be paying no attention ..." declared air historians. After flying away from the cruiser, the Hudson continued to patrol around the ship for a while, then departed for base.[8]

Earlier, the *Suffolk* had sighted the *Seal* at 4:14 and five minutes later catapulted a "spotting" Walrus. A few minutes after that, *Suffolk's* captain observed rockets and anti-aircraft fire from the direction of the airfield, preventing identification of the flare that the Hudson had dropped to indicate the position of the target. By then, dawn was beginning to break, snow was falling, and land was barely visible. At 4:45 *Suffolk* reduced speed to fifteen knots and catapulted the second Walrus aircraft. "Unfortunately," wrote naval historians, "wireless communication with the aircraft could not be established, and in consequence the bombardment did not start until 0513. ... In three runs the *Suffolk* fired 217 rounds, causing casualties to the German naval air contingent and destruction of two gasoline dumps." Not much of a victory, it seems.[9]

However, while the *Suffolk* blasted away at the small base, German troops stationed at the facility sent a message to Berlin. General Jodl noted in his diary: "Stavanger is calling for help." Apparently no aid arrived, and the German troops managed to hold out.[10]

After completing the bombardment of 217 rounds at 5:58, Durnsford noticed two enemy aircraft shadowing him, started zig-zagging, and increased *Suffolk's* speed to thirty knots – almost full ahead. Forty minutes later he reduced speed to twenty-five knots, then increased to full once more, when at 8:25 the first bombs fell around the ship. "*Suffolk* apparently steamed west for some 35 miles before altering course to North. ... She was thus much further to south-west than would have been the case had she steamed northward from her bombardment position, as might have been expected from instructions given in the Admiralty signal, ..." noted the RAF. Actually Captain Durnsford and the four destroyers had steamed northward to intercept five enemy destroyers. Durnsford then sent a cypher message giving his position, course and speed to Headquarters, Coastal Command, but it was not received until five hours later. The same message reached Rosyth almost seventeen hours later, resulting in catastrophe.[11]

At 8:26 *Suffolk* telegraphers issued a message: "Enemy are dropping bombs," but gave no position, course or speed. This SOS did go through, and three Hudsons took off at 10:20. At 9:40 Captain Durnsford sent out a second plea describing persistent bombing attacks and gave his position, course and speed. Once more he signalled her exact course, and forty-five minutes later the air force notified the three Hudsons, who headed for the *Suffolk*. As navy historians described it, "the Suffolk was under continuous attack – both high level and dive bombing – for six hours and 47 minutes. ... At 1037 the ship suffered a direct hit by a heavy [1,000 pound] bomb, which caused very severe damage, put 'X' and 'Y' turrets out of action, reduced her speed to 18 knots and caused flooding to the extent of some 1,500 tons of water in 20 minutes. Repeated requests for fighter support, giving the position, failed to have any apparent effect."[12]

Finally, at 11:19 A.M. the Commander in Chief, Home Fleet, who was at sea, heard the bad news and ordered all Skuas at Harston, as well as two battlecruisers, to *Suffolk*'s assistance. At 11:40 Rosyth informed the *Suffolk*'s skipper that three Blenheims and three Hudsons should reach him by 12:30. As it turned out, the first three Blenheims failed to take off until 4:45 that afternoon. One of them and two of the Hudsons could not locate the *Suffolk*, "owing to lack of information as to her movements." RAF reports state further that "The reinforcing flight of three Blenheims failed to locate its objective and returned after searching for an hour and a quarter."[13]

Unremitting bomb blasts on the *Suffolk* continued. By 1:05 P.M. both steering motors were out of action, then repaired twenty minutes later; near misses blew in the lower deck scuttles and pierced the ship's side, causing further flooding. Six hours after the Germans initiated bombing of *Suffolk*, the three Hudsons made it to the scene, but before they arrived, three Junkers 88s zoomed in and attacked them; however, the Hudsons drove them off. When the fighters reached the spot where the *Suffolk* was being heavily attacked, they found themselves being shot at by the cruiser. "The Navy did not accept our recognition signals. This was probably due to the number of enemy aircraft in the vicinity," explained the RAF.[14]

Undaunted by the feisty German planes and friendly fire, the Hudsons stayed and chased away two Dorniers. Next arrived three British Skuas to relieve the Hudsons, who headed home. (At that time the fighters had limited fuel and range and had to relieve each other.) Additional British fighters appeared – nine in all by 2:30 – but they could not prevent four further attacks on the cruiser. Captain Durnsford later remarked that "the fighters in pursuit of the enemy appeared to have left the overhead area unguarded." One could hardly blame the pilots, who were being shot at by the *Suffolk*.[15]

In all, the *Suffolk* endured thirty-three attacks with eighty-two bombs; and at the last, with the engine room flooded, she was steering by screw and attempting to get back to Scapa Flow. Seventeen sailors had been killed.[16]

To Captain Durnsford's relief, the two battlecruisers *Renown* and *Repulse* finally came into sight, prompting the exit of German bombers and the start of *Suffolk*'s trip home. "Eventually the *Suffolk* managed to struggle into Scapa on 18th April with her quarterdeck awash," wrote Commander in Chief, Home Fleet, Admiral Sir Charles Forbes.[17]

Understandably, the Royal Navy and the Royal Air Force criticised each other for the disaster of "Operation Duck," afterwards labelled by the RAF as "The Tragedy of Donald Duck." In reports about the whole mess, the air force wrote: "Both the ship and the telegraphist in the Hudson complained of the ineffectiveness of wireless connection and the difficulty of getting signals through. This may have been due to the fact that the telegraphists were naval personnel and not familiar with the layout and operation of the W/T set in the Hudson." In the early months of World War II the different branches of the British armed forces had not learned to cooperate closely and at the same time had not learned much about each other's technical functions, such as wireless equipment, but they soon did. Lack of sea-air cooperation, according to author S. W. Roskill, "contributed to bringing us, for the second time in the present century, to the very edge of the abyss of defeat at sea. ..." As the war progressed, the Navy and Air Force "joined hands ... in a spirit which ... grew more and more comradely – and they did so just in time."[18]

By 1936 Hitler had built a large, superb air force with fast and accurate fighters and bombers, overpowering the few that Britain could muster to aid the *Suffolk* in April of 1940.

Rupert Lonsdale, who waited in the *Seal* while a madhouse took place overhead, remarked in his war diary that there was "a marked falling off of air activity after the raid on the 17th." By his sonar he could hear "grunts without number ... and it was thought that they came from explosions in the sea and on the shore." One wonders what he was thinking during all the noise. In his war diary recommendations Lonsdale wrote that he thought German supplies were reaching Stavanger either by sea or by rail from Egersund. As for the railway, he thought it could be cut where it passed close to Ogne Bugten. "It is hoped," said Lonsdale, "that *Seal* may be given the object of achieving this as soon as possible. With practice beforehand and suitable conditions of Moon and Sea it is thought that a demolition party could be landed in this vicinity from the Submarine." This looked like an excellent opportunity for the submarine crew to perform some worthwhile and exciting sabotage.

After thinking about Lonsdale's proposal, Captain Monzies of the Second Submarine Flotilla rendered the opinion that if details could be had from large-scale maps, any railroad bridges might be destroyed from seaward, bombarded by a submarine "who could get the range accurately by shore fix and who could dive if subjected to air attacks." His suggestion was vetoed by Vice Admiral Submarines Horton, who replied on 28 April that he had investigated destruction of a portion of the railway, but that the country in the vicinity of Ogne Bugten was flat and it was thought that the railway crossed no bridge of any appreciable size. "It appears, therefore, that this operation would be unlikely to result in any but a very temporary interruption of traffic. While I appreciate the desire of the Commanding Officer of *Seal* to carry out this enterprise, it is already evident that *Seal* will in all probability be employed on important minelaying operations during the next few weeks." Horton concluded the report by saying that he considered Lonsdale's patrol "excellently carried out" and that he commended the commanding officer for his skill and initiative.[19]

It seems almost negligent of Horton not to have attempted to cut a vital railway line used by the enemy, but the armed services owned pitifully few detailed maps, especially those of the intricate coast of Norway, with its numberless fjords and islands. "It appears that our main resource was the town plans in Baedecker's *Scandinavia.* ..." wrote T. K. Derry.[20]

So *Seal*, in spite of all efforts, did not succeed in hindering the Germans in Norway until her next patrol. Her assignment would be to stand in for a sister submarine, *Cachalot*, which had been rammed and nearly sunk, on a hazardous minelaying expedition in the Kattegat. At that time, the Germans occupied Danish and Norwegian shores, were heavily patrolling the Kattegat with planes and boats, and had laid a huge minefield there. With no escort for protection, a British submarine mission in this well-guarded enemy territory would have been close to suicidal: in fact, the commanding officer of *Seal*'s flotilla tried to persuade Max Horton to change his mind. Former sub commander Horton listened but would not budge from his position, which surprised no one, as he had gained a reputation for being a relentless hardliner. Horton's many ship sinkings in World War I had made him famous; and he was the first to raise a Jolly Roger flag (with skull and crossbones and number of sinkings) on his boat – bringing him the nickname "The Pirate."[21]

Lonsdale and his crew then departed Rosyth and steamed to Immingham, where they began the loading of fifty mines. Lonsdale alone realised what they were about to get into.

Notes

1. Manchester, *The Last Lion*, 638.
2. RNSM, Patrol Report HMS *Seal*, 6 April–19 April 1940.
3. NA, ADM 234/333, *Naval Staff History*, 44.
4. Previous sections from NA, AIR 15/202, Bombardment of Stavanger Aerodrome.
5. NA, AIR 15/202; Patrol Report HMS *Seal*, 6 April–19 April 1940.
6. RNSM, Patrol Report HMS *Seal*, 6 April–19 April 1940.
7. NA, AIR 15/202, Analysis of Air Cooperation provided for H.M.S. SUFFOLK—17/4/40, 6.
8. NA, AIR 15/202, Analysis of Operation "Duck", 9.
9. NA, ADM 234/333, *Naval Staff History*, 64, 65.
10. Hubatsch, "Tagebuch Jodl," in *Die Welt als Geschichte*, 376, as quoted in Kersaudy, *Norway 1940*, 144.
11. NA, AIR 15/202, Analysis of Operation "Duck", 14.
12. NA, ADM 234/333, *Naval Staff History*, 65.
13. NA, AIR 15/202, Analysis of Operation "Duck", 6.
14. Ibid., 5.
15. NA, ADM 234/333, *Naval Staff History*, 65, f.n. 3.
16. NA, ADM 199/2033, 17 April 1940, "Operation Duck."
17. NA, ADM 199/362, Despatch of the Commander-in-Chief, Home Fleet, 1 March–15 June 1940.
18. NA, AIR 14/202, Analysis of Operation "Duck"; Roskill, *The War at Sea*, 39.
19. RNSM, Patrol Report, HMS *Seal*, 6 April–19 April 1940.
20. Derry, *The Campaign in Norway*, 54.
21. *Navy News*, "Century of the Silent Service," Part Three, 1.

CHAPTER IV

Catastrophe

Lacking easy access to the Atlantic, German navy ships normally followed a route from Kiel northward, through the scattered islands of Denmark, then into the Kattegat and Skagerrak – waters south of Sweden and Norway. Laying mines in this enemy thoroughfare posed a daunting task for a highly visible British submarine. Two hundred and eighty-nine feet long and almost thirty feet wide, with six bow torpedo tubes and one Mark 12 gun on the aft deck, the *Seal* presented a target about half a football field in length and as high as a two-storey building. In order to place fifty mines, Lonsdale had to remain on the surface in mine-infested seas, constantly watching for planes and patrol boats.

"It was a very big submarine," said Stoker "Happy" Eckersall, "and we carried the mines in the casing – like a cupboard six to eight foot tall – enclosed within the outer hull. It was a long tunnel with rails, and the mines ran on the rails down to the stern of the boat. At a given time, when you're ready to lay them, you take in a bit of water to make up for the weight of each one as it goes off the end."[1]

Equipped with a plumb line and attached weight, the mines were dropped from the boat's stern; they sank towards the sea bed, and when the weight hit the ocean floor it stopped the descent of the mine, placing it about eight or ten feet below the surface.

Before leaving base, the *Seal* had undergone minor repairs in Blyth and taken on supplies: as part of the provisioning, certain luxuries in the food line, known as "comforts," were stowed aboard. "We had small luxuries like tinned fruit and things like that," explained Ernie Truman. "One little thing that was always good when we were out on patrols was a cup of soup in mid-morning. It was very nice." Ernie said they lived better on the boat than they did at home, where food shortages were growing acute.[2]

On 29 April 1940 *Seal* set out on what was to be her final voyage, a journey of five hundred miles. Once the boat had left port, Lonsdale informed his crew of their mission, and they responded with enthusiasm, hoping that this patrol would at last give them a chance to prove themselves at war. "We was at Immingham, all of us, in the control room," said Stoker First Class Taff

Harper, "and we had the mines aboard, all primed and ready for exploding, and the skipper said, 'Now, this is death or glory. I won't try to hide anything from you.'" Lonsdale explained to his men that they would be heading to an area where the *Narwhal* was laying mines, and that their sister sub had already been spotted by the Germans, creating double danger for the *Seal*. Everybody knew that the Kattegat would be teeming with patrol boats, planes, and minesweepers, and that if a torpedo, depth charge, shell, or bomb hit them, the fifty mines would blow them sky high. Each mine had power enough to sink a 30,000-ton ship. "Lonsdale was a great fellow, a smashing fellow," recalled Harper. "He thought more of his crew than he did himself, and he was a religious man. I think the rest of the crew would have followed him anywhere, 'cos mind, he called a spade a spade."[3]

ERA (Engine Room Artificer) Ernie Truman, head of the minelaying crew, commented: "Actually, it was just like an ordinary day. True, it was the first time we had ever taken in mines really seriously, but there didn't seem to be anything extraordinary. We were all ready to go off on patrol, and that was it."[4]

After four days sailing, *Seal* arrived on 3 May at a location off the northern tip of Denmark, called the Skaw. Here they awaited news of the *Narwhal*, due to be heading back from her minelaying expedition in the Kattegat. No signal came in from her as dawn approached, so Lonsdale continued east early on 4 May.

After a short time, *Seal* lookouts spotted a submarine approaching: it turned out to be the *Narwhal*, who radioed the Admiralty that she had fired six torpedoes and made six hits. When they heard her message, the crew decided that *Narwhal* had been quite lucky, but at the same time had stirred up trouble for them, as the Germans would now be on guard. Using her Asdic equipment, *Narwhal* tapped out a Morse code message to *Seal*: "Good luck. You'll need it." After travelling on the surface to this point, Lonsdale decided to take the boat under; but before he could do so, he heard the ominous roar of approaching aircraft.[5]

Seal plunged into an emergency dive and had reached only thirty feet when a massive explosion shook the boat. "We got bombed by one of their planes," explained Harper. After a couple of seconds the crew realised that their boat was still descending, and at ninety feet the *Seal* stopped. Damage had been done, but not too serious: there were two leaks in the pressure hull – one over the main engines – and the forward hydroplane motor field coil had shifted. Luckily, the explosion hit safely away from the stern, where the mines were stored, and in five-and-a-half hours the crew managed to finish up the repairs. Lady Luck had saved them once again.[6]

"Then we carried on after the bomb attack," said Eckersall. "We had two [possible] places to put the mines: they generally give you two or three positions. We went to Position One to lay the mines, but a few minesweepers was running around, so we kept away from them and went to the next position, which was Number Two." Minelaying went without a hitch, according to Ernie Truman, but releasing the mines entailed a certain hazard, in that any accidental blow to the top of a mine could cause it to explode. But the crew knew their job well and did it expertly. "We laid our full complement of mines, hoping that Jerry [the Germans] would find them when he least expected or desired," commented Ernie.[7]

Remarkably, the *Seal* succeeded in placing fifty of the explosive devices between 9:00 and 9:45 in the morning, with German anti-submarine trawlers (converted fishing vessels) running all over the Kattegat. Immediately after the operation, Lonsdale headed the boat homeward, slowly and surreptitiously creeping along on a course different from the one he had earlier taken. Unfortunately, the return trip was to route *Seal* right through two lines of German mines, placed at forty-nine feet and ninety-eight feet below the surface, but *Seal*'s crew had no idea of their existence.

Using hydrophone listening equipment, the German trawlers, now searching for the submarine, occasionally stopped to hear more clearly, but *Seal* had Asdic as well as hydrophones and could tell when the trawlers stopped. An oscillator fitted inside a special dome under the hull emitted supersonic sound waves to locate objects in the water and ascertain their approximate distances for up to two miles. This could be done at almost 360 degrees around the boat – a big advantage for the British sailors, for the Germans had only noise-detecting hydrophones. Actually, the British submariners were using the earliest form of sonar.[8]

Accordingly, the *Seal* stopped at the same time as the overhead enemy and started at the same moment. By taking quick looks through the periscope, Lonsdale could ascertain, as the hours wore on, that the circle of enemy boats was narrowing. At three in the afternoon the captain sighted nine German torpedo boats, a more dangerous foe than the trawlers: these "E Boats" were equipped with torpedo tubes and carried depth charges as well as a depth charge thrower. In an attempt to evade the growing armada on the surface, Lonsdale steered the *Seal* towards the east, then north, then west, changing speed as he went.

At 6 P.M. the situation looked so threatening that Lonsdale ordered the boat down to about a hundred feet into a salt layer, then stopped the electric motors and all other noise-making equipment. A few minutes later, for no apparent reason, the boat began to move a few feet upward, then slightly downward. Back in the motor room Able Seaman Mickey Reynolds heard an odd scratching sound, somewhat like a wire scraping the boat. Reynolds passed the message forward to the control room, and a minute or so later the *Seal* once again became steady.

At 6.30 Ernie Truman, on watch in the control room, waited for his relief to show up, envisioning a hearty supper. "Owing, however, to the previous action, this meal was late and so was my relief. As these thoughts passed through my mind, there was a terrific explosion. Everybody wondered what had happened."[9]

"As we gathered in the after mess," said Mickey Reynolds, "there were plates and food on the tables, and everything ready – BANG. Everyone stood thinking for a split second it was a depth charge, but then to our dismay we heard the rush of air from the mining compartment and through the escape chamber, being compressed by the water rushing in where we had been holed." Tom Vidler, tired and hungry, had been looking forward to the main meal of the day: roast beef, two vegetables, prunes and custard. "I never got any food. Before I could grab a plate, WHAM! I was flung off balance and pitched right across the mess. The noise was nerve-shaking, and the explosion gashed a great gaping hole in the mining compartment, where I had been seconds before."[10]

"All ears were anxiously listening for the next one, everybody assuming that we were being depth-charged by the E Boats," explained Ernie. "However, none came, and the hydrophones could detect no surface craft in the vicinity." Suddenly there was pandemonium from aft, and the news was passed through that we were making water rapidly in the mining compartment."[11]

"Then the flood started to rise," explained Vidler, "and oilskin suits, rubber boots, loaves of bread – all began to float around the mess." Most of the crowd scrambled into the engine room, leaving Tom yelling for assistance to close the escape chamber hatch. Heavyweight boxing champion Happy Eckersall, standing in the engine room, ran aft to help Vidler and Reynolds, who were struggling with the several-hundred-pound door. "We wasn't weaklings," said Eckersall. "Vidler was a wrestler; I was a boxer. We was strong people, but we just couldn't make it shut. There was three of us at first, then five or six or seven, but we just couldn't get it because there was so much pressure there."[12]

"We got the hatch to within a half inch of latching, but that was the limit," added Vidler. "Then we let go of the hatch." At the same moment everyone else scrambled through the filthy, oily, debris-filled water into the motor room in the next compartment.

Attempting to escape along with his mates, Vidler started to climb through the door of the flooding mess, but mounting air pressure banged it shut on his chest, hurling him into the bread storage bin. The water surged higher as Vidler struggled out of the bread barge; then it picked him up and carried him feet first into a fierce whirlpool heading through an open hatch down to the machinery space below. Realising that he would be killed if the water sucked him into the lower area, Vidler hung on. "With a superhuman effort, finding handholds where I could, I managed to stay on the right side of that hatch. My arms ached."

A new tidal wave poured in, pulling off one of Vidler's boots and carrying an unknown fellow seaman along with it. "Until then, I thought I was alone, but Mickey Reynolds also had been trapped with me."

Just after giving up the attempt to shut the door to the mining compartment, Reynolds, aware that everyone else had rushed forward, concluded that he was the only one left in the mess area. "At least I thought so, and water was still coming in and the boat settling by the stern. The bulkhead door to the main motor room being closed, I looked around and said to myself, 'Well, you are trapped here.' I can still see in my mind's eye the whole of my family passing in front of my eyes, just like a slow-motion picture ..." Reynolds told himself that if he had to die, he would prefer to go ahead and drown, and "I tried to hold myself to the deck [floor], but the swirling waters brought me to the surface."

Vidler could see that the flood had carried Reynolds up almost to the maze of ceiling pipes, but then it hurled him against the rear bulkhead and pinned him there. "He was trying to keep his head above the foam."

Reynolds heard a voice yelling, "Are you okay, Mickey?" Reynolds shouted back that he was trapped, "and I saw it was Tom Vidler standing partially inside the manhole into the machinery space and heard him yell, 'Give me your hand.'" Reaching over, Vidler pulled Reynolds towards him, "but by this time we were settled in the mud by the stern," explained Mickey, "and the water was below the level of the bulkhead door." As Vidler described it, "We both threshed through the water, spluttering up towards the [motor room] door. With our eardrums bursting, we managed to get it open. The deserted motor room was dry."

Realising that they had to close the door they had just climbed through, the two soaked, exhausted men pulled with all their strength and by a miracle got the door, hanging downward, shut. "We were pretty well finished," said Vidler, "and we half-crawled up the incline to the engine room door but were much too weak to open it. We knocked feebly, and incredibly, the others heard us and opened the door."

"Some of the boys on the engine room side heard us," recalled Reynolds, "and helped us into the control room, where most of the crew were."

Lonsdale, amazed to see the two haggard and dripping sailors, greeted them and asked if the *Seal* was badly damaged – to give him some details. "The first part," related Reynolds, "we could only guess from the rush of water, and our second guess was a mine because of the amount of high explosive fumes with the rush of air and the silt which came in."

"Then Vidler and I were stripped, rubbed down, and wrapped in blankets from the wardroom – someone getting us some gear to put on. We also got a good tot of rum to warm us up. Maybe there were tears in my eyes, maybe I cried; I just can't remember, but we were all together and had a fighting chance."

As the two sailors tried to recover, they could hear torpedo boats thrashing the surface overhead. Reynolds thought that the Germans surely had heard the mine explosion and would watch to see if any bodies floated up, then finish them off with depth charges. "We listened tensely as they passed over us, waiting for the depth charges, but all we heard was the chug, chug of the engines, all the time being plotted by our Asdic. No one dared to make a sound, in case it would be heard by those above."[13]

"Conjecture now arose," said Ernie Truman, "as to what had happened, and it was finally decided that we had selected that one spot on the ocean bed to sit on a submerged mine." Apparently the *Seal* had snagged a mine mooring cable, and after she stopped, the mine floated forward and hit the boat. "The mine exploded underneath the ship, damaging the propeller and the rudder, and the force of the explosion blew all the silt away, which then came down on top of us. That's why she was trapped by the stern." Had Lonsdale kept going, he probably could have lost the deadly device. Happy Eckersall commented that "It was lucky we didn't have any mines on board."[14]

"It was then that we decided to wait for darkness before attempting to surface, in case the enemy should still be in the vicinity," added Truman. Every activity was extremely difficult in the sloped position, but the *Seal* remained there for two hours. By 7:00 P.M. they had been submerged for sixteen hours, and most of the crew lay in their bunks to conserve energy, preserve quiet, and reduce their intake of oxygen, which was beginning to diminish. The hydrophone operator had stopped hearing sounds of torpedo boats – an enormous relief for everyone. "When our Captain was sure that they had moved on, he ordered up spirits, which was very welcome, and I had quite a few snifters from the boys," said Reynolds. "The Captain then told us to rest and preserve what little air was still in the boat, and we would try in an hour or so to surface."[15]

As the men sat or lay quietly they began to notice the stench – a noxious mixture of sweat, cooked food, diesel fumes, human waste, and disinfectant. Additionally, they were starting to feel the debilitating effects of excess carbon dioxide and low oxygen. "I had hardly any breath and no energy," recalled Tom Vidler. To get their minds off their terrifying predicament, the men tried to occupy themselves as best they could. "You know how submariners are," said Reynolds, "they like a gamble; so some played cards, and some just rested, but no one was allowed to sleep."[16]

At around eight o'clock Lonsdale told the crew that he would make a surfacing attempt at about ten, to be sure that they emerged before dawn, which was about three o'clock in the morning. Lonsdale ordered all code and cypher books placed into a weighted bag, ready to be taken up to the bridge at the last moment. "One of the officers, with amazing devotion to duty, tried to burn the ship's confidential papers in the middle of the engine room," explained Vidler. "Someone tried to strike a match, but it would not light in the oxygen-starved air."

At 10:30 with everyone in position, the skipper gave the order to surface using full power with the main motors, as well as blowing ballast from the main ballast tanks. As the engines roared, the *Seal* began to slowly lift, but the angle only increased, and Lonsdale ordered motors and blowing stopped, at which time the *Seal* resumed a slightly better angle. "The after compartment was completely flooded, and at the same time, we were buried in silt," explained Truman. "That's why we couldn't surface by just blowing tanks."[17]

The crew by this time were struggling to breathe, and any movements were now requiring hard physical effort. Water in the aft section had increased the air pressure, condensation was forming, and carbon dioxide levels were rising. As Vidler recalled, "It was past midnight, and the mental effect of these failures, coupled with the lack of air, made all of us sleepy and dazed." However, no one wavered in his belief that Lonsdale would get them out of the crisis.

Thinking that other methods might succeed, their skipper ordered a second surface attempt. He planned to blow the little air that was left into various tanks and to release the drop keel. Removal of the eleven-ton weight would aid the boat's surfacing in a dire emergency; but after the keel fell off, the boat would have no way to submerge again.[18]

"At 2200 hours diving stations were called," said Truman. "Every effort was made to lighten the boat. The drop keel was released and ancillary tanks blown, but still we did not move in the desired direction. These actions took us the best part of three hours to accomplish and at 0100 hours on May 5th, things seemed pretty hopeless." The *Seal* had merely shifted into a more precarious angle of about forty-five degrees.[19]

Throughout the ordeal Lonsdale remained unruffled, though the boat's position had become more difficult than ever. Believing that one last effort could be attempted, he sent two men down into the engine room to connect a couple of small reserve air tanks to the main blowing system. The pair made a valiant attempt to accomplish the task, but their exertions failed. Now that nothing remained to surface the boat, gloom set in. "The Skipper called the crew together in the control room," recalled Reynolds, "and told us we had been in some tight spots before and had come through, and with God's help would do so again. So he thought it was time to say the Lord's Prayer together. I don't believe there was one man there who did not say it, and maybe another with it."[20]

After the prayer Lonsdale had an idea – something that should have been obvious. He ordered all unoccupied men to the torpedo room in the forward end of the boat, in desperate hopes of forcing down the bow and dislodging the *Seal* from the mud. "By this time," said Reynolds, "the air was so bad, it was impossible to breathe properly. You could exhale all right, but breathing – you were just gasping, or at least that is how I remember it."

Mickey, along with his mates, recalled his struggle to climb to the torpedo room. "The angle of the boat being such ... it was impossible to walk to the far end without aid, so someone in the torpedo space dropped a heaving line down to us, and by this means most of us were able to move forward. As he struggled up the rope, Reynolds noticed that one of his mates had fallen beside the doorway of the officers' toilet and heard him say, "if I have to die, I will die here."[21]

"We rigged this rope," explained Taff Harper, "from the bow to the control room. I got halfway up from the bow, between the control room and the forward end. I couldn't go any further – I was too puffed." It took Taff half an hour of climbing to get there, "breathing, breathing, breathing, and with all this foul air." After the explosion, the normal submarine stink had grown even worse: along with cooked cabbage, diesel oil and battery aromas, there was now cordite from the explosion and evidence of humans passing wind. "They had had nothing to eat for twenty-four hours," added Taff, who had climbed to a position opposite the freezer. The sight of it reminded him that there was a big hunk of beef inside. "Beef was very scarce in those days, and I was wondering what the devil we could do with this when we resurfaced. I was going to find the cook, give him the beef, and let him prepare it for the whole crew." Taff could practically taste the meal.

Along with thoughts of roasted meat, the exhausted sailor started to worry about his wife, for they had been married less than a year. Taff did not know whether he had left his young bride pregnant, and he grew concerned about what would happen to her if she had a child. "We had no fear that we weren't going to surface, but the thought was there: 'All right, if we don't, we don't.' We were all professional submariners and had had experiences on various subs, so there was no panic."[22]

But as the minutes dragged by, hope diminished, and many began to think that death was inevitable.

Ernie Truman, ever ebullient, envisioned putting on his dress uniform and meeting Greta Garbo when the submarine made it to Sweden. "I felt convinced we would be fine."[23]

As the crew sat and lay sprawled in the forward end, Lonsdale gave orders for motors to go slow, then half-speed, then full ahead, at the same time blowing the remaining bit of air into the saddle tanks. Said Reynolds, "I think we all knew it was the final effort." Taff Harper recalled that "We were on the last gasp of high pressure air when we started seeing the movement on the depth gauge. It seemed like hours and hours for it to shift just half an inch. Then it started moving a bit quicker: you can just imagine the relief of everybody."[24]

Astonishingly, the huge submarine shook, shuddered, broke loose from the sea floor, and levelled herself. However, all the water in the lower levels of the stern rushed forward, submerging parts of the main motors. "Here she hung in the balance, seeming neither to rise nor to sink," said Truman. "Anxious moments, as we had now used our last high pressure air, and if she slipped back now we were finished." Even so, the boat gradually rose until she reached the top, to the intense joy of everyone. "It must have been like a whale surfacing," said Happy Eckersall. "You know how they spout up." Taff Harper and his friend Martin Fitzgerald stood waiting in the engine room for Lonsdale to open the upper hatch in the conning tower; and after he pushed it outward, Taff asked, "What's that funny smell, Fitz?" His friend replied, "Taffy, my little Welsh friend, that funny smell is fresh air." As the sea-scented air surged into the boat, it brought relief, excitement, and in some cases violent headaches and nausea.

Signalman Waddington and the lookouts followed Lonsdale onto the bridge, and Telegraphist Charlie Futer quickly sent a high priority message to Vice Admiral Submarines Horton, then received his acknowledgement and switched off the wireless transmitter. The message read:

MOST IMMEDIATE – CONFIDENTIAL
My position MBAQ 4711. Submarine filled with water stern to 129 Bulkhead, caused by mine or depth charge. FD7 laid in 057 degrees 033 degrees 30" North, 011 degrees 035 degrees 30" East. Confidential books destroyed. No casualties. Am making for the Swedish Coast and will try for Goteborg.[25]

Henderson then grabbed the three bags of code books and Signal Publications, toted them to the bridge and heaved them over the side. At the same time, a group of sailors dismantled the Asdic equipment, then demolished the pieces with hammers and threw them into the sea.

"Now our position was this," said Truman. "We had our engines in working order, but our steering gear, being in the flooded compartment, was useless. Our bows were pointing the wrong way towards Denmark, so our only hope was to go astern to Sweden, which we could see about ten to fifteen miles distant."[26]

"We were in a position so the engines could go in reverse (we had reverse engines on the *Seal*)," said Eckersall. "So they changed over the crankshaft and started the engines up, and we carried on, but we had one engine running fairly fast and one just running slowly. We was trying to make for Göteborg." Eckersall recalled that after they surfaced, everybody went back to more or less minimal routine. "I'd say there was no panic anywhere. Everybody had the same idea that the captain would get us out of it – they had so much faith in him."

Once the engines were again humming, Happy made his way back aft to the crew's living quarters, which were fairly accessible by then; he took from his locker a wallet containing photographs of his wife and baby boy and put it in his pocket. "I had a little bottle of rum in there, as well, and I put that in also." Then an announcement came that a few men could go to the bridge for fresh air, but they must take either a life belt or a Davis

Submarine Escape Apparatus. Happy climbed to the bridge and brought out his bottle of rum, offering some to Smith, who was leaning on the starboard side of the bridge rail, facing inboard. "The next thing I saw was the plane coming at us from the bow. He let fly straight away with tracer bullets. As you know, with a tracer there's one tracer bullet and then six bullets, and then another tracer. They just whistled past our ears."[27]

Everyone on the bridge ducked or ran for cover, and Lonsdale grabbed a Lewis machine gun and started firing at the plane; Gunner Jaunty Mayes snatched a second one and followed suit. After a few moments, though, Lonsdale's gun jammed, so he ran over to the deck gun and fired it several times, missing the plane. Jaunty's gun had ceased to function as well.

Along with the others, Eckersall frantically searched for a sheltered place to hide. "I dropped into an oil fuel galley, then into the pressure hull after the plane made the first strike. I was fairly safe there. Then another plane came over, and inside the bush of the propeller he had a cannon: he fired a couple of shots, and of course, it went through us like paper." Hitting the superstructure noisily, the shells and bullets flew in all directions. Of the ten people on deck, two were wounded, but Smith, who was leaning on the rail, simply disappeared. "He must have caught it in the back," commented Eckersall. "We never saw any more of him." A bullet hit First Lieutenant Terence Butler in the leg, forcing him to lie on the bridge for a few moments before he painfully crawled down below. Able Seaman Jack Murray crumpled to the deck with a long piece of shrapnel in his thigh. Two bombs from the Arado bashed the sea but missed the *Seal* and the plane's cannon shells whipped into the conning tower.[28]

A second Arado buzzed in to continue the onslaught, dropping two more bombs closer to the wallowing submarine and riddling the tower with machine-gun and cannon fire. At the same time, German subchaser UJ 128 hove into view and fired a warning shot far in front of *Seal*'s bow. The heavily listing boat's engines had frozen up, and she had no steering or power of any kind. To add to the desperate situation, a third plane arrived, let loose more bombs, and punctured the saddle tanks with a barrage of cannon shells. As Lonsdale considered his hopeless situation, he started to believe that the time had come to give up; then he heard one of his men saying that surrender was now in order. With that, the commander requested the white wardroom tablecloth, climbed with it up to the deck, and waved it. "We could all have wept," said Tom Vidler, "as the skipper asked for the white tablecloth ... but he had no choice."[29]

"In my opinion," said Mickey Reynolds, "it was a miracle that the Captain was not shot, as the voice pipe he used to keep in touch with the control room was cut clean in two by cannon fire. I think the Captain was an inspiration to everyone on board by his coolness and his never-say-die spirit."[30]

With desperate speed the men jumped into a second round of equipment destruction, smashing the navigation and communication apparatus and anything else that might prove valuable to the Germans. Though the entire crew believed that their boat would soon sink, they energetically wrecked everything possible, then climbed topside to await their fate.

Notes

1. Happy Eckersall, telephone interview with author, 1 May 2000.
2. Ernie Truman, interview with author, Bournemouth, England, 22 September 2000.
3. Harper interview, 3 February 2002.
4. Ernie Truman, telephone interview with author, 24 August 2001.
5. Happy Eckersall, interview with author, Portsmouth, England, 9 July 2000.
6. Warren and Benson, *Will Not We Fear*, 46–61; Harper interview, 3 February 2002.
7. Eckersall interview, 9 July 2000; RNSM, Ernie Truman, "The Epic of the Seal."
8. Lipscomb, *The British Submarine*, 16.
9. Truman, "Epic."
10. Tom Vidler, "True Life Drama," *Weekend* magazine, 5–9 December 1962; Mickey Reynolds, "HMS *Seal*."
11. Truman interview, 22 September 2000.
12. Vidler, "True Life Drama"; Eckersall interview, 9 July 2000.
13. Reynolds, "HMS *Seal*"; Vidler, "True Life Drama."
14. Truman, "Epic."
15. Truman, "Epic"; Reynolds, "HMS *Seal*."
16. Reynolds, "HMS *Seal*"; Vidler, "True Life Drama."
17. Truman, "Epic."
18. Eckersall interview, 9 July 2000.
19. Truman, "Epic."
20. Reynolds, "HMS *Seal*."
21. Ibid.
22. Taff Harper, interview with author, 18 November 2000.
23. *Bournemouth Daily Echo*, 19 August 2000.
24. Reynolds, "HSM *Seal*"; Harper interview, 18 November 2000.
25. NA, ADM 156/283, Exhibit "D."
26. Truman, "Epic."
27. Eckersall interview, 9 July 2000.
28. Ibid.
29. Vidler, "True Life Drama."
30. Reynolds, "HMS *Seal*."

CHAPTER V

The Germans Arrive

"The next thing we saw was a ship," Happy continued. "We had tried to use the gun to put drogues on [buckets hanging over the sides in the water to pull a boat the other way]. But the gun swivelled partly around to the starboard, and this ship that came up was a subchaser, and he put a shot across our bow because our gun was pointed at him." (The captain had actually fired a routine warning shot.)[1]

While patrolling for enemy submarines Captain Lang of UJ 128 had caught sight of an Arado seaplane at about 5:00 A.M. at dawn on 5 May. As the plane approached, a radio message came in from the Arado's captain: "Please help me. I have a surfaced submarine, and I'm going to show you where it is." Lang replied, "I will follow you."

Lang began to run at full speed in the direction of the plane and at the same time sent a message to the group commander: "Airplane reported a surfaced enemy submarine. I'm going after it." At 5:40 Lang noticed a big oil slick about a thousand feet in diameter on the starboard side of the minesweeper. (The *Seal* crew had earlier blown out some fuel in hopes of getting off the seabed.) Immediately afterwards, the captain spotted two planes circling and headed towards his target. "At approximately 70 degrees a big submarine on the surface. We sounded the submarine alarm. At the same time we spotted that often observed Swedish plane, a Junkers 86, and at the next opportunity we are going to attack it, since our experience has shown that it always shows up when British submarines are nearby…"

Lang could see machine-gun fire and little clouds of exploding ammunition near the German planes and guessed that the sub was defending herself. "It seems that there was a white flag pulled up on the periscope of the submarine. We approached … in such a manner that we were always looking at it from the side. We were trying to get into such a position that it could not fire a torpedo." *Seal*'s number, 37M, and her name could be easily read by the German crew, making it obvious that she was British.

By now most of *Seal*'s crew stood on deck in their life preservers waiting to be rescued. "We already had prepared the line to tow the submarine, so we could immediately start to salvage it," wrote Lang. "A group of people, commandos, under direction of Lieutenant Nolte ... was sent at 6:50 to board the submarine with instructions to fasten the tow rope." Nolte had orders to bring six men at a time over to the subchaser, guarding the remainder to prevent them from scuttling their boat. "The last ten men were to be instructed that if they tried to sink the boat, they would be certain to die with it."[2]

Young Leutnant zur See Nolte, first watch officer of UJ 128, who was sent over to the *Seal* as head of a commando unit, wrote his own account of his activities: "I received orders from my captain to go with a party of three men to the English submarine in a motor dinghy, board her, and save the English crew. We were supposed to do everything in our power to prevent the sinking of that submarine. To make sure that none of the English people were sinking their boat, we were supposed to keep ten [of their] crew members down in the submarine."

Nolte picked as his team three sailors: Dunekake, Banduhu and Wilkes. "We were equipped with pistols. As we boarded the English boat, we found out that it was leaning a little to the port side, and the stern of the ship was somewhat underwater. The biggest part of the crew had gathered on deck, and they were wearing life preservers as well as breathing devices." Nolte asked them to point out the chief engineer and went to speak to him. Clark informed Nolte that there were two wounded men on the deck.

Nolte located the two – Butler and Murray – and after talking to them, ascertained that one (Butler) was the first watch officer. "I ordered the boarding party to save these two first, and then I proceeded with the chief engineer to the inside of the boat." First Nolte made a quick trip around the submarine, sending any crew members that he found to the top and ordering all officers to go on the inspection with him. "I had to assume that the British plan of sinking the boat would be done by the officers, and therefore I wanted to keep an eye on them." Nolte then ordered his commandos, except Dunekake, to return to UJ 128.

In a quick assessment of the sub's condition, Nolte decided that it was "completely undamaged, and they even had a few torpedoes on board." He asked the chief engineer why the rear engine room hatch was closed and was told that there was water behind it, as they had hit a mine. "By now I had all the officers gathered around me, with the exception of the first watch officer, who was wounded, and who in the meantime had transferred to the subchaser. I decided that at this time I was going to ... take the officers and meet with them in the control room. I wanted to keep an eye on this room, from which the sinking of the boat could be most easily arranged."

"In the control room I found, lo and behold, a technical chief petty officer and other petty officers busily turning some valves and such, evidently at the instructions of the chief engineer." As far as Nolte was concerned they were turning valves to flood the *Seal*. He had already noticed that the submarine was leaning more and more to the port side.

"I took a good look around in the control room and noticed a light signal system above the valve they were manipulating. Evidently these were to indicate whether the valves were open or closed." Nolte ordered the chief engineer (Clark) to close the two tanks on the port side.

While Nolte worked in the control room he ordered Dunekake down into the control room and told him to search the boat's interior to be sure no one was hiding. "Now one of the [*Seal's*] officers approached with a bottle of rum, and he asked me whether I would go in the mess deck and have a drink with them. It was navy rum, supposed to be very good in England." Nolte declined the invitation to go into the mess area, as he knew that his chief task was to prevent any scuttling attempts. "But, however, I had nothing against a glass of rum. We had a taste in the control room, and it tasted very, very good." (Taff Harper explained that it was "Pusser's" brand navy rum – ninety percent proof.)

Dunekake returned, reporting to Nolte that there were no other people inside the boat except those in the control room. "I sent him up to the deck again with specific orders not to allow anyone inside the boat."

Meanwhile, *Seal* continued to list to the port side, despite the closing of the valves. "A British sailor hollered down that the German ship was now alongside, and we were to come up on deck and transfer to the subchaser. The British officers and petty officers wanted to get to the deck through the tower hatch, but I would not let them. The chief engineer told me that the sub would be capsizing in about ten minutes and asked whether I wanted to go down with her, so I told him, 'In that case, we will all drown together.'"

Then Nolte inquired whether the electric motors were operable and was told that they were sitting in water and had shorted out. "According to my observations from a while ago, that was probably the truth, because they were situated in the aft compartment, and that was full of water." Clark told Nolte that the diesels wouldn't work either, because after the mine exploded, the crew had tried to use the diesels, but the engines couldn't get any oil because the lubrication tank was flooded. "Evidently, there was nothing we could do with the engines."

Nolte told Clark to put air pressure into the port tanks, but the lieutenant replied that there was almost no air left in the high pressure air tanks. "Meanwhile, the boat tipped a little more, so that I actually slipped off my seat. They smiled and asked, 'Should we go up topside now?'" Instead of replying, the youthful German officer demanded that they blow air into the flooded tanks in spite of the low pressure, and this was done. "It was enough to right the boat by several degrees; the captain of the UJ 128 observed this and prepared to tow the sub."

Nolte had decided to wait for a bit longer "to make sure that the boat was kept at the same even keel. During this time I allowed the officers to pack some of their things from a nearby closet: they put everything into suitcases." While the officers loaded their bags, Nolte asked them about the mine accident and was told that they had hit a mine at about a hundred feet of depth. Evidently the anchor cable of the mine had been snagged by their rudder, they explained, because some of them had heard a scraping noise. "When the mine exploded, water came into the electric motor room and into the aft lubrication oil tank."

The officers told Nolte that at the time of the accident there were two men in the motor room, and when the crew closed the hatches they accidentally locked them inside. The pair was later able to escape and had the good sense to close the hatch after leaving the motor room. "They were down on the sea floor until 3:00, and all attempts to rise to the surface were futile. They had given up all hope of saving themselves. As a last resort, they were able to blow all the fuel to the outside, and that made the boat so much lighter that all of a sudden, they rose to the surface at about a thirty-degree angle. They then tried to get the diesels going and escape into Swedish territory." (Blowing the fuel had in fact been done when the keel was dropped, but the boat refused to rise.) Continuing their explanation, the officers declared that their efforts to get going failed because one diesel shorted out, and the other was able to function only in reverse at a slow speed, causing the boat to run in a circle; then German seaplanes had spotted them and attacked. At that moment the two sailors were wounded by bullets. "One of the planes took the commander off the submarine, and another took a petty officer with them, just before the subchaser came on the scene. Airplanes again shot at them, just before the subchaser arrived." Nolte noted that the sailors' story jibed with what he had observed.

In the control room Nolte saw scraps of dirty paper strewn all over the deck, and he assumed that these were secret codes and information. "Without coaching, they told me they had had plenty of time to destroy whatever secrets were on the boat and that we would not find anything of any importance. That made sense to me; however, as we found out later on, it was not true."

In his inspection of the control room Nolte saw that the torpedo aiming device had been damaged with a hammer, "but it was still very recognisable. The British had had enough time to destroy all the other instruments I could see from here. I could not make an exact estimate, because I did not want to leave the control room."

Seal's officers asked Nolte what he planned to do with their submarine and declared that towing would be impossible, for in about two hours it would sink. "My answer to that was something I remembered from my study of English in school: 'Wait and see.'" As they all stood in the control room, Nolte noticed that one of the intact depth gauges was holding pretty steady, and at that time decided to get the rest of the crew off the boat. Before giving orders to leave, Nolte had them blow the remainder of the high-pressure air into the port diesel tanks. "The British were very polite, and they offered to let me leave the sub first, but I decided that it was not necessary, because I felt quite at home here now. I again assured myself that the tanks were closed and then left the boat, as well."[3]

Watching *Seal* from the bridge, Captain Lang remarked, "We could see that the submarine was leaning more and more towards one side, so it could be in danger of tipping over. For this reason we moved alongside the sub and took the crew that were standing on deck. They were separated by enlisted men, petty officers, and officers." The transferring of the *Seal* crew to UJ 128 was then accomplished.

When all had boarded the subchaser, Lang sent one last commando equipped with special tools to close the damaged hatch in the tower and to attach a buoy to the *Seal*'s tower hatch with ninety metres of line. As work progressed, the boat tilted more and more. "The tower manoeuvre had to be executed with a great deal of care, since the rudder of this very heavy submarine was jammed at the starboard position. In addition, some wrecked equipment, maybe the starboard planes, were visible under water. In spite of that, it was possible to slowly increase the towing speed, so that with revolutions of nine sea miles [per hour] we were actually making five sea miles ..." At 6:55 A.M. the journey towards Denmark had begun.[4]

"We was all tired and had a stinking headache," recalled Happy Eckersall. "The German crew was quite decent to us, though." As soon as the *Seal* mates had scrambled aboard the German boat, they were treated to some hot soup and bread, then they collapsed in their quarters to sleep. "I went up to the toilets, up on the upper deck, and one of the Germans came with me," added Eckersall. "I looked out, and they was towing the *Seal*, and she was over on the port side, and there was about five foot of the conning tower showing – that's all. She was right down at the stern, and she was being towed along: the German seamen had a big axe ready to cut through the rope if it should go anywhere."[5]

Nolte, meanwhile, had been ordered by the captain to look after the crew and to get as much information from them as possible. After allowing the haggard sailors to eat, he separated the officers, petty officers, and remainder of the crew into different compartments and later offered them some beer and liquor, "because I had discussed that with the captain and acted accordingly."

Nolte then outlined what the prisoners told their interrogator. "Evidently there were two other boats of the same class in action somewhere around here, one man told us. But he was slightly under the influence of alcohol." Others testified that after they arrived in the mined area, they managed to lay their own mines. "There was some argument about that; however, that would be highly possible, because we found no mines on board. They said that the mine that they hit was German, because they knew the effects of their own mines."

"The officers insisted that they travelled by day submerged, and at night it was very difficult to stay on the surface, because the nights are very light here. Everyone had a great deal of respect for our airplanes, but they insisted that German army reports about ship sinkings and damage by airplanes was highly exaggerated." To prove their point, the officers said that they had seen ships at sea that had been described by German propaganda as having been sunk.

Nolte wrote that the *Seal* men had much respect for German depth charges, "but that is probably true with all submarine people around the world. On their own, they started talking about our magnetic mines, and they insisted that they also had magnetic mines, but they admitted that the Germans' were much better." However, the British officers informed Nolte that soon they would be using equally good magnetic mines, because they had salvaged a German one, taken it apart, and examined it.

"About German losses they were not too well informed: for instance, they insisted that England had never thought about occupying Norway. The only thing they wanted to do was to go into Norwegian waters and lay mines." (An accurate statement, as Britain had attempted to thwart German ore ships.) Nolte's report said that the prisoners admired the way the Germans were conducting the war, "especially since we had the guts to go against what was always the rules of the sea. ... That, they had never figured on."

Nolte said the officers considered Chamberlain a "grand old man," but they didn't have much sympathy for Churchill, although "he had a lot of energy and probably was the right man." One of the prisoners' complaints against the Germans had to do with the English-speaking radio announcer (Lord Haw-Haw) who broadcast only partial lists of captured British military personnel and pronounced their names incorrectly. Not only did the Germans not give the information often enough, they griped, but "it was not fair and a cheap way to tie the British to the German radio." Continuing their argument, the officers told Nolte that the British announced POW information differently: if they mentioned only a few names of German prisoners, it was because they had captured just a few.

"All prisoners," wrote Nolte, "were surprised by the good, fair treatment they received on board. To the officers I pointed out the *Cossack* incident [seizure of the *Altmark*], where the British behaved differently, and they all fell into an embarrassed silence. Then they tried to convince me that the fierce German propaganda by Dr Göbbels was not true at all."

"All were of one mind: they had counted on a fourteen-day furlough when they arrived in Britain, but now the furlough was messed up. They explained that they had not had any free time for a very long while."[6]

Lang, attempting to increase UJ 128's speed, found it impossible, as the bulky sub kept veering to the left, endangering the towrope. He was worried that British submarines might be approaching and ordered his entire crew to battle stations. After fighting a heavy current that was taking him near Swedish neutral waters, he steered away from the swift areas and continued his course towards Tönneberg Bank, the nearest shallow region. At 8:19 Lang sent a radio message to BSO (Befehlshaber der Sicherung der Ostsee, Commander of Baltic Operations) informing them of his prize and requesting escorts.

Shortly after 10:00 A.M., a four-person patrol boat and two other boats from the 13th Patrol Flotilla came rushing in at full speed to get in on the action. As the small flotilla slowly steamed along, Lang's lookouts spotted a periscope, and the three patrol boats dropped eight depth charges: at the same time two planes appeared and were told that UJ 128 was being attacked by a submarine. They could see no sign of the sub, which had disappeared, and they continued to fly overhead.

At 10:35 the escort boats asked Lang if they could place lines under the submarine to keep it from sinking but "we denied them, since we thought that this was a manoeuvre with big problems, and the submarine was a large vessel. Another thing was that we had not observed any changes in the condition of the submarine, so it would mean that these patrol boats would be in great danger by executing a manoeuvre like that. Also, it would have been very time-consuming." Lang added in his report that the manoeuvres and helpfulness of the boats and planes were "very commendable."

Twenty minutes later the salvage vessel arrived, equipped with a portable air pump, and Lang radioed her to stay close, while the escort boats remained vigilant for Allied submarines.

"During the course of the next hour, several other minesweepers, patrol boats, and so forth, joined us – altogether seventeen vessels. Largely due to unseamanlike manoeuvring, they were jeopardising the tow procedure. M 1106, a minesweeper, in spite of my urgent signal, could not be persuaded to slow down when it got close to the submarine." Highly irritated, Lang sent him a message saying, "Please make sure you cease your reckless procedures near me."

Suddenly, a whaling boat arrived with a message for Lang to follow a certain course and speed, but the captain disagreed. "For one thing, it was not possible to go at that speed, because I was towing the submarine. Only on my boat could one actually judge what the best speed would be." As for the course, it would take them into deep water, where there would be danger of losing their prize, and Kortvettenkapitän Rösing, who previously had arrived on board, concurred with Lang's reasoning. "Based on these observations ... I did not obey those orders." It seems that everybody wanted to get in on the act of towing *Seal*.[7]

Korvettenkapitän Hans Rösing, submarine expert and commanding officer of the 7th U-Flotilla, had arrived via a seaplane and was transferred to UJ 128 in a lifeboat. "He agreed [in regard to the submarine] that nothing should be changed. Because the wind and sea were increasing, it was decided to go into Frederikshavn, and a message was sent to BSO to that effect, saying, '*Seal* will arrive 1600 at Frederikshavn. Please clear a dock. Boat is in good shape. Signed, Rösing.'" The entry into Frederikshavn harbour proceeded smoothly. "At 1645, shortly before entering port, we transferred Kpt. Rösing and his sailors to the submarine, and after we set the German flag on top of the white flag and British flag on the periscope, we turned over the towing to a towboat." At 5:55 P.M. on 5 May, Lang's boat tied up alongside the *Rugard*, where a bevy of excited reporters waited to memorialise the astonishing event.[8]

By the time *Seal*'s towing ship arrived at the dock in Denmark, word of her capture had flashed throughout Germany, and newsmen rushed to interview two of the Arado pilots the minute they landed at Aalborg, a short distance from Frederikshavn.

Karl Schmidt, captain of the first attacking Arado, told a radio reporter about his contact with the *Seal* and his taking of Captain Rupert Lonsdale into custody. The next day, 6 May 1940, German radio (as picked up by the BBC) announced that "a British submarine, which had been damaged by a mine, was discovered by two German planes on May 5 in the Kattegat. ... You hear now a report from the German naval airmen ... who took part in the action and how the submarine, which could not submerge due to mine damage, was captured and how the commander was made prisoner. Thus the enemy was prevented from scuttling his ship."

"After they had discovered the submarine he [Schmidt] fired from his machine-gun ... and after he had fired one round of bullets a man suddenly appeared on the conning tower waving a white piece of cloth – it was a white shirt. Then three or four other men appeared." Schmidt continued: "I said to my pilot, 'Let's land and see what's going on here.'" They darted down onto the water and fired a second time with the machine gun, "in order to keep them from getting any strange ideas, because a plane landing beside a submarine is in danger – it is quite defenceless and helpless – but they did nothing of the sort, only raised their arms and waved their white pieces of cloth."

Schmidt told reporters that he tried to make himself understood by yelling in English, shouting that he wanted the commander to jump into the water and swim over to his plane, because he wanted to take him separately. "They hesitated a bit. The water is very cold, after all; but finally one of them put on his life belt and jumped into the water." At a distance of about twenty metres from the submarine, Schmidt pointed his machine gun towards the conning tower, but saw nothing threatening. "Then I descended onto the float and dragged the man, who was trembling from the cold and could hardly swim any longer, onto the float. That was the commander; I put him into the back of our plane." Schmidt wrapped the freezing man in a coat and gave him his cap and gloves. "He was quite happy to be saved." The captain asked Schmidt what would happen to the other members of his crew, and Schmidt told him they would be rescued by the German navy and other planes. During the interview Schmidt, following military regulations, made no mention of Lonsdale's name, nor did he identify the sub.

With the captain aboard, Schmidt could safely proceed on his way, as two other planes were circling above him. "We now started and set course for our home aerodrome. In the plane he told me that he had never flown before in his life and that it was quite fun. He was no longer depressed." Schmidt said that this captain told him that several of his crew were injured, but that he thought none of them were dead. On the return flight Schmidt noticed several auxiliary vessels proceeding toward the *Seal*, and upon reaching his airfield at Aalborg, he waved and made signals that "this time something has happened. The waving announced success."[9]

Events did transpire according to Schmidt's story, except that he described the white tablecloth as a "shirt" and pretended not to have realised that the surrender signal had definitely been given. He even said that "they raised their arms and waved their white pieces of cloth," as though such motions meant nothing; and his glorious tale made no mention of the subchaser's vital assistance nor the fact that the second Arado had picked up Petty Officer Marcus Cousin.

Of course, the captors had to gloat a little: one of the naval war diary entries on 5 May said: "The submarine *Seal* was evidently damaged from the UMA Sperre [mine blockade], so it was unable to dive. Capturing this boat has been a very happy success story. It is absolutely unbelievable that the crew of the boat was not able to sink it in time. ... an unfortunate indication of British determination and preparedness for action!!"[10]

Notes

1. Eckersall interview, 1 May 2000.
2. Previous sections from NARA, T1022, Roll 3908, PG 396691/3, Akten des Befehlshabers der Sicherung der Ostsee (B.S.O.) – Akte K9, Kampfhandlungen, Bd. II, 80–2.
3. Ibid., 83–6.
4. Ibid., 80–2.

5. Eckersall Interview, 1 May 2000.
6. NARA, T1022, Roll 3908, PG 396691/3, Akten des Befehlshabers der Sicherung der Ostsee (B.S.O.) – Akte K9, Kampfhandlungen, Bd. 11, 83–6.
7. Ibid., 80–2.
8. Hans Rösing, taped narration, 21 December 1999.
9. RNSM, Information Section N.I.D., "Extract from B.B.C. Digest May 6–7."
10. Previous sections from NARA, T 1662, PG 32029, KTB 1/Skl, TeilA, Heft 9, May 1940, 45, 46.

CHAPTER VI

Freedom Ends

For Korvettenkapitän Hans Rösing, a handsome, dark-haired officer with years of experience in submarine construction, the summons to inspect *Seal* came at a somewhat inopportune moment. "After a hard week with my flotilla, I was hoping to get some rest when the phone rang. Captain von Friedeburg, who was in charge of nonoperational submarine matters, told me that a British submarine had been captured in the Kattegat and that I had to go out there on the double by hydroplane." Rösing immediately selected two non-com officers and set off. After a short flight they saw a German patrol boat towing the *Seal*, and as the weather was clear, they had no trouble landing near subchaser UJ 128. "We transferred over to the subchaser in a boat they sent for us, and the commanding officer said they had been towing the submarine for some hours and that it had not changed floating position. Therefore, I did not interrupt the towing and went down into the hold to see the British crew."

Right away one of *Seal*'s officers informed Rösing that the submarine was about to explode, but the news failed to trouble the German officer. "Later, I saw what he meant, because we found an activated depth charge in the bulkhead of the bow compartment, triggered for a depth of about twenty metres. Of course, we wanted to get rid of the bomb, but there was insufficient lifting capacity at the docks to safely heave the bomb, so I decided to leave it where it was."

At Frederikshavn Rösing and his assistants inspected their trophy, "searching mainly for documents of a confidential nature, which naturally had been thrown overboard, but we found a complete set of technical blueprints, which were very useful. The outer hull had many shot holes from the airplane crew, who had discovered *Seal* floating and unmanoeuvrable after being hit in the stern by a mine, jamming the rudders and damaging the propellers."

On the following day workers patched dozens of shot holes in the tower and blew the ballast tanks by using the still-charged batteries. "The sub lifted but remained down by the stern, owing to the mine hit; the aftermost compartment was flooded. The bulkhead held and we never tried to open the door. We had assistance from a German salvage tug and its crew." For the next three or four days the German team inspected the *Seal*, worked on repairs, and prepared her for towing to Kiel.[1]

Meanwhile, the two Arado seaplane pilots had flown Commander Rupert Lonsdale and crewman Marcus Cousin to the German air base at Aalborg, Denmark, causing a big stir. Herbert Uhlig, a pilot with the squadron, typed a letter to his fiancée Vera (he normally wrote letters by hand, but in this special case he typed): "I want to tell you that it was our air unit that seized that U-boat so it could be towed to Frederikshavn. It is historically an unparalleled event that an enemy submarine fell into German hands. You can't imagine the valuable equipment that fell into our possession. Anyway, it is a tremendous occasion. Both of the involved crews have received the EK 1 [Iron Cross First Class]! ..." Uhlig went on to say that he had driven to Frederikshavn to take a look at the newly captured vessel. "It was more than interesting to me," he enthused. "I took several little souvenirs with me; they will be in a packet, and I am sending them to you shortly." One of the items Uhlig sent his betrothed was a red signal pennant; the other, a key from the Morse telegraph machine.

Still ebullient from the capture, Uhlig wrote to Vera on 16 May: "Please try to get the 'V.B.' [*Völkischer Beobachter*, a Nazi newspaper] dated 10 May because therein is a good drawing of the 'Seal' and of our two Arados. ... I beg you to collect all of the material, which some day will be of interest." After keeping the flag for four years and having no real use for it, Vera realised that it was made of fine, linen-like material that was impossible to find in 1944; and she cut up the flag and sewed a couple of little red shirts for her two-and-a-half-year-old son Peter.[2]

The evening before departure for Kiel, Hans Rösing remained alone on board the *Seal*, making sure that "every valve and other opening were tightly closed – the safest way, since no engine whatsoever was to be activated under tow." A week passed in Frederikshavn, then the triumphant journey back to Germany began. "We had a former whale hunting boat for towing and could do no more than three knots, due to the jammed rudder on the *Seal*. We were, of course, protected by a strong escort, since we could assume that the British would try to attack the submarine under way." Expecting enemy planes at any time, the Germans were surprised that none appeared. "Apparently the enemy aircraft seemed to have been occupied otherwise."

Rösing recalled that the weather cooperated nicely and the seas were fairly calm, allowing a slow and easy passage for the flotilla. "After about seventy-two hours in tow and without any incidents, the convoy entered Kiel Harbour."

High-ranking navy officials eagerly awaited a chance to inspect the captured *Seal*, and Admiral Carls, commanding admiral of the Baltic, was one of the first to greet Rösing. "He asked me for suggestions for later employment of the *Seal*, and my answer was to refit it for trials so as to get knowledge of a modern British submarine, then scrap it. For instance, there were large quantities of non-iron material built into the ship; the whole conning tower was built of massive bronze because of the magnetic compass within the conning tower."

"He became very angry, since some weeks previously I had delivered a very derogatory judgment on Norwegian submarines we had found in southern Norway. I explained to the admiral that we had no torpedoes that would fit into the [*Seal's*] torpedo tubes ... nor had we mines that would fit into her minelaying mechanism. Later, even Hitler meddled in the matter, and it was decided that *Seal* would be fitted out for missions." Even top submarine expert Rösing could not convince the German navy of *Seal's* uselessness to them for warfare.

However, cooler minds prevailed and the decision came down that the newly-claimed vessel would be sent to the western Atlantic for radio and weather observations. "Fortunately for the crew," said Rösing, "she was not sent on a mission and after about two years was scrapped." During the *Seal's* stay at the Krupp shipyard, an officer from U-27, whose boat had gone in for repairs, climbed aboard the captured sub and looked around. He remarked to friends that he was impressed by the mahogany panelling in the radio room.[3]

But as Rösing remembered, "We were, of course, eager to learn about British submarines, and *Seal* had been launched in 1938; but we didn't find anything of great importance to us. While the British, as a result of World War I experiences, were leading in antisubmarine warfare, we had our nose ahead in subs. But Germany, by the Peace Treaty of Versailles ... was prohibited from building and running submarines, so German sub experts constructed and tested submarines for other countries." In the early thirties Rösing and some other officers had spent time in Spain, Finland, and Turkey making test runs on submarines designed by Germans in the Netherlands; some of the boats had been built in Germany, others in Finland or Spain.[4]

As soon as they could, German inspectors gathered fifteen bags of trash from *Seal* and on 10 May sent the "booty" by courier to navy headquarters, where it was sifted through and analysed. The navy listed such items as patrol reports; sea charts; a few engine blueprints; copies of radio messages; general instructions for services; radio material and signal procedures; engine logs and other notebooks; some photographs from foreign navies and air forces; and a great deal of private correspondence. Someone had torn out the front pages of the Asdic notebook, leading the Germans to conclude that the missing pages "might be found in the pile of torn-up materials." The report said that "for notes of a secret nature they mostly used pink paper, and these have been sorted out." Within the notices about radio traffic there was a series of mine notifications (warnings to British subs about mine fields) "from which we immediately sent the ones that had a newer date to Kiel and to the high command, as well as BdU and Wilhelmshaven."

Analysts gained information about the time and place that *Seal* was constructed, as well as her engine power and surface speed. From her patrol reports they could tell where she went on every mission, but the reports had been written with radio messages listed by number – no actual words. Lonsdale had put vague information about *Seal*'s precise locations but did mention ship sightings. When the Germans scrutinised the short passage about Lonsdale's entry into Skudesnes Fjord, guarded by German boats, they puzzled over how he managed such a feat and concluded that the *Seal* must have been submerged and that Asdic somehow had been a factor. They were right, but they knew nothing about how Asdic functioned. Here was something of vital importance to them, but they never inveigled a single clue about Asdic from any crew member during interrogations.

"We have not been able to find out how the boats were communicating with each other. The radio messages probably went exclusively through land stations," they wrote. They could not guess that British subs used Asdic to transmit underwater Morse code messages in plain text to each other, and that the messages went only one direction. In this way, the *Narwhal* had sent a "good luck" signal to *Seal* on her way to the Kattegat. U-boats had absolutely no means of communicating with each other, and in fact, many training catastrophes occurred in the Baltic with underwater boat collisions and deaths of entire crews.

On 10 May the German navy zipped a telegram to BSO (Befehlshaber der Sicherung der Ostsee, or commander of Baltic operations) announcing their prize:

> The English boat *Seal* was brought in on 5/5. Further interrogation and examining some salvaged papers. Results as follows: One should figure that *Seal* was heavily damaged, surfaced, and was able to send a signal to the Admiralty in London, Whitehall, on 5/5. It was heavily damaged by a German plane. Their radio room was badly damaged, destroyed, in fact, and is completely useless. On 18 April *Seal*, before its return trip from Norwegian seas to Rosyth, was able to shell the airfield at Stavanger with artillery.[5]

The Germans made no mention of mines laid by *Seal*, and they erred when they assumed that the submarine had shelled Stavanger, not realising that it had been the cruiser *Suffolk* firing at the air base. Since the Germans saw nothing specific about Lonsdale's firing towards Sola Airfield in his war diary, they guessed wrongly that he did it – an odd assumption, since they had heavily bombed the *Suffolk* on the day of the attack.

As Germany studied *Seal* and argued about what to do with her, Lonsdale's crew began their captivity. Mickey Reynolds remembered that after they landed at Frederikshavn, "we were billeted in a very large hall, where we thought, 'well, here we will get a little rest,' but it was not for long, as a crowd of German soldiers came in. After a lot of shouting, they got us lined up against the walls about three feet apart, and everyone had to put all their personal belongings in front of them, including watches and rings, cigarettes, and anything we had. I, personally, had nothing – not even the clothes I was wearing." Reynolds realised that he must have looked a sight, dressed in huge, baggy pants that he had borrowed and Tubby Lister's oversized sweater.

"That night," explained Happy Eckersall, "we stayed in a school, and we slept on straw in one of those big rooms, like a hall." Mickey said they finally managed a bit of sleep, and at 5:30 A.M. came yells of "'rouse! 'rouse! Kaffee!" calling their attention to pots of German coffee that the guards had set inside the doorway. "I don't think much was taken. Then we were issued canned loaves of German brown bread stamped 1933 or 1935 and a tin of meat, but I don't think there was much of either taken then. But in later years it would have been very welcome." After a brief interval the guards again yelled, "Rouse!" and ordered the prisoners to line up outside and to proceed on foot to the railway station. "There were more soldiers than POWs," recalled Reynolds. "At the station we were loaded into carriages to go to Kiel."

As Eckersall described it: "The station people was staring at us: 'Oh, what a motley crowd.' We wasn't dressed in our best suits, you know. My clothes was in a mess from all the oil and water in the machinery space, where we tried to pump it out. Anyway, when we got to Kiel we stayed there for a while."[6]

On the morning of 6 May the crew marched into the Kiel Friedrichsort naval barracks, "and here we were well looked after by the German navy," said Mickey Reynolds. "What a change: here we had maybe twelve or fourteen to a room, with beds and clean bedding, but not a smoke between us. Our first thoughts were, 'Better watch what you say – there may be microphones concealed in the rooms.'" Taff Harper described it as well: "In the navy barracks they treated us like themselves; we had the freedom of the depot." The enlisted men could walk around inside their fenced area, and they saw their superiors only when the officers were allowed out for exercise. "They were kept away from the rest of the crew and had a guard with them. We never heard how the interrogation went."[7]

"Two of us were being interrogated every day," explained Reynolds, "and those who were questioned had to move to another area so as to be out of contact with the rest." Ernie Truman remembered the questioning as being civilised, but probing. "They were quite gentlemanly about it. They asked me how the British could see in the dark, and I replied: 'carrots.'" Ernie believed that the interrogators did not get anything out of them at all. "One of the first questions they asked you when you first went in was,

'What was your job on the submarine?' And it was amazing the number of people we had who worked the engine room telegraphs." Naturally, no crew member had the slightest idea about how the Asdic functioned.[8]

By the Geneva Convention of 1929, prisoners of war were bound to tell only their name and rank or regimental number. "No coercion may be used on prisoners to secure information" the rules stated. "Prisoners who refuse to answer may not be threatened, insulted, or exposed to unpleasant or disadvantageous treatment of any kind whatever." Apparently the German navy officers conducted their interrogations of *Seal* crewmen completely in accordance with the Convention, to their credit.[9]

By 18 May the German naval staff had enough information from the boat's "booty" and its crew to draw up a lengthy report covering many of *Seal's* activities. Their findings indicated that it was very possible that *Seal* had all its mines aboard, about fifty of them, on 4 May at 02:30 A.M. when the first German plane attacked. Then, they believed that *Seal*, travelling at two to three sea miles submerged, discharged her mines from 10:00 and 12:00 in a block approximately four to five sea miles long, with spacing between the mines of approximately 150 metres. "From 1830 on, the submarine was lying on the ground, and we estimate that possibly between the time of surfacing and the second plane attack, it was able to cover about fifteen to twenty sea miles in the direction of the Swedish coast. It is therefore surmised that the [mine] barrier lies on the Danish side of the Kattegat." Lastly, the Germans mentioned that the minelayer *Narwhal* had conducted a similar mission and started its return trip the day before.[10]

How correct were they? Somewhat, as Lonsdale did place the mines on the Danish side of the Kattegat; but the minelaying on 4 May had started a bit before 9:00 in the morning and ended at about 9:45. Following that, *Seal* plunged to the seabed to escape trawlers and hit the German mine at about 7:00 that night. Before dawn the next day, at 1:30 or 2:00, the crew at last brought their boat to the surface and were then captured. German investigators made conclusions about the minefield location based on Lonsdale's war diary, radio messages they had picked up, and possibly a few innocuous remarks by crew members. Even having approximately located the minefield, the investigators failed to prevent four ships from passing through it with disastrous results.

Much later, after a great deal of investigating, analysing, and arguing, the German navy had found almost nothing they could use from the captured boat. The only idea they came up with concerned underwater refuelling: while two submerged U-boats travelled together, they used a telephone to maintain constant course and speed. Steaming ahead of the submarine to be refuelled, the first one released a buoy with a towing hawser, an air-filled hose, and a telephone cable. From the *Seal* the German engineers removed a pressure-tight socket and installed it in a U-boat to waterproof the telephone cable that went into the second sub. These methods came into play in late 1942, while the "milch cows" were refuelling the smaller U-boats, but by mid-1943 the Allies had sunk all the big supply subs. One can imagine how the imprisoned *Seal* men would have guffawed if they had heard news of the Germans using their "socket."[11]

As the prisoners were being interrogated, word went around that Lord Haw-Haw on German radio was announcing some of the names of British military who had been captured or killed. Eckersall said that he anxiously anticipated news of their capture, but "it never came over this night."[12]

Seal prisoners in Kiel hoped that Lord Haw-Haw would reveal all their names immediately, so that their families could have the relief of knowing that they were alive; but the wily propagandist on 12 May gave out only twenty-four names and deliberately mispronounced several. Then on 31 May and 1 June he trickled out two more batches, but about twenty sailors remained unaccounted for. Families of *Seal* submariners were forced to wait for final verification of those captured until they received postcards from them.[13]

After about four weeks of questioning, imprisonment began for the entire fifty-nine-man crew, except for Able Seaman Smith, who had disappeared when the German planes attacked. *Seal* crew members privately thought that Smith might have jumped overboard during the fighting and tried to make it to land, as he had been a champion navy swimmer.

"For some reason, I did not get interrogated," declared Taff Harper. After the questioning had ended, dispersal began, first with the officers, then part of the crew, leaving behind five who had not been quizzed. Taff Harper, Martin Fitzgerald, Jaunty Mayes, Bungy Williams, and (first name unknown) Cambridge were the last to leave the navy base and were told, "You can go now and join your comrades in an army camp."[14]

Lonsdale, Clark, and the rest of the officers were shipped off to an officers' castle prison, Oflag IX A/H at Spangenberg; the rest of the crew, except for the five mentioned above, departed for an unknown destination.

"We were put on a train for Poland, a place called Thorn," recalled Mickey Reynolds, "and this was the start of many journeys." Ernie Truman remembered travelling for three days on a "very uncomfortable train" and arriving at a Polish town on the Vistula river. "We were then marched for about two miles to a disused old fortress, which was to be our home. ..." Stalag XX A, an imposing castle complex, was surrounded by a thirty-foot-wide moat with heavily guarded gates at each end of the moat bridge. "We were kept waiting on the bridge for quite a time, and from the windows of the fort came words of encouragement from the British P.O.W.'s who had been captured in Norway," wrote Signalman John Waddington.[15]

Truman said that "the place was already occupied by prisoners from the army, RAF, some French troops, and quite a number of Polish prisoners. "Quite a mixed bag but very interesting."[16]

Mickey Reynolds said that they were put to work at various jobs, and "some of us were sent up the Vistula river to construct dams at different parts." Other crew members, soon after arriving at the brick barracks, repaired a dilapidated boiler and hand pump that fed water into overhead perforated pipes for quick group showers – a welcome refresher. After spending nights on dirty, bug-infested floors, the men needed to clean themselves in order to survive. Sometimes they took their filthy white submarine sweaters into the showers to wash them as best they could.

Happy Eckersall and others were sent to work at the laundry, where they stacked coke and coal in the compound; and after completing their duties, they managed to construct a machine for delousing themselves. "We got an old boiler from the Germans, rigged it up, ground the valves like you do on a car engine, and got it working. It was a steam delouser, and while the chaps was having a shower, we used to get their clothing and put it inside the steam delouser, shut the lid, put high pressure on the steam, and this more or less cooked 'em; all the lice was supposed to die." If any of the prisoners found a potato in the fields as they trudged back from work camps in nearby towns, they grabbed it and stuffed it into their white prison suit pocket. "And then they'd come in and someone would say, 'See Happy on the boiler: he'll cook it for you.'"

"There was very little food there – I mean in Poland itself," explained Eckersall. Loaves of brown bread were distributed, and "you was lucky if you got even an Oxo-sized [bouillon] cube of it in the middle that wasn't green or mouldy. And the water had not been used for so long at the fort that it was sour, and we had to keep pumping the water, let it run." During their miserable stay at the Stalag, some of the prisoners died of dysentery, but *Seal*'s crew somehow survived.[17]

"The stay at Thorn was fairly tough," recalled Ernie Truman, "but for me it became quite important. I met a young soldier who held religious beliefs similar to mine, and between us we started visiting the sick berth each evening." The suffering patients expressed such thankfulness for Ernie's concern and attention that when fellow prisoners heard about his efforts, they joined the visiting party. "So much was it appreciated that I requested the German Commandant to allow us to hold Sunday church services. He was very pleased to agree, and from then on, he always addressed me as 'Pastor,' even calling on me to conduct the funeral of one of the soldiers who unfortunately had died." A thousand more prisoners of war, captured at Dunkirk, then arrived at the fortress, increasing Ernie's work but giving him great satisfaction.[18]

While most of *Seal*'s crew struggled to exist at Thorn, the five others who arrived later, Herbert "Taff" Harper, Jaunty Mayes, Martin Fitzgerald, Cambridge, and Bungy Williams landed in a large, flimsy tent outside the main fortress, where overflow prisoners were put. "We had a very, very hard time; there was no Red Cross or anything like that, and I remember that we lived in a big, marquee tent, and the toilet was a big trench with a tree trunk across it that you sat on – no shelter or cover over it." No beds existed – not even straw – and the five were forced to sleep on the hard ground in their clothes. "There was no blankets or anything like that, and that was the primitive condition we was in."

A field kitchen had been set up, and food rations consisted of old bread, handed out about every three days, and a bowl of "soup" that consisted of clear water with a rotten potato in the bottom. "You was lucky if you got just half a slice of bread – very black, years old." After three months of wrenching hunger, Taff and mates began scavenging through a dump site. "If you saw a potato you couldn't put your finger through, you'd pick it up. We used to get that just to chew on and ate them raw. Sometimes the men sneaked out of camp to raid the fields of turnips and parsnips, if they could find them. There was a lot of people went down with dysentery and what have you." The ravenous men would risk their lives to go and "pinch" a bit of food.

"Twice I tried to escape, but I was caught. Didn't get anywhere. I was put in solitary for a week or fortnight, but it was just one of those things that happened." Taff knew they were too far inland to make it very far, and most of the men had little or no knowledge of the German language. "I picked up German pretty quickly, because we was in working parties. I could speak it fairly good, but it didn't get me anywhere. Sometimes you could get escape gear, because I was in the escape club, and they had clothes and what have you."[19]

The Germans had hastily set up Stalag XX A in May 1940, just before the arrival of *Seal*'s crew and other captives, and the camp consisted of five or six old castles on the edge of Thorn, in German-occupied Poland. Hundreds of new prisoners of war were sent straight there to be sorted by rank and nationality, then transferred elsewhere; but those who stayed had to endure a bleak existence for the first two years. In 1943 conditions improved, but by that time, *Seal*'s crew had been shipped to other camps. In the beginning, prisoners suffered from lack of food, water, and adequate clothing; working crews received only a shirt and pants – nothing for warmth. "The main persistent bad aspects were poor footwear, overcrowding in some working camps and in the main camp hospital, bad water supply and lighting in the main camps," said a report written after the war.

Fortunately for the prisoners, Swiss delegates from the International Committee of the Red Cross made periodic visits to see whether the prisoners were being treated according to the Geneva Convention. If not, they complained to the German military authorities. "We now had the protection of the Red Cross," wrote prisoner W. C. Law, "a very important thing for us, as Germany now had to account for anything that might happen to us." Perhaps the internees believed that their lives would be at least comfortable in the camps, but things did not work out that way.[20]

"The German guards," said the Red Cross report, "were soldierly and unbribable – they firmly believed what they were told, that Germans were in England now." Guards aged 25 and older dealt with the prisoners fairly, but "the younger Germans tended to be brutal." Sometimes the guards arbitrarily shot the prisoners, especially in the early years, and at least twenty-two died by this cruelty. Such behaviour went directly against international rules.

In July 1940 camp overseers sorted the men out by trades and sent groups out to their many working camps, which numbered from 180 to 200. Red Cross observers thought that conditions at these outlying camps were "much harder than at the Main camp," but in truth, the prisoners sometimes fared a bit better in them.[21]

"Health at main camp very unsatisfactory," wrote camp inspectors. "Cases of diphtheria, grippe, and other undiagnosed diseases of which chief symptoms edema, which many have due to malnutrition. Berlin authorities are being advised."[22]

But in spite of all the hardships, "the morale of the prisoners of war at XX A, judging by escapers and other reports," said inspectors, "seems always to have stood high. … The camp was fortunate in its British Officer and W.O. officials. Also, the early German Commandant was a fair man and did his best for the prisoners of war, as their letters showed." Years later Taff Harper commented: "On par, I think it was half and half – good and bad." The men could get moral support from their elected Man of Confidence, who maintained discipline and handled complaints, while the Escape Committee approved and aided plans to get out.[23]

Fifteen men managed to escape from Thorn prison by the end of 1940, including Petty Officer Maurice Barnes of the *Seal*. While labouring at a work camp Barnes and an army friend joined about thirteen other prisoners in a night-time getaway on 27 July 1940. As soon as all had trekked safely away from the camp, Barnes and friend took off in a different direction from the others, heading south-east towards Warsaw and probably following the Vistula river. For two weeks they walked by night through the dense Polish forests; then Barnes's thin patent leather boots wore out, leaving him with sore, blistered feet.

Terribly hungry and weak, the pair chanced to meet some friendly Poles, who told them about the Polish underground system and helped them get on a train for Warsaw. Upon arrival in the city, an ambulance met them at the station, took care of their needs, and turned them over to local underground members. For three weeks Barnes and his friend rested and waited in Polish homes, and Barnes received a pair of sturdy new boots. Then the hosts bade their guests goodbye and advised them about how to get to the Russian border, which lay about a hundred miles to the east.

Travelling once more on foot at night, the escapees followed the suggested route and came upon a Russian border hut on 9 September. No one seemed to be around, so they pounded on the door. Suddenly a group of grubby, armed soldiers surrounded the pair, menacing them. The two tried to tell them that they were English POWs, but none of the soldiers seemed to understand English or to care. Seizing Barnes and his buddy, the Russians confiscated the men's wristwatches and small change given them by the Warsaw underground; then their captors indicated that the escapees were to take off all their clothes and run fast, before getting shot at. Terrified, the two prisoners stripped naked and tore off at full speed, hoping to get away in time; but without hesitation the guards fired two shots, wounding Barnes, who fell in the road. The British army man, unhurt, succeeded in escaping and later managed to reach England; but Maurice Barnes was never seen again.[24]

British military rules stated that every prisoner had a duty to try to escape, but before making any attempts, he must consult the Escape Committee, which in turn received items from England to help the cause. In December 1939 the British government had set up MI9 (Military Intelligence) in a London hotel room to facilitate POW escapes in all the armed services. They published a pamphlet and issued copies to all companies and units called "Conduct of British Personnel in the Event of Capture." In gift parcels MI9 secreted items such as silk maps, compasses, and money, but the Germans found and confiscated most of them when inspecting the boxes.[25]

According to returned escapees, most of the escape aids that MI9 mailed were probably useless; and they pointed out that "Special mechanical gadgets are not necessary, as the men can procure these articles themselves. What we needed most ... was money, passes, and ration cards." Plans of North Sea ports proved invaluable, and money could provide bribes for guards and fees to pay German officials. One escapee reported that "nearly all successful escapes were due to money aid."[26]

To obtain getaway equipment, food, clothing, and other items, the club members used their contacts with the German public while they worked in various locations outside the Stalag. The Geneva Convention prohibited the forcing of officers and non-commissioned officers to perform any labour; but the German guards ordered most of the junior ratings to leave camp (if they did not volunteer) and to do gruelling jobs. At first Taff and his friends refused to raise their hands for work parties until they noticed that a group of French prisoners was going out every day, and "they used to come back with little bits of food in their pockets. We said, 'If they're going to get fed for going on working parties, we'll do the same.' Of course we was really green in those days; we was just newly prisoners of war."

Once the parties began to travel beyond Thorn, they had no trouble sponging tidbits from friendly Poles or inveigling pieces of civilian clothing for escape purposes. Each civilian carried an Ausweis card, or licence to work and travel around in German territory, and sometimes the prisoners managed to obtain one; if not, the escape club forger created it. Explained Taff Harper: "It was an identity card that allowed you to travel and look for work over and above where you were staying." Even civilians could not freely travel and were restricted to certain areas. "You needed that passport to take you from town to town, providing you was looking for work."

At first the *Seal* crewmen mingled openly with Polish civilians, but as time passed, the German guards noticed that a few sailors were getting "too friendly" with their new acquaintances, who were giving them food or tobacco or other treats. To separate the British prisoners from civilians, the Germans put the POWs to work in factories, and "it was fine, because you was working under shelter, and you used to share some food with the Jerries," said Taff.[27]

Inside Thorn fortress Ernie Truman and friends often suffered harsh treatment from the guards. "They were in the Hermann Göring Panzer Division, and if you ever knew of a more arrogant bunch than that ..." The guards never spoke normally to the prisoners – they constantly shouted, all the while aiming their rifles at the labouring men. While digging ditches, Taff Harper more than once received rifle butt blows on his head, in his stomach, or elsewhere for not doing what the guards wanted – "to teach you to do as you're told." It seemed to Harper that the army guards punished them constantly, even for the way the prisoners looked at them or didn't look.[28]

Every morning the internees lined up for roll call. "They'd see that you were all there and nobody had escaped during the night-time," declared Taff, "and you got picked for working parties. They'd get about thirty of you with about twelve guards. Then they'd march you to the site where they wanted you to go." On one occasion they arrived at the location of a new factory building, where deep trenches were being dug for foundations. "For some reason or other, we wasn't working fast enough, and there was one of the workers, an ex-policeman, who stood up to these guards and told them we couldn't work any faster. You know, lack of food and what have you, and the heavy job, because we was pretty deep then. He told them, 'You've got to give us more time,' in German, because he could speak a bit of German." At that point the guard jerked the prisoner's shovel out of his hand, whammed him over the head with it and watched the prisoner crumple to the bottom of the trench. "Heraus! Heraus!" ("Get out! Get out!") he screamed, and seeing no movement from the fallen man, grabbed his rifle and shot him through the heart.

"Fortunately," said Taff, "Amos had a cigarette case and his disc [identity tag] in the breast pocket of his jacket, and that stopped him from being killed. The bullet hit both of these, dented them up and bruised him very badly." During their year of confinement at Thorn, the *Seal* men concluded that the arrogance of their guards stemmed from the fact that "they were so confident that they were going to rule the world, and they could do anything they wanted."[29]

Notes

1. Hans Rösing narration, 21 December 1999.
2. Prof. Dr. Ralph Uhlig to author, 14 April 2001 and 24 March 2002.
3. Rösing narration, 21 December 1999; Hans Esken to author, 27 February 2001.
4. Rösing narration, 21 December 1999; Rössler, *The U-boat*, 91, 92, 98.
5. NARA, Roll T 1022, PG 39691/3, Akten des Befehlshabers der Sicherung der Ostsee, 72–7.
6. Eckersall interview, 1 May 2000.
7. Reynolds, "HMS *Seal*"; Harper interview, 2 February 2002.
8. Truman interview, 22 September 2000.
9. Yale University, "The Avalon Project at Yale Law School," ("Convention Between the United States of America and Other Powers, Relating to Prisoners of War; July 27, 1929"), available on *http://www.yale.edu/lawweb/avalon/lawofwar/geneva02.htm* on INTERNET.
10. NARA, T1022, Roll 3908, PG 39691/3, 65.
11. Rössler, *The U-boat*, 162.
12. Reynolds, "HMS *Seal*"; Eckersall interview, 1 May 2000.
13. NA, ADM 116/4121.
14. Harper interview, 3 February 2002.
15. Reynolds, "HMS *Seal*"; Warren and Benson, *Will Not We Fear*, 184.
16. Ernie Truman to author, 14 December 2001.
17. Eckersall interview, 1 May 2000.
18. Ernie Truman to author, 14 December 2001.
19. Taff Harper, telephone interview with author, 18 November 2000.
20. Diary of Private W. C. Law, 2 Gloucester Regiment, available on *http://www.wartime-memories.fsnet.co.uk/pow/stalag20a.html* on INTERNET.
21. NA, WO 208/3281.
22. NA, FO 916/32.
23. Harper interview, 18 November 2000; NA, WO 208/3281.
24. Warren and Benson, *Will Not We Fear*, 185, 186; RNSM, Secret Message from Head of Naval Mission, Moscow, 11 November 1941.
25. NA, WO 208/3247.
26. Ibid.
27. Taff Harper, telephone interview with author, 17 December 2000.
28. Ibid.
29. Harper interview, 18 November 2000.

CHAPTER VII

Hitler Gloats

During one of their sudden barracks searches at a work camp near Thorn, German guards had discovered four homemade radios, confiscated them, and put each owner into solitary confinement in a tin hut for a few days. Now the prisoners had no access to BBC news: they heard merely the incessant blaring of German propaganda on the loudspeakers. Taff Harper remembered one prison comrade at that time who was about thirty years old and extremely clever with his hands. One day the friend asked, "Heard any news, Taff?" Harper replied, "No, nothing at all." So the friend grumbled, "I'm sick and tired of not having any news. The next time you're out on a working party, could you get me a thermos flask?" Puzzled about the request, Taff told him he had never seen one outside the camp, but the friend was undeterred. "Oh, I think the German workmen are bound to have a flask."

On his next assignment Taff and crew were constructing a brick water tank and planting grass around it. "We used to share a hut at mealtimes with the German workers, carpenters and so on, and I saw this thermos flask on a worker." By that time Harper could speak a few words of German, and he said to the labourer, "I'll give you a package of cigarettes for your flask." "Nein, nein, nein," replied the man. Taff offered two packs, then five chocolates and two cigarette packs; the worker accepted the better offer and the two men made the exchange.

"I took it back to the camp – smuggled it in, you know. We were very, very fortunate because we had a friendly guard with us on these working parties, and we used to bribe him." Underfed and underpaid, the German guards sometimes accepted cigarettes and food items in return for favours and equipment. Normally they searched every prisoner when work parties departed and returned from camp, but on this occasion, things were different. "I showed 'Fritz' [the guard] the flask, hinted that I wanted to take it in, gave him a package of cigarettes, and he searched me very quickly, passing over the flask. I had on a big army coat."

At the hut, Harper turned over the container to his talented friend. "What do you want it for?" he inquired. "I'll tell you later," said his buddy.

Taff knew that other comrades were collecting items for the project, as well, when they went out on working parties.

"Anyhow, he made a radio and hid it in this flask," recalled Taff. "It worked fine, and he got the news from it." When a prisoner manufactured a wireless set, he would secretly listen to BBC broadcasts, then tell trusted friends, who passed the information around the camp. "They [guards] used to make raids," said Harper, "to see if there was any contraband or anything." When the Germans marched into the huts, all the prisoners had to hustle outside and stand around in the prison yard while the guards looked for hidden items such as radios or escape gear. "They turned our bunks upside-down and everything else; stuff from our lockers used to get strewn around." The hut was furnished with triple-deck bunks with a shelf attached to the wall next to the upper bunk, where the radio man placed his treasure. "The flask just stood there," said Taff, "and the Jerries never did pick it up, as far as I know, because it was still working when I left that camp."[1]

Private W. C. Law, a British army prisoner, ended up at Thorn prison in June 1940, about the same time the *Seal* group arrived. During that month France had capitulated to Hitler's armies, and Private Law had been caught hiding with his men in an old house and taken captive, then shipped over to Thorn. "In the first few months," he pointed out, "our lives were very dull, as we had nothing to do but walk round and round on the small grass hill in the centre of the fort; and the Germans printed a small paper in English about once a week ... which told us of some terrifying things that was happening to Britain – Coventry flattened, London bombed every night, Bristol in rubble, then the navy sunk. All this happening to our families and we can do nothing but walk around in small circles!" In addition to such depressing reports, the broadcasters proclaimed that after Germany had won the war, the POWs would not be allowed to go home until they had rebuilt everything damaged by British bombers.

Law described Thorn as "a town made up of forts with damp dungeon-type passages inside." He said the cuisine there was "regular, not very much – just a bowl of soup a day with a bit of bread, about three slices, and a small knob of margarine and a spoonful of jam once or twice a week." At intervals the prisoners could go into the prison barbershop to get a shave (none possessed razors) and a head shaving for lice prevention. "It was a big problem keeping down the lice." He recalled that they occasionally got deloused and had a welcome shower. For footwear, they were issued wooden clogs after their original boots had worn out, and pieces of rag for socks. "As winter approached, everyone was given an overcoat and hat, from what the Germans had taken from Polish forces." Law commented that in the spring of 1941 he was sent to a different POW camp that had working parties, and that life was better there, because the men could get food and news from the Poles.[2]

Food, according to the Geneva rules, "shall be equal in quantity and quality to that of troops at base camps." Shortages of all edibles in Germany, where a severe depression had been causing problems for years, made it difficult for the camp overseers to adequately feed the German guards, much less the prisoners. "Furthermore," the rules stated, "prisoners shall receive facilities for preparing, themselves, additional food which they might have." Since the POWs received no cooking utensils, some of them dreamed up clever ways of using tin cans to make little stoves for heating a spot of tea or a tidbit they might have saved.

Red Cross parcels from Canada and Great Britain slowly trickled into Germany for the first couple of years of the war, and the food boxes saved hundreds of thousands of POWs from starvation. After September 1939, shipping had become extremely difficult because of German blockades and attacks; and aid had to be routed through Switzerland. Help would come from America after the U.S. entered the war in December 1941. The Geneva Convention stated that each parcel was to be addressed to a specific prisoner, but in early 1940 Germany had captured so many of the Allies that German POW administrators lagged behind in giving lists to the Swiss representatives, creating another delay.

Each Red Cross parcel, about the size of two shoeboxes, contained dried milk, a semi-sweet chocolate bar, sugar, liver paste, Spam, cheese, whole-wheat crackers, and a few other things like cigarettes. "Many of the items," remarked Harley Tuck, "were from U.S. Army Food stores, sent with the help of the U.S. Army. We'd line up by barracks, generally on Saturday, to receive our parcel. The Germans would stab each canned item with a bayonet so it would spoil soon, in order to prevent us from saving up food to escape." Harley used his cigarettes as a medium of exchange with other prisoners for more packets of cheese. "We maintained health with these food parcels and the hot water and raw vegetables that were provided by the Germans."

Harley grew used to the sourness of the black bread and began to enjoy it, but he missed eating meat, since they only received about a tablespoon per week. "I caught myself looking with anticipation at a cat wandering by, but some other man got to it first." As time went on, care packages, boxes of clothing from home, parcels from the Swiss YWCA, and a few other necessaries reached the deprived men. "The guards always suspected the British prisoners of receiving things they shouldn't have, so they went through all the things the Englishmen got very carefully. The Americans didn't have that reputation at first, so for a long time we were getting things like cameras, tools, special foods, and other things useful for escape attempts."[3]

Taff Harper often conjured up escape ideas and helped in several tunnel digs; but he never made a successful breakout. Sometimes in moments of boredom he reminisced about his earlier experiences on the *Seal* and shared them with his camp mates. Taff had served on the big minelayer from the start, making every patrol until the catastrophe on 5 May. Soon after the crew reported for duty in January 1939, they discovered that Herbert Harper came from Wales, so they dubbed him "Taff." Harper believed that all Welshmen were nicknamed "Taff" because of some connection to the Taff river in Wales.

From February to May the new submarine underwent many tests and inspections, then sea trials, and she passed them all with flying colours. In May 1939 the *Seal* entered His Majesty's Service. Following the ceremony Lonsdale took his big, impressive boat out for deep diving tests in June. As they headed out, news reached the *Seal* that their fellow new sub, the *Thetis*, had disappeared in Liverpool Bay while undergoing sea trials. She had sailed from Birkenhead on 1 June at 1:30 P.M. for her first dive and had failed to come up after the normal three hours. About seven hours later, after midnight, the Admiralty started the search with a cruiser, eight destroyers, seven minesweepers, seaplanes, and every other craft available, but by 3:00 A.M. they had had no success.

Finally, just before dawn on the 2nd, as tides receded and *Thetis*'s air supply would have been about half depleted, the destroyer *Brazen* sighted an object protruding from the water about sixteen miles north of Great Ormsby Head and put the engines at full speed. At the scene they found *Thetis* with her stern jutting up almost vertically into the air, and at once they sent officers over to her in lifeboats. With hammers the officers tapped on the submarine in Morse code telling the trapped men that help had arrived. Great was the excitement when the officers heard taps coming from within the *Thetis* saying that the crew was still alive.

The *Brazen*, meanwhile, was calling for assistance, and as other vessels began to arrive on the scene, *Brazen* crew saw two submariners wearing escape equipment bob to the surface, and a few minutes later two others showed up. After they were hauled to safety, the four crewmen kept staring at the sea in hopes that more comrades would appear, but the sea remained empty. Though suffering from carbon dioxide poisoning, they managed to tell their rescuers that everyone was still alive inside the sub, but that some of the older men were in dire straits. They explained that they had waited to emerge until they knew that help was at hand.

One of the escapers, Captain H. P. K. Oram, Commander of the Fifth Submarine Flotilla, said that the trapped men had held a conference and decided that the civilians on board should be paired up with crew members to make their escapes, since navy members knew how to use the Davis Escape Apparatus. In the darkness of the exit compartment, civilians would not be able to make their way out without assistance. Why only four people were able to free themselves was never known, but it was theorised that a non-navy man became stuck in the narrow escape tube and blocked passage for the rest of the crew.

Another successful escaper, a mechanic named F. Shaw, told reporters that two men trying to get through the exit hatch had drowned and
another one "went mad and died." He went on to say, "When I left, the air
was getting worse. The men were sprawled about in the compartments,
but there was no panic. It was dark, and in a few minutes I would have
been too weak to escape."

At 12:30 on the afternoon of the 2nd, emergency workers rowed over
to the stranded vessel, climbed onto the stern, and with blowtorches tried
to burn a hole. By four o'clock they had accomplished nothing; suddenly
a big wave rushed toward them and they were forced to scramble off the
boat just as it surged over the *Thetis*, completely submerging her. At that
point salvage ships placed cables beneath the boat with pontoons, hoping
to lift her and keep her from sinking deeper and to continue working on
the escape hole, but this failed when the cables broke. Because of the surging tide, there was no way to attach air hoses to the emergency valves,
ringed with white circles on the hull – or so the navy said. "The rescue
squads seemed baffled at every turn," said a reporter for the *New York
Times*.[4]

When the tide again receded at 6:00 P.M. and darkness set in, there was
no sign of *Thetis*. Additional heavy salvage boats arrived on the scene,
but their efforts came to nothing, and at dawn on 3 June, the Admiralty
announced that all hope was lost. They did not explain the messages that
had been tapped out by the crew members before they died, and they told
grieving relatives that they possessed no rescue bell like the one that had
made possible the saving of thirty-three men from the USS *Squalus* off
Portsmouth, New Hampshire, the previous week. Later investigations did
reveal that one of *Thetis*'s torpedo tube caps had been inadvertently left
off, causing the boat to sink soon after diving.[5]

Three of *Seal*'s crew, Ernie Truman, Mickey Reynolds, and Tubby Lister
had been assigned to *Thetis* but ended up on *Seal*. Tubby had traded positions with another sailor, and Ernie's appointment got changed at the last
minute. Mickey was supposed to have gone out on either the *Thetis* or the
Seal, and at the time the *Thetis* tragedy was announced, Reynolds' parents
did not know which submarine he was on. After some agonising time
passed, they finally ascertained that he had not died on the sunken boat.
Every man on British submarines mourned the tragic loss of *Thetis* and
then tried to forget it as they continued their duties.[6]

When he learned of the disaster, Taff Harper could not help but remember another ghastly submarine accident that had taken place in 1932. An
M2, or "Mutton boat," had been refitted with a small deck hangar and carried a two-seater Parnall Peto spotter aircraft: submarine commander Max
Horton had dreamed up the idea. In 1927 one of the first test pilots and
his observer, both weighing a great deal more than ordinary, took off in
the tiny biplane. Failing to make a rapid ascent, the Peto began to wobble

over a fashionable beach at Lee-on-the Solent. By now the two tubby pilots were so low that one of their floats hit a cabana, knocked it down, and revealed a startled bather wrapped in a pink towel. This incident caused a bit of embarrassment for the Royal Navy, as anyone could imagine.[7]

Several years later, in 1932, the top-heavy submarine sailed out of Weymouth to try to speed up her plane launching procedures. At that time Taff Harper, a sailor on one of the destroyers out of nearby Portland, remembered that the M2 had gone out for tests and never returned. "We were called off shore leave and told to take taxis, cars, anything we could find to get back to Portland and get out to sea for a search party. It was broadcast over the radio for all naval personnel to return to ships and depot immediately. A mate of mine and I caught a taxi back; the driver didn't charge anything, of course." Once the news went out by radio, in theatres and restaurants, and by word of mouth, the public offered as much help as they could to the sailors who were rushing to assist rescue efforts.

"So we got back and went out [to sea]. The rumour was that she had been doing a crash dive – you know, that's to see how fast they can go down in case they sight an enemy, and apparently they opened the hangar doors just before she surfaced, and she flooded right throughout the boat." It was true, the crew *had* opened the pressure hull hatch to the seaplane hangar, as well as the watertight hangar doors while the boat was still partially submerged. The Royal Navy located the wreckage eight days later and found that the plane had been forced to the rear of its container by tons of water, crushing two seamen, whose bodies they recovered. Intensive efforts to salvage the M2 continued for eleven months without success, and the boat was left sitting upright on the sea bed 110 feet down with the rest of the crew (fifty-eight men) inside. "There was very little news about it," remarked Taff. "It was a terrible time."[8]

In the 1920s and 1930s the British Navy had not yet formed a clear idea of a submarine's role in war and were still experimenting with various functions for boats, such as convoy escorting, surveillance, minelaying, aircraft carrying, and occasional attacking. The M3, a big minelayer that carried eighty mines, had trouble diving and was condemned for war; however, experience with the cumbersome vessel led to the development of Porpoise-class minelayers, of which *Seal* was one. Loss of crews on the M2 and *Thetis* revealed the awful fact that the Admiralty had not worked much on submarine rescues; everybody knew it, and newspapers made jabs at the navy for negligence. Editorials asked why the *Thetis* crashed; why the sea trials were done in an area filled with sunken wrecks; and why no naval escort vessel accompanied the new-type boat. "Why, five hours after that stern had been above water … had not a hole been made?" inquired the London *Daily Mirror*. "There are devices for burning a hole through steel plates through which men can crawl." To these questions no real answers ever came.[9]

Submariners in those times had no choice but to continue with their duties and hope that they could survive.

After the *Thetis* tragedy the *Seal* headed for China to join the British flotilla stationed there, with everybody hoping to enjoy a warmer climate and getting some shore leave. One of the officers even loaded his golf clubs. "We was going out there," recalled Taff, "to relieve the only minelayer, the *Narwhal*, who was due to come home after two-and-a-half years. That was the commission: you went for two-and-a-half years." *Seal* departed on 4 August and headed down to Malta, where she took on oil and stores, then headed for the Suez Canal. After a safe passage through the canal Lonsdale announced on 3 September that Great Britain had declared war on Germany: this put a whole new face on the submarine's situation. "Now we had to patrol the Suez Canal," said Taff, " in order to keep it clear of enemy mines."

Sailing up and down the canal became a drag on the men's strength and spirits: everyone suffered from the blazing heat, and "we were sick and tired of being there. It was red-hot, and there was no humidifiers in the sub." Finally the Admiralty gave permission for the *Seal* crew to take a recuperation leave for about a week, but the only place to go was a wretched location on the island of Barim, off the south-west tip of Yemen. "It was one of the hottest places in the world, and you couldn't even stand on the casing of the sub, even with shoes on." Their "resort" consisted of a kind of barge used as relaxation quarters for navy crews, but no one was allowed to go onto the island. The men could swim in a small pool built inside a rock harbour, where they would be safe from sharks.

"We got in a dinghy and went over for a swim. There was about seven of us," said Taff, "and I was looking forward to it. The water felt lovely, and we was having a smashing time." All of a sudden the swimmers felt a crawly feeling on their skin, and Taff asked Fitzgerald, "Fitz, are you feeling queer?" Fitz replied, "Aye. Let's go." Everyone rushed out of the pool and jumped into the dinghy, where they discovered that their bodies looked as if they had been poked all over with pins – every part of them that had been submerged. Back at the *Seal*, they asked the coxswain, Joe Higgins, for medical help, and he gave them some disinfectant, then told them to take a saltwater shower. "The skipper seemed to think it might have been a kind of jellyfish," mused Taff, "but we never really found out what it was."

After the swimming debacle, Lonsdale took the boat to Port Said to finish the "recuperation," and there the men could finally enjoy themselves. "That was good," remarked Taff, "because there were pubs there, brothels, and whatever real sailors want, you know. So five days we were there, and then back to the routine of the Suez."

"And then, the most peculiar sight I'd ever seen: a sandstorm. It was just like a wall of sand coming at you." Unable to see ahead, Lonsdale searched along the shore for somewhere to secure the boat. He spotted a lone palm tree and headed straight for it, then tied the *Seal* to the tree trunk. Luckily, the sandstorm passed fairly rapidly, and the sub continued her travels. At the end of October *Seal* was back at home and away once more for several uneventful patrols – until the fateful trip in May.[10]

The day after the Germans seized the *Seal* (6 May 1940), Göbbels' radio programmers beamed broadcasts to their countrymen, announcing that German forces had captured a large British submarine in the Kattegat. That same day the BBC picked up that report plus a second one sent by Germans by short wave to Portugal "and her Colonies" informing them that the captured sub's commander and a petty officer had been taken aboard one of the German planes on the scene. "The capture of the submarine by the German crew was effected very rapidly, and this prevented the British from carrying out the measures they had already prepared for scuttling the submarine."[11]

Six months later, Vice Admiral Submarines Max Horton was handed a typed transcription of the latest news from German Radio. In stilted English, the announcer described the scene in a German naval port: "In front of us we see a huge U-boat which today is to be commissioned." This revelation meant that the German navy had apparently converted the *Seal* to their own use. "It happened for the first time in the course of the ... war that it was possible to capture and tow into a German port an English submarine of this size. Today this submarine lies in front of us. However, it looks somewhat different on closer scrutiny, for months have passed and these months were used to make the English U-boat serviceable for German purposes."

Continuing his exaggerated narrative, the announcer bragged that everyone had clearly seen that originally the boat did not live up to the requirements of German U-boat commanders and crews, but that now they were putting it into service. "She lies in front of us at the Pier, we can see her, brightly shining in the sun. It looks almost like a new boat." Using a quote from Schiller, the ceremony speaker then crowed: "The arrow bounces off ... the archer."

Next came an address by the boat's commander, Fregattenkapitän Bruno Mahn: "Comrades, we have fallen in at this spot today in order to put a submarine into the service of the German navy. This is an event which by no means happens every day. ... The ship was destined to fight against Germany, but the fortunes of war made it happen otherwise. Now it is to serve German interests."

Captain Mahn gave orders for placing the vessel, now named UB, in service, and the band struck up a lively tune. The youngest crew member of the U-boat forces saluted Hitler, the crew's supreme commander, and yelled, "Sieg heil!"[12]

To be sure that the victorious account of the capture and refitting of a British sub spread throughout the world, Hitler sent an additional radio broadcast to East Asia and North America on 28 December 1940. "In May this year," the statement glowed, "an item of news aroused great admiration throughout the world. It was that the Germans had succeeded in capturing the British submarine, *Seal*, in the open sea. ... The submarine has now been reconditioned in a German shipyard and can today be used under a German flag in the struggle against the British."[13]

In the *New York Times* a two-inch notice appeared on page six of the 29 December issue saying that a "Seized British Submarine" was now manned by Nazis with a German crew and would fight against the British. "The 2,500-ton former British submarine ... was technically inferior in equipment to this type of German underwater craft, so it was reconditioned within. The outside, except the German war flag at the mast, is the same as before the capture." *Times* editors apparently felt that the event deserved far less attention than the Germans gave it.[14]

At the end of December, German Propaganda sent a photograph of the *Seal* to the Italian fascist newspaper *La Stampa* in Turin, and the editor published it with the caption, "The English submersible 'Seal,' captured by the Germans and placed in service with the new banner of the German navy."[15]

More trumpeting reached the ears of German people on 14 January 1941 with news that the first officer of a motor torpedo boat (Nolte of UJ 128) had been responsible for the capture of the *Seal*. "He and two men went on board ... as prize crew, and by his resolute bearing prevented commander and crew of the Seal from scuttling their ship. Since then he wears the Iron Cross First Class."[16]

By now, word of *Seal*'s conversion to a German warship had flashed around the globe. How Max Horton took the information will never be known: the British Navy avoided expressing thoughts or opinions in their written accounts, giving only facts. However, it was the bull-headed Horton who had ordered Lonsdale to carry out the well-nigh-impossible task of laying mines in deadly enemy waters.

The Admiralty, aware since early June 1940 that *Seal* had been seen under tow to Denmark and later in Kiel with her stern blown away, made a big decision. In a letter written 28 February 1941, they said: "Their Lordships have decided that Lieut. Commander Rupert P. Lonsdale, RN, is to be tried by Court-Martial in connection with the loss of the H.M.S. Seal on his return to this country."[17]

Lonsdale's last radio message to the Admiralty had described his perilous situation: the submarine was filled with water; he had destroyed the confidential books and Asdic, and was attempting to reach the Swedish coast. He had rejected the idea of scuttling *Seal* so as to protect the crew: inside the boat a depth charge had been set to go off at fifty feet, and the explosion could have killed many of the men as they tried to swim away. To Lonsdale's situation message Max Horton had replied, "Your 0150 understood and agreed with. Best of luck. Well done." A few minutes later Horton radioed a second message: "Safety of personnel should be your first consideration after destruction of the Asdics." Neither message reached the sub, leaving Lonsdale to wonder whether his actions had been approved. The Admiralty, knowing full well that Lonsdale had made a desperate attempt to evade capture and had told him he was doing the correct thing, nevertheless decided to hold a trial when the *Seal* crew made it home, but only after they had heard and read Hitler's boastings.[18]

News of the *Seal*'s capture came at a terrible moment for the British people, who had just endured seven months of massive, devastating German bomb attacks, known as the "Blitz." In February 1941 the future looked dark for England, as it did for the interned *Seal* crewmen in Germany.

Notes

1. Harper interview, 3 February 2002.
2. Diary of Private W. C. Law, INTERNET.
3. Harley Tuck's War Diary: Prisoner of War, available at *http://www.nmia. com/gwydion/WWII_S17b/powfin~1.htm* on INTERNET.
4. *New York Times*, 3 June 1939, 1.
5. *New York Times*, 2 and 3 June 1939, 1.
6. Compton-Hall, "Century of the Silent Service," Part Two; Imperial War Museum.
7. Ibid.
8. Harper interview, 17 December 2000; Compton-Hall, "Century of the Silent Service," Part Two.
9. *New York Times*, 3 June 1939, 3.
10. Harper interview, 3 February 2002.
11. RNSM, A1940/003, Report from B.B.C. Digest May 6–7.
12. RNSM, A1940/003, Radio broadcast 7 December 1940.
13. RNSM, A1940/003, Radio broadcast 28 December 1940.
14. *New York Times*, 29 December 1940, 6.
15. RNSM, A1940/003, Message to M.I. 3, 31 December 1940.
16. RNSM, A1940, 003, "Capturer of *Seal* Decorated," 14 January 1940.
17. NA, ADM 156/283.
18. Ibid.

CHAPTER VIII

The Wireless War

"When we got sunk and captured," explained Taff, "Lord Haw-Haw broadcast to England in beautiful, perfect English: 'Today the *Seal* has been sunk, and if there are any survivors, I will announce it at a certain time on a certain day of the week.' Of course that meant that everybody in England was listening for the survivors' names. I think there was about twelve of them announced, that's all." After the broadcast in England and one week after the capture of *Seal*, the Admiralty sent telegrams to relatives of all the sailors. Taff's wife Joan in Portsmouth read her message: "Deeply regret to inform you that your husband Herbert E Harper stoker D/K X 80738 is missing on war service believed to be a prisoner of war. Commodore Devonport." Then on 8 June came a second telegram from the British navy saying, "It is now established that your husband … is alive and a prisoner of war." A green postcard labelled "Kriegsgefangenenpost" (prison camp postcard) arrived from Taff on 6 July with a printed message in German telling her that he was alive and well; an attached memo from the Royal Navy informed her that his prison was Stalag XX A3A in Germany.[1]

Happy Eckersall's wife Dolly received news on 12 May from the British Admiralty that the *Seal* was missing. On the night that Lord Haw-Haw was supposed to announce a few survivors' names, an air raid hit Portsmouth, and in all the chaos, fires and explosions, she had no way to tune in to the broadcast. Then in August came a small green postcard with "I am well" checked and a signature. "I had to take it down to the naval barracks," Dolly recalled, "and they said, 'Can you guarantee that's your husband's signature?'" She verified his writing, and on 20 August 1940, the young wife knew with certainty that her husband was a prisoner of war.[2]

In Ireland, Mickey Reynolds' mother read in the *Ballymena Observer* in May that the *Seal* was overdue and presumed lost. About a week earlier she had had a terrible dream that her son was in danger – that he had climbed high onto a steep rock, then shouted, "Oh, Daddy, come and help me." The next day she felt that bad news about Mickey was coming, and that afternoon a telegram arrived from the Admiralty saying, "Sorry to inform you that your son is missing. Believed to be a prisoner of war. …"

A local news report said that "Mrs. Reynolds is only recovering from a serious illness, and the news that her son is missing has left her prostrate with grief."[3]

"My first wife was in Gosport with our two young children," said Ernie Truman, "and one evening she had put the children to bed and for some reason switched on the radio and got Lord Haw-Haw. At the start of the broadcast he said, 'This is Germany calling. At the end of this broadcast we will give you the names of ten survivors of the Submarine *Seal*.'" Everybody was already aware that *Seal* had been reported lost, but that evening was the first time Ernie's wife Kathleen received news that anyone was still alive. "At the end of the broadcast," added Truman, "he read out ten names, and one of them was mine, another was one of my colleagues who lived just down the road from us."

Even though it was midnight, Kathleen jumped up and ran out of the house to tell her friend Olive that Olive's husband Jack, Ernie's fellow crewman, was safe. Olive had already sprinted down the road to tell Kathleen, and the two ran past each other in the darkness. Stopping in their tracks, they shared the wonderful news.[4]

Information had trickled into the Admiralty from various sources confirming *Seal*'s unhappy fate. From Naval Intelligence on 2 June came the terse words: "*Seal* is in Kiel with her stern blown away. Definite information." Four days later a secret message arrived from the Swedish Naval Attaché, London, who received it from the Swedish Commander in Chief Navy. It read:

> On May 5th at 3.30–3.55 a.m. a Submarine was attacked with bombs by an aeroplane about 9' 215° from Pater Noster. Several Aeroplanes and a German trawler reached the spot at about 5.30 a.m.
>
> At about 6.00 a.m. a Submarine was seen waterlogged about 8' 300° from Vinga lighthouse. The Submarine's stern was under water, with a heavy list, a large white flag fixed to the mast or the after periscope, and was marked "37 M" on the sides of the conning tower. By the side of the Submarine there was a German armed trawler, which was occupied partly with taking off the Submarine's crew (the survivors numbered about 25 men), who stood lined up on the Submarine's deck forward of the conning tower – and partly with towing the Submarine. They succeeded in this after a good deal of trouble and the U-boat was towed in the direction of Frederikshavn.[5]

This intelligence probably had been gathered by the pilot of the Swedish Junkers 86 that UJ 128's captain saw flying around the disabled *Seal*. In any case, the British quickly ascertained that their big minelayer had been captured by the enemy – a bitter piece of news: no UK warship had surrendered since the *Reindeer* capitulated to the American *Wasp* in the War of 1812.

At the time Admiralty learned of the *Seal* disaster, things were not going well in the war. Great Britain had failed to protect Norway from invasion, and on 10 May the Germans marched into the Netherlands and France. Hitler was storming across Europe when Winston Churchill became Prime Minister on 10 May, and gloom prevailed as the British people accelerated preparations to fend off a German invasion of their own shores.

Hitler had indeed planned to tackle Great Britain in "Operation Sea Lion," and was assembling troops and planes in France for the purpose. Just after the fall of France in June, Hitler decided to first destroy British air defences and then to ferry a large army across the English Channel; he then initiated the "Battle of Britain," a fierce air war that lasted from 10 July to 31 October 1940. In the seacoast town of Portsmouth, home of Britain's largest Royal Navy base and arsenal, bombs blasted the area just as *Seal* wives received notices that their husbands had been taken prisoner.[6]

In 1939 the people in large cities in the south of England were already expecting German troops and had sent their children to stay in private homes in the country, but as nothing seemed to be happening, they brought the young ones back. Unfortunately, the first bombs hit Portsmouth on 11 July 1940, killing eighteen people and injuring eighty. Right away, workers hustled to build shelters outside towns so that citizens carrying their bedding could get there quickly on buses and spend the night, as bombing became heavier after dark. Three more devastating raids crashed into England in August and four in September; then more from October to December; and on Christmas Day the Luftwaffe used high explosive and incendiary bombs, destroying massive areas of businesses, industries, and homes. Hitler's strategy to terrorise the British citizenry into submission seemed to be succeeding. "A regular feature of raiding has been the machine-gunning of working services and of roads leading from bombed towns. Casualties were only slight, but demoralisation possibly greater than actual raids," a British official reported.[7]

A hellish blitz rained down on Portsmouth on 10 January 1941. "Arrangements were made to evacuate the women and children who were homeless," the government wrote. "They embarked in buses, carrying a few possessions and were accommodated in schools and halls in outlying districts."

All in all, sixty-seven bomb attacks devastated Portsmouth, Southampton, and Gosport, killing a total of 180,000 out of a population of 253,000. Ninety-three percent of the homes were damaged or gutted; and the stately 1890 guildhall, main shopping areas, and many public buildings lay in ruins.[8]

During the terror and chaos, explosions and fires, Taff Harper's wife Joan carried on with true British grit. "She went right through it," declared Taff. "She acted as a firefighter, as a matter of fact." The Harpers lost their first home – the one they had purchased a couple of months after they were married. "It was bombed right to the ground. There was nothing saved from it, but we had a bit of furniture in store, fortunately, so she got another place, and of course that got bombed."

From the second home – destroyed after two months – Joan saved a few sticks of furniture, and they used the two wardrobes, a dressing table, and other small pieces for several years after the war. "At that time you couldn't buy any furniture, just the cheap stuff made of cardboard and plywood," recalled Taff. "So we kept the old things, with all the steel bomb splinters in them; you couldn't even dig them out, and you had to be very careful with them. You couldn't polish the furniture because you'd cut your hands up."

In Thorn prison camp everybody knew that Portsmouth and other towns were being hit by bombing raids. "The Jerries were boasting about it: all the dirty details came over the German radio, which blared out German music and German news at you all day." Fearing for his wife's safety, Taff wrote letters pleading with her to get out of Portsmouth and go to Burry Port in South Wales to live with his mother. "It was very quiet down there, not much bombing." Joan eventually packed up her clothes and travelled westwards to live with her mother-in-law.

"Of course my Mum made her very welcome, because Mum had three sons in the war – me, my brother who was in cargo ships, and the younger one in the army, in the desert." One day a letter arrived for Joan from the Ministry of War inquiring as to why she was not employed in war efforts. Right away Joan (not having any choice in the matter) went to work in an ammunition factory about three miles away at Pembrey. The entire installation, constructed in World War I, had been totally covered with sand dunes. "They had big sliding doors that went into them," explained Taff, "and there was nothing showing on top. The Germans were looking for the factory and bombed Burry Port once or twice, but they never did find it." Joan worked in the hidden facility for several years. "She made good friends at the plant and could speak Welsh better than they could. She was very good with languages."

Towards the end of the war the factory passed a new regulation barring any light-skinned persons from working in certain departments. "But for some reason," went on Taff, "somebody made a mistake and let Joan, who was blonde, into one of those, and she was there for a month. She turned very, very bright yellow, with blazing red hair; it had perforated her skin, you see, and it took her two years to get rid of it." Joan and Taff figured that was lucky, because "they kicked her out of the factory."[9]

During the bombing of southern England and London, Lord Haw-Haw gloated in his broadcasts from Germany, announcing false forthcoming air raids that would hit prominent stores, buildings, airports, and other vital locations. " Haw-Haw rumours are again becoming more prevalent. Such rumours are so varied and numerous that occasionally one of them happens to coincide with a local occurrence, with the natural consequence that greater credence is placed on those that follow," bemoaned the British Southern Command of the Home Forces, a civilian defence organisation. "Every effort should be made to ridicule and deny these rumours, and every opportunity should be taken in lectures and talks … to drive home the fact that investigation invariably proves that the rumoured announcements have never, in fact, been made."[10]

Another disclosure on 10 August 1940 came from a commander of the Home Forces: "The 'Haw-Haw' … broadcasts are listened to in Public Houses from time to time, but no other propaganda services have been heard of. At the beginning of the war the 'Haw-Haw' Broadcasts were listened to more frequently, reactions being amusement mixed with derision. The novelty of these broadcasts has now worn off, Haw-Haw being regarded as a bore instead of a comedian." As for the troops, they had very little chance to tune in to German propaganda and cared nothing about it.[11]

Under a paragraph entitled "Deductions," the commander wrote that "the subject matter and the method of presentation … are based on the illusion that there is a wide gulf between the British government and the British people and that the British people are lukewarm and unconvinced in their attitude of resistance to Nazi Germany."

In September 1939, a couple of weeks after the broadcasts started, Jonah Barrington, radio editor of the London *Daily Express*, had penned an amusing article about the mysterious Hamburg announcer, nicknaming him "Lord Haw-Haw" and likening him to P. G. Wodehouse's Bertie Wooster. "From his accent," said Barrington, "I imagine Lord Haw-Haw as having a receding chin, a questing nose, thin yellow hair brushed back, a monocle, a vacant eye, and a gardenia in his buttonhole." Three weeks later Lord Haw-Haw had become an international figure.[12]

Apparently Lord Haw-Haw's broadcasts caused the British Home Service a fair amount of concern: their reports summarised the situation saying, "Germany seeks to undermine morale and create confusion among the public … seeks to confuse and mislead military authorities as to the nature of German military plans." Home defenders decided that the propaganda broadcasts to England had a second purpose: to create general confusion, suspicion and distrust, and to undermine confidence in the government and armed forces. This was accomplished by false stories of inefficiency; shortages; damage; corruption; class conflicts; attacks on personalities (especially the Prime Minister); giving misleading advice (to evacuate in the event of invasion); the spreading of rumours (such as parachute landings); and incitements to revolution. Four programmes from the "New British Broadcasting Station," the "Workers' Challenge Station," the "Christian Peace Movement Station," and "Radio Caledonia" rattled out incessant propaganda from Germany in the voice of Lord Haw-Haw and other British traitors.[13]

Misleading remarks on the German programmes did indeed produce many unfounded rumours among the people of southern England, who were trying to defend themselves against high explosive and incendiary bombs with barely trained civilians, a few big guns, and courageous RAF pilots. Realising the seriousness of the situation, Winston Churchill, from his office-bedroom in the underground Cabinet War Rooms, made four speeches via the BBC to the citizens of Great Britain, the Commonwealth, and occupied Europe, denouncing Hitler and urging the Allies to keep up their spirits. King George VI and Queen Elizabeth, wearing elegant attire, visited bombed neighbourhoods in London, Portsmouth, and other cities, and offered sympathy and encouragement to their suffering subjects. Along with the royal visits and Churchill's efforts, someone wrote a song that became a big hit: "Lord Haw-Haw the Humbug from Hamburg."[14]

In December 1939 the Ministry of Information conducted a survey to find out how Hamburg (Haw-Haw) broadcasts affected the public. Results showed that one in six adults listened to Haw-Haw, but four out of six regularly listened to BBC News. Most people tuned in to Hamburg at 9:15 every night. "This is Germany calling, Germany calling," intoned his confident British voice. "Good evening, everybody." Then followed outrageous charges against Churchill, short plays, English music hall jokes, and burlesque skits depicting Englishmen as pompous, overbearing and monocle-wearing. In short, the announcer amused the Brits, sending them into gales of laughter.[15]

But listening increased in the early months of 1940. "The blackout, the novelty of hearing the enemy, the desire to hear both sides, the insatiable appetite for news and the desire to be in the swim have all played their part both in building up Hamburg's audience and in holding it together," the Ministry admitted. "An extremely important primary cause of listening to shows from Hamburg is, undoubtedly, curiosity, with which must be coupled the novel 'thrill' of hearing, from the comfortable security of one's fireside, the voice of one's would-be destroyer."

Some of the results of a written questionnaire explained the public's reasons for tuning in to Lord Haw-Haw: many thought that "Lord Haw-Haw's version of the news was so fantastic that it was funny; some tuned in because so many other people were listening to him; a few, because they liked to hear the German point of view; others, because his anecdotes made people laugh and because the BBC news was so dull; and a handful because he was clever."[16]

To rebut Haw-Haw's endless lies, the government initiated a crusade to ridicule and counter their wireless foe. At the start of the war with Germany, BBC programming consisted of long, boring, and innocuous presentations. "I'd rather face German guns than hear any more organ music," complained one listener; others called in to gripe that the BBC was dominated by organ recitals and public announcements. Even Winston

Churchill, in the beginning of radio in the 1920s, disliked the broadcasters and labelled them "The enemy within the gates." However, as German bombs began to rain on his country, he sang a different tune, realising that this wireless medium could be a powerful war weapon. Listeners heard his encouraging broadcasts and were fortified.[17]

The BBC paid attention to public criticism of their programming and came up with a new comedy show, "It's That Man Again," featuring Colonel Chinstrap ("I don't mind if I do") and Mrs. Mopp ("Can I do yer now, sir?"). Comedian Tommy Handley as Chinstrap and his fellow actors attracted sixteen million listeners each week with their antics; and three war correspondents helped bring in more audiences with their nightly "War Report" at the end of the main evening news.

But people listened to Haw-Haw, too; they were tickled and at the same time disgusted with his absurd show, "Views on the News," that came on just after the BBC nightly news (at the same time as "War Report"). Some considered him first-class entertainment and others thought his broadcasts contained a grain of truth. The fight for wireless audiences was on, with the BBC barely in the lead: Josef Göbbels, Hitler's head of propaganda, was said to have admitted that BBC Radio had won "the intellectual invasion of Europe."[18]

As the war ground on, everybody in Great Britain puzzled about the identity of Lord Haw-Haw, and many wrote to London newspapers asking the editors to please solve the mystery. At last, on 17 December 1939, the *Sunday Pictorial* announced, "Lord Haw-Haw's Wife Tells: He's an Englishman!" Most people had already assumed he was English because of his impeccable English accent, but now they learned his name: William Joyce. News reporters had interviewed his ex-wife the previous night, and she verified that she recognised Joyce's voice the first time she heard it. "One night I turned on the wireless while they [her two children] were in the room. Joyce was speaking. My eldest daughter turned pale, and when I asked her what was the matter, she said, 'That's W. J., isn't it?' – she always called her father W. J."

The ex-wife went on to tell reporters that she had heard that Joyce had moved to Berlin in late August, a few days before England declared war on Germany (3 September 1939). She described her ex-husband as a brilliant linguist who could speak four languages and that his friends had forecast a great future for him. "But," she continued, "I'm afraid he has a queer twist in his makeup." A fanatical Fascist in 1933 when Hitler came into power, Joyce went on to found the National Socialist League, and his violent temper landed him in jail numerous times. A long, ugly scar on his right cheek was reported to have come from one of his brawls.[19]

By February 1941 Military Intelligence had been working on solving Haw-Haw's identity, and they obtained valuable information from a Major G. N. Preston of OS 17. Preston wrote a memo to Captain Liddell in MI5 saying that he had known Joyce as a Latin tutor in 1929 or 1930 and that Joyce was considered clever, sarcastic, and supercilious, was an ardent Fascist, and had a large scar on his lower cheek. "There is one curious point that might interest a psychologist – Joyce was an inveterate 'doodler'! He could never come within reach of pencil and paper without drawing a coronated devil's head, as under [drawing], and this never varied. Later, it might be possible to establish his identity by reason of this curious habit alone." Preston told MI5 that he had not the slightest doubt that the broadcaster from Germany was William Joyce, as his voice, manner, and radio personality were identical to the man he had known.[20]

On 3 April 1941 an article appeared in the *Daily Herald*: "Haw-Haw Says: I Am." Beneath a photograph of dimple-chinned, scarred, slick-haired Joyce were the words, "Lord Haw-Haw, broadcasting from Bremen last night, admitted for the first time that he was William Joyce and that he had been imprisoned in England six times for his political opinions. … He said that he left England and abandoned all his personal possessions because he was convinced of a German victory." A Military Intelligence report verified the revelation: "On April 2nd 1941, Joyce disclosed his identity over the German Radio in a broadcast monitored by the BBC, and if thought necessary, evidence can be adduced to prove this."[21]

Years later, in 1944, Joyce broadcast on 28 August about the reasons that he had terminated his residence in England. "One of those rare but long-life visions is that of the last few moments in which I beheld the land to which I had devoted myself until I saw that it had, in essence, become a colony of Palestine."[22]

Corporal Francis Maton, a British POW, went to work in the German radio service as a member of the "British Free Corps." The Germans selected certain war prisoners like Maton and made their lives wretched with solitary confinement, lack of food and warm clothing, beatings, and other tortures, to force them into working against the British in locations outside the prison camps. Maton, one of twenty-one "Free Corps" members and secretly assisting British Intelligence, met William Joyce and other former British citizens who had gone over to the German side at Radio National. "All these people," he wrote to MI5, "who I have mentioned as broadcasting for Germany I have actually seen with my own eyes, and while most of them have quite magnetic personalities, I think the most outstanding … of them is surely William Joyce. Joyce is a man who many people have tried to describe, and … he is both universally known and hated over here."

Maton went on to say that Joyce was a complete idealist, second only to Hitler himself and was often moody and nervous. "He also beats his wife, who is rather a fast woman and has had affairs in Berlin with a large number of men. Joyce surprised me by the amount of courage he showed during some of the worst raids, and while most of us stood shivering down in the air raid shelters, Joyce stood alone on top of the Reichsportsfeld making a recording of the raid."

Joyce's broadcasts, declared Maton, had formerly been from written manuscripts (guided by Göbbels) but in about 1944 he apparently discarded them. "Joyce has risen into the position where is kingpin of the whole show. ... I have myself seen him sit down in front of a radio, listen to the BBC news, walk straight over to a microphone and broadcast his well known 'Views on the News.'"[23]

At the age of 33, Lord Haw-Haw had created a successful new life as a Hitler worshipper, hater of Jews, and broadcaster. Even the noted foreign correspondent and author William L. Shirer was fascinated by his personality when he met Joyce in Berlin in the autumn of 1941. "I had just finished my broadcast in Berlin. It was one o'clock in the morning and the British bombers were over us again," he wrote for the newspapers. In a dark air raid shelter Shirer found himself in company with the noted William Joyce and his second wife Margaret, who urged that they leave the shelter by sneaking past the guards, and this they did. Finding an unused tunnel, the three shared a bottle of schnapps brought by "Lady Haw-Haw," as Margaret called herself.

"Haw-Haw can drink as straight as any man, and if you can get over your initial revulsion at his being a traitor, you find him an amusing and even intelligent fellow," Shirer claimed. After finishing their libations, the trio went up some stairs into Haw-Haw's office and there opened the blinds to watch the bombs and raging fires in Berlin. "To the south of the city the guns were hammering away, lighting up the sky. Sitting there in the black of the room, I had a long talk with the man."

Shirer explained that Joyce's nickname in Germany was "Froelich," or "Joyful" and that Haw-Haw denied being a traitor: Joyce claimed that he was no more a traitor than the thousands of British and Americans who had renounced their citizenship to become comrades in the Soviet Union or Germans who defected to the United States in 1848. "This doesn't satisfy me," wrote Shirer. "He kept talking about 'we' and 'us,' and I asked him which people he meant. 'We Germans, of course,' he snapped."

Shirer described Joyce as a heavily built man, about five foot nine, with Irish eyes "that twinkle," and a scarred face. "He has a titanic hatred for Jews and an equally titanic one for capitalists." Joyce thought that the Nazi movement would free the world from the bonds of "plutocratic capitalists" and saw himself as a liberator of the working class.

From Joyce's booklet entitled "Twilight over England" William Shirer learned that the traitor had been born in New York of English parents in 1906. Joyce's father and mother had left their home and settled in New York; and Joyce blamed their move on "loss of fortunes by reason of their devotion to the British crown." In 1909 the Joyce family returned to the British Isles, this time making their home in Ireland. Joyce, a bright student, attended the University of London in 1923, studying literature, history and psychology. This was to be the year of Hitler's unsuccessful "Putsch" in Munich, and Joyce, thrilled by Nazi ideas, joined the British Fascists.

Ten years later, when the Führer took over Germany, Joyce became a member of Oswald Mosley's British Union of Fascists and soon was one of its principal spokesmen and writers. He spent three years as Mosley's chief of propaganda but was kicked out of the party in 1937; Joyce and a former member of parliament then organised the National Socialist League. In attempts to promulgate his beliefs that England would lose the forthcoming war, Joyce grew more violent and was arrested twice on charges of assault and disturbing the peace.

Already convinced of Hitler's invincibility, Joyce proclaimed in "Twilight over England" that he had no trouble making a decision to abandon his country. "To me it was clear on the morning of August 25 [1939] that the greatest struggle in history was doomed to take place. I felt that if, for perfect reasons of conscience, I could not fight for her, I must give her up forever." On that date Joyce and his second wife Margaret boarded a boat for Ostend, Belgium, "to take part in the sacred struggle to free the world."

Of course the burgeoning German radio, under Josef Göbbels, happily welcomed British traitors into its service. The only problem with Joyce, though, was his nasal voice, and at first the Propaganda Minister considered him entirely unfit for an announcing position. However, Göbbels finally realised that Joyce's wit and intelligence would be excellent for his efforts to ignite feelings of racial hatred at home and fear among the British, so he let the traitor have a microphone. In the beginning, too, Joyce complained about "the inane things which Göbbels makes me say."[24]

As soon as Hitler came to power in 1933, he selected Göbbels as his new "Reich Minister for Public Entertainment and Propaganda"; thus, Göbbels totally controlled film-making, drama and other arts, publishing, and radio. By coincidence, the "wireless" became quite popular during the same years as the Nazi era, and from the start, radio ownership in Germany grew rapidly. When Hitler seized control, 4.5 million citizens owned wireless sets; by 1942 about sixteen million, or seventy percent, enjoyed radio, making the medium a splendid form of mass communication. The affordable Deutscher Kleinempfänger (German mini-receiver) sold for approximately one week's wages of an average worker; everybody had a radio, and entire families gathered in the evenings to listen. In case a few did not have access to a set, the Führer installed loudspeakers in restaurants, factories, and all public places to make sure everybody could hear his incessant yelling, Göbbels' propaganda, and happy, schmaltzy music. But he made it crystal clear that *nobody* would be allowed to listen to the British Broadcasting Company, on penalty of death.[25]

Naturally, the Führer ordered placement of loudspeakers within the newly constructed prisoner of war camps in Germany, even if the camps had barely any food, bedding, or clothing for the internees. But before long, the prisoners devised ways to secretly tune in to the BBC, while German families clandestinely listened to the British broadcasts, as well. Indeed, the wireless war had begun.

Notes

1. Harper interview, 18 November 2000; Harper collection.
2. Eckersall interview, 27 September 2000.
3. Lawrence Reynolds collection.
4. Truman interview, 22 September 2000.
5. RNSM, Telegram from NID, 2/6; RNSM, Secret message 6 June 1940.
6. *Encyclopedia Britannica*, 1963, s.v. "Battle of Britain," and "Portsmouth."
7. NA, HO 199/451.
8. *The Portsmouth News*, "Smitten City"; *Encyclopedia Britannica*, 1963, "Portsmouth"; NA, HO 186/2939.
9. Taff Harper, telephone interview with author, 3 April 2002.
10. NA, HO 186/313, 32A.
11. Ibid., 21A.
12. *New York Times*, Magazine section, 25 February 1940, 3.
13. NA, HO 186/313, 31B.
14. NA, HO 186/313.
15. *New York Times*, Magazine section, 25 February 1940, 3.
16. NA, HO 186/313, "Hamburg Broadcast Propaganda."
17. Imperial War Museum, *The Cabinet War Rooms*, 14.
18. BBC Past, Present and Future Written Archives, "BBC History"; available from *http://www.bbc.co.uk/thenandnow/history/1940sn.shtml* on INTERNET.
19. NA, KV 2/245, *Sunday Pictorial* (London), 17 December 1939.
20. NA, KV 2/245.
21. NA, KV 2/245, *Daily Herald* (London), 3 April 1941; HO 45/25780,"M.I.5 Report."
22. NA, KV 2/245.
23. Ibid.
24. Previous quotes from NA, KV 2/245, *Sunday Chronicle* (London), "I Meet Haw-Haw," by William L. Shirer. (Shirer authored the books *Berlin Diary* and *The Rise and Fall of the Third Reich.)*
25. Grunberger, *The 12-Year Reich*, 401, 402.

1. HMS *Seal*, early Porpoise-class minelayer, July 1939. The stern has a flat 'clamshell' door that opens for laying mines (Royal Navy Submarine Museum).

2. Prison ship *Altmark* trapped in ice at Jøssing Fjord, Norway, 17 February 1940. *Seal* helped in chasing her down (Imperial War Museum, HU 5206).

3. Lieutenant Commander Rupert Lonsdale, captain of HMS *Seal* (Mrs Rupert Lonsdale).

4. *Seal* crew members, 28 January 1939. Happy Eckersall on left, holding seabag (Lawrence Reynolds).

5. Quartet of *Seal* sailors: left to right, Maurice Oley, Sam Brown, Albert ("Happy") Eckersall, and Bill Hurst (Albert Eckersall).

6. Able Seaman Hugh ("Mickey") Reynolds, from Ballymena, Northern Ireland, taken on 16 June 1939, with a note of his medals (Lawrence Reynolds).

7. *Seal* with German boarding party approaching. A group of *Seal* crew members on deck (Bibliothek für Zeitgeschichte, Stuttgart, 389/20).

8. German Arado seaplane of same type and squadron that captured *Seal* on 5 May 1940 (Prof. Dr Ralph Uhlig).

9. JU 128 towing *Seal* toward Frederikshavn, Denmark. White surrender flag can be seen on *Seal*'s periscope (Bibliothek für Zeitgeschichte, Stuttgart 389/17).

10. German war flag flies atop British surrender tablecloth and British war flag as *Seal* is towed into Kiel (Bibliothek für Zeitgeschichte, Stuttgart 389/11).

11. Kapitän zur See Hans Rösing, German submarine expert who inspected and evaluated *Seal* (© Hans Rösing).

12. German officers inspect shot holes in *Seal*'s tower. Frederikshavn, Denmark, in May 1940 (Bibliothek für Zeitgeschichte, Stuttgart 389/21).

13. *Seal* undergoing repairs at Frederikshavn, Denmark, May 1940 (U-Boot Archiv, Cuxhaven).

14. *Seal* entering Krupp Shipyard (Germaniawerft) at Kiel (Bibliothek für Zeitgeschichte, Stuttgart 389/8).

15. Krupp Shipyard with *Seal* ready to be refurbished as a German submarine (Bibliothek für Zeitgeschichte, Stuttgart 389/14).

16. Lt. Trevor Beet leads *Seal* crewmen through Frederikshavn to schoolhouse prison (Imperial War Museum, 35968).

17. *Seal* crew having a small meal in schoolhouse prison yard at Frederikshavn (Imperial War Museum HU 35946).

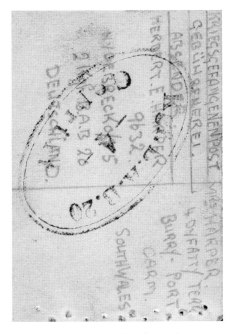

18a. A miniature photograph (40mm x 60mm) of Taff Harper taken by a German guard. Taff paid the guard five cigarettes and wears a British army uniform allocated to POWs (Taff Harper).

18b. The back of the miniature photograph of Taff Harper addressed to his wife which, despite its size, she received in the post.

19. Most of *Seal*'s crew at first prison camp, Stalag XX A, Thorn, Poland, 1940 (Albert Eckersall).

20. First German crew to man UB, formerly *Seal*. The photograph was probably taken at the commissioning ceremony (Bibliothek für Zeitgeschichte, Stuttgart 589/13).

21. The German crew takes UB out for a trial run. The submarine was never used as a warship against the British (Bibliothek für Zeitgeschichte, Stuttgart 389/12).

22. British traitor and broadcaster William Joyce, alias Lord Haw-Haw, dressed in Fascist uniform (Imperial War Museum PL 68682).

23. Nightclub scene on Marlag-Milag stage. Photographs were taken of plays and sporting events and mailed to POW families by the Germans (Lawrence Reynolds).

24. *The Pirates of Penzance*, staged by POWs at Marlag-Milag prison camp. Men often played women's roles (Lawrence Reynolds).

25. Marlag-Milag theatre production depicting an air raid shelter (Lawrence Reynolds).

26. Postcard photograph of a POW football team of twelve men wearing underwear uniforms. Snow falls as the men pose. Mickey Reynolds is second from left, front row (Lawrence Reynolds).

27. Prison camp boxing match. Prisoners were allowed to play sports in many camps (Lawrence Reynolds).

28. Aerial view of Colditz Castle, an 'escape proof' prison for officers (Museum der Stadt Colditz).

29. Tubby Lister of HMS *Seal* and Wally Hammond of HMS *Shark* after escaping from a German work camp to Switzerland in December 1942 (Royal Navy Submarine Museum).

30. Fifty-million-Mark note found by Taff Harper after the Germans surrendered (Taff Harper).

31. King George VI, Queen Elizabeth and Princess Elizabeth greet Mickey Reynolds, one of a group of wounded sailors, at a victory ceremony in Londonderry, Northern Ireland, 1945 (Lawrence Reynolds).

32. First *Seal* reunion, 11 July 1946, at Seal Village, England. Rupert Lonsdale fourth from right, second row; Taff Harper, front row on left (Lawrence Reynolds).

CHAPTER IX

Marlag-Milag

Seal's crew, except for Taff Harper and his three mates, survived for seven months at Thorn, Poland; meanwhile, the Germans were busy building prisoner of war camps as fast as possible to handle the enormous number of Allied captives and forced labourers being transported into the country. From the beginning of the war in early September 1939, Hitler's forces were making swift, ferocious attacks on neighbouring countries, seizing one after another. As POWs poured in, Hitler incarcerated high-ranking Allied officers in nine ancient castles and fortresses located on high mountain peaks and housed the rest of the masses in approximately forty-four Stalags throughout Germany and Poland.

The Geneva Convention had earlier laid out rules for prisoner groupings: "Belligerents shall, so far as possible, avoid assembling in a single camp prisoners of different races or nationalities." Apparently this was done, in that after the Germans commenced building separate camps, they kept the French, Russians, Poles, and other unfortunates in separate compounds. However, Russia had never signed the Geneva Convention, and their intransigence caused the Russian prisoners to receive brutal treatment – far worse than other groups. Except for the Russian POWs, German officials acted fairly well within the rules of the Convention, as some of the prisoners later testified.[1]

Luckily for the *Seal* men, their chiefs, petty officers and ratings were able to leave Thorn after about seven months and go to a new camp at Sandbostel, built for navy prisoners and called "Marlag." Seventeen miles north of Bremen, the navy compound seemed in many ways to be a vast improvement over Thorn prison. "Life became quite civilised," recalled Ernie Truman, "because there's that camaraderie amongst seamen – mariners – that exists. From then on, we were high and dry. With navy officers in charge at Marlag, life became much more bearable: they ran the place like a ship." The 400 German guards came from Naval Artillery Units and ranged in age from 45 to 55: all were unfit for front line service.[2]

"This was a very large camp, and, joy of joys," Ernie exclaimed, "our officers rejoined us, and we were pleased to see them." Naval prisoners from around the world came streaming into Marlag, and many of them were submariners the *Seal* men had known prior to being captured. "The reunions were great and the stories interesting. We also received a real chaplain, which took a load from my shoulders."[3]

"The camp was quite a good one," said Happy Eckersall. "Kapitänleutnant zur See Spiess, who was a U-boat captain in World War I, was very fair. He wasn't a typical Nazi." Some of the people Happy met in the camp were merchant mariners, and others were navy men whose names had been mentioned in newspapers as having been captured. "When it came to cleaning the camp, people had different jobs – picking up paper, cigarettes, matchsticks, anything like that. We kept it clean."[4]

One of Happy's chores had to do with sanitation. "For toilets, there was a cess pit, and the toilets was built on top of it, and everything went down into this big tub. We had this thing we called 'Smelly Nelly,' which was a handcart with a big tank on top, and we used to pump it [effluence] up into this Smelly Nelly." Once they had filled the cart, the sailors wheeled it out to a nearby field, opened the sluice at the back, and then ran around spreading it on the ground. "Fertiliser," said Happy.

When the men began to get organised in the big Marlag camp, they decided to have some football games. While escapers busily dug away at tunnels, the players took the dirt in small batches and spread it on the football field. "We had some good football matches – ship to ship – playing one another," recalled Eckersall. "We had quite a good team: there was myself and Algar, one of my chums, and Spoff Middleton – he was chief stoker. At one time Algar was a welterweight champion; I was a middleweight and Spoff was a heavyweight."

During the Sandbostel period, Eckersall said that the Germans brought in many Russians, straight from where they had been captured, "and they was in a sorry state. We went past them in a crowd one day, and some was alongside the road, dying. We was supposed to get Red Cross parcels, and it made us feel so bad." Later, Eckersall saw the Germans bring in horse carts, throw the Russians' bodies on them, and wheel them back into camp. "And then they would pull off their clothes and throw them in a big, deep pit, about twelve foot deep, then put lime on them. That was the end of them. If they even looked dead, they'd put them in."

At Sandbostel the first Red Cross parcels started coming in, to everyone's delight. "We got organised, with four in a group," continued Happy. "We got one bunch of parcels on a Monday, and another on Wednesday for the other chaps. So he shared your parcel, and you shared his. You would have one parcel between the two of you. We would have been dead if we hadn't got the Red Cross parcels."[5]

As the prison population increased with POWs from the European and Russian fronts, the Germans decided to move the camp to nearby Westertimke and create two separate camps: Marlag for the Royal Navy,

Milag for the Merchant Navy. In 1943 they added Dulag for transits. In Marlag the navy officers and ratings lived in separate areas – the officers in "O" and the ratings (non-officers) and petty officers in "M." Swiss Legation and International Red Cross reports said that "there were very few complaints from P/Ws themselves. … The conditions in Marlag 'O' and 'M' were satisfactory, and for a P/W camp, the running, which was done in naval style, and the morale were outstanding. The food was good, and sufficient with the aid of Red Cross parcels, which began to arrive in 1942; sanitation was fair; the clothing situation not very satisfactory; and mail delivery slow – held up due to a shortage of censors." In 1940 the World's Committee of the YMCA joined the International Committee of the Red Cross in inspecting camps, supplying leisure equipment like books and games, musical instruments, and other items for the prisoners.

"From one of the guards," explained Happy Eckersall, "we found out that we were going to be moved from Sandbostel to another area nearby." To be sure that no one pulled a shenanigan, the German guards searched each man as he was leaving, then marked an "X" on his back. "The only thing they didn't know," chuckled Happy, "was that we also had some white chalk, so we finished things up, and everybody had 'OXO' on their back. ["Oxo" brand bouillon cubes had long been a staple in Britain.] That upset them a little bit."

When they arrived at the Westertimke camp a few miles away, the men learned that their belongings had not been inspected and were stored in a barracks with a front and a back door. "When we got there, we found two guards at the front and none in the rear. One of the chaps who noticed the unguarded back door said to the guards, 'Hey, your back door is open.' So the guard told him that nobody was supposed to go in that way; but then everybody went around in the back, got their kit and took it away with them." The sailors had a big laugh, because the German guards strictly followed their orders to keep watch on the front entry. "They wouldn't think of looking the other way."[6]

At Marlag "M," Ernie Truman recalled, "We found a hutted [barracks] camp with better facilities and much more space for recreational services." At Thorn, the only exercise the men could get was to walk around a path at the top of the fortress for about a quarter of a mile: at Marlag they could participate in sports such as football, cricket, and softball. Ernie said that the men had a chance to attend study classes and visit the library, stocked with books from the YMCA. "A complete barrack block was provided for a theatre, and with help from the authorities, was fitted out with proper stage lighting and even an orchestra pit." Both the ratings' and officers' compounds had a theatre: in the case of "O," Lieutenant Commander Clark designed the remodelling of a condemned living quarters, and with some other officers and materials provided by the Germans, converted it into a performance hall. In prison camps, the authorities placed great emphasis on high morale, trying to keep the internees content and their thoughts off mischief and escaping. Since war rules prohibited forced labour for POWs, the Germans kept everyone busy, and on the whole, their methods seemed to work well.

Truman labelled the theatres "a blessing to all." Orchestras were formed, with some of the instruments handmade by the prisoners and others donated by the YMCA. Everybody liked the concerts, and "There were several occasions on which various people performed portions of Gilbert and Sullivan operas and other works, so we collected those who showed interest to see whether we could do something rather special," Ernie explained. Wondering if they might be infringing on any copyrights by performing the excerpts, the musicians decided to ask the composer. "I managed to write to Sir Rupert D'Oyly Carte [producer of Gilbert and Sullivan operas] for guidance. The result was a lovely letter from Sir Rupert giving us permission, his blessing, and the scores and libretti of several operas. The response from the big man himself gave us a great lift."

The new playhouse had proper stage lighting and even an orchestra pit, and "we were able to proceed with our wish to produce full Gilbert and Sullivan operas. ... We had no female talent to call on, so female parts would have to be played by sailors, but to our surprise we found many willing and able takers for all parts." After much consideration, the cast chose *HMS Pinafore* for their first production, "an obvious choice. It was about the Navy – by the Navy and for the Navy. And so *Pinafore* was launched."

Ernie said that the jolly operetta was a huge success and ran for six performances, including one for the German authorities, "who received it very well. We were very encouraged, and so we formed the Marlag Amateur Operatic Society and planned further shows." To set up and produce each opera, it took the men about ten or eleven weeks, and they succeeded in presenting six of Gilbert and Sullivan and other works: *HMS Pinafore*, *The Gondoliers*, *The Pirates of Penzance*, *The Mikado*, *The Student Prince*, and *Merrie England*. Scores for the latter two came through exchange of scores with other prison camps. During times between operas, other drama producers presented various comedies and dramas, plus orchestral concerts.

"The theatre was therefore a very important and much appreciated facility," concluded Ernie, who produced and played major roles in many performances. Since childhood the handsome young sailor had been a talented singer, making his first public appearance at the age of 7.[7]

Happy Eckersall said that "One of the funny sides of it [prison camp life] was the shows we organised, such as *Pirates of Penzance*. We made do: for instance, I lent my blanket for a dress, because it was serge colour or something, but I had to sleep on it that night, so we'd only put big stitches in it and clip it together because we had to take it to pieces again and do it all over again the next night." The actors fashioned wigs from bits of string off Red Cross parcels, "and they were marvellous," said Happy. "They were also good enough for escaping."[8]

The small stage, about twenty-five feet wide and twelve feet deep, had a support post near the front, slightly off-centre. In this tiny space the cast and stagehands created clever settings: a nightclub, a boxing ring, a street with storefronts, a small office, a bomb shelter, a garden, a living room, a hotel lobby, and many other make-believe places. The men outfitted themselves in authentic-looking costumes such as pirates with head scarves and striped tee shirts; women in print dresses and curly wigs; London bobbies; wealthy gentlemen in top hats; businessmen in suits and ties; tennis players with racquets; British soldiers with uniforms and helmets; maids in uniform; and female nightclub singers.

Ernie Truman once rigged himself up as "Bessie Throckmorton" in *Merrie England*, looking every bit the elegant Elizabethan lady in a long, white gown with high ruffled neckline and green lace edging on the skirt. To complete the outfit he wore a lovely brown wig topped by a prim green and white hat. "There was always a problem getting makeup – greasepaint," recalled Ernie.

For *HMS Pinafore*, Ernie played an Able Seaman and helped design an attractive programme with an old sailing ship drawing on the cover and several pages announcing the date (20 April 1943); full credit to Rupert D'Oyly Carte, Esq.; the cast of characters; and Ernie's name as producer.[9]

German officials allowed Rupert Lonsdale to go over to the ratings' camp to see *Merrie England*, and he described the production in a letter to Seal village (the small English town that had adopted *Seal* when she was commissioned): "I do wish you could all have seen it. The cast … is a big one, and the singing absolutely first class. Truman himself has the best tenor in the camp. …" Lonsdale went on to say that the dresses had been created from coloured crepe paper, the jewels from coloured glass and tin, that the cast wore wigs, makeup, ruffs, and carried fans. He declared that every bit of the show had been designed in great detail.[10]

Further enjoyment for the POWs arrived in the form of gift boxes from the people of Seal village in England. Believing that the crew had been killed when the boat disappeared, and not having been informed otherwise by the Admiralty, the chief organiser, Miss Dorothy Coleman, learned six months after the fact that the men were prisoners of war. With that, she jumped into action and rounded up every family in town to help. Willing villagers began to write letters and contribute money; they knitted great amounts of warm clothing and collected personal items such as razors and toiletries, blankets, large towels, and "comfort" foods for their quarterly packages to Marlag-Milag.

In 1942 the flow of parcels from the Red Cross increased, supplementing the ever-dwindling food supplies and providing other benefits. "I passed my time," recalled Mickey Reynolds, "making football nets out of Red Cross parcel string and creating new footballs by taking the best panels from old ones and sewing them back together again. Anything for entertainment and to while away the time."[11]

With many activities and decent meals, the Marlag prisoners led a fairly comfortable life, and some managed to become familiar with their German overseers. Getting chummy with the guards actually came easily, according to Truman, especially when the Red Cross parcels started arriving, and the men had cigarettes and soap to trade or bribe with. "The Germans couldn't get any decent soap at all," said Ernie. "A wonderful guard, who was one of the dog handlers, got quite pally." Every evening just before turn-in time, Ernie and friends enjoyed a cup of cocoa and a biscuit from their parcels, and the friendly guard showed up regularly at that hour with his dog, a powerful German shepherd. "Of course, we were a little bit scared of this animal, and I said to the guard, 'Can I give the dog a biscuit?' And he said, 'Go on, it's all right.'" Ernie placed a biscuit on the floor, but the shepherd refused to take it. "He doesn't want it," Truman told the guard, who replied, "Put it on your hand and offer it to him." It worked, and a new friend was made.

Now and then the Gestapo arrived to make lightning searches in the middle of the night, as they knew or suspected that Ernie's hut had a radio hidden somewhere, "because we used to tell them all the news. We used to tell them how the Germans were getting along on the front line and all that, but they couldn't find our radio set." Ernie's crew knew exactly when the Gestapo were coming: their friendly dog handler helped them. One night Ernie felt something licking his face, opened his eyes, and saw the German shepherd and his handler. The guard whispered, "Hide the radio. Hide the radio."

"We hid it somewhere outside the hut," said Ernie. "We dug a pit, lined it, and made a nice, convenient wooden lid, covered it with turf, and kept it in there."[12]

A Swiss Legation report said that sometimes Marlag overseers tuned into the BBC on the loudspeakers – an odd occurrence – and no one knew whether it stemmed from bribery or friendliness. No doubt the internees thoroughly enjoyed the occasion. Marlag "O" did not get a radio until 1944; Marlag "M" had several wireless sets for messages and news; and Milag (Merchant Navy) owned at one time seventeen sets. As all the radios were electric, the men could listen to the BBC only in the evening, when camp electricity was turned on. Milag, first to have radio sets, received special coded messages from military intelligence, as well as news broadcasts. They circulated the news within their own compound by word of mouth, and later, when Marlag "M" obtained wirelesses, Milag sent them the coded messages, though there was the constant fear of stool pigeons and the danger of the radios being confiscated. One of the repatriated prisoners in England told Military Intelligence that they should duplicate any really important messages – one to Marlag, another to Milag.[13]

"Military information was collected in various ways and dispatched from Marlag 'O' [officers' compound]," explained the Swiss Legation report. "A good deal of useful information came from Marlag 'M' and Milag, as the prisoners of war had more chance on working parties to converse with the local inhabitants, some of whom were quite ready and eager to talk." Sometimes the prisoners bribed guards to get information from them, but often newly arrived prisoners brought messages from other camps and observations they had made en route. "Captured escapers gave hints and advice for future attempts, and newly captured prisoners reported on the sinking of their ships and the possible compromise of crypto-broadcasts." In November 1944 the men with radios sent the War Office an enormously valuable piece of news about the Lancasters' air attack and sinking of the *Tirpitz*. "In this way, a good organisation of codes in a naval camp probably had its greatest value, being often the only way the Admiralty could obtain a clear and concise description of action."[14]

From Military Intelligence the men received not only news; they obtained advice about escaping – something almost every man dreamed of. However, getting out and making it back to England presented an enormous challenge: each camp was surrounded by two twelve-foot-high barbed wire fences five feet apart, with coiled barbed wire between them. Trip wires lay inside the fences, and all four corners of the compound had watch towers. Many perimeter lights completely lit up the space between the fences, and searchlights swept around from high towers. Sentries with rifles marched along the fences in the daytime, and at night two guards made rounds with dogs. If a guard spotted a prisoner trying to escape, he had orders to yell three times at him to halt; then, if the escaper kept going, the guard could shoot him.[15]

Despite the hazards, escape plans continued night and day. In Marlag "O," Commander Beale headed the Escape Committee, and each of the four other huts had a representative in the group. When a prisoner had thought out an escape plan, he presented it to Commander Beale, and the committee considered its possibilities. If it did not come up to the requirements, the committee rejected it; if they approved, they gave the escapers all possible assistance: contact names, maps, passes, and local intelligence.

In July 1942 British Military Intelligence, under the cover name IS9, Intelligence School 9, began sending small items hidden in parcels from home, after hearing from successful escapers about what was needed. The most requested items were maps, lists of contacts, names and maps of the best ports, courses of action, and facts about frontier crossings. Further, the escapers wanted blankets for making overcoats, dyes, materials for forging workers' passes, and radio parts such as wire and condensers.

Intelligence sent other small items, as well: pens, paper, metal files, money, German workers' caps, false identity documents, and midget wireless receivers.

When the boxes arrived in Germany, they were taken immediately to the German Kommandantur (camp overseer's headquarters) to be searched. Soon the searchers discovered the hiding places in game parcels; and in March 1943 a German officer showed Captain Cavaye a green baize game board with money and maps inside. "You complain about your parcels being broken up," the officer remarked, "but here is the reason why." The censors normally did not inspect food parcels, so IS9 had the most success in smuggling escape items in them.

When intact IS9 boxes arrived in the Marlag parcel store, the Escape Committee members could easily remove them unobserved. In the boxes, tinned milk and gramophone records usually held secret items, and some boxes had false bottoms. Altogether, the internees received a great deal of help from the outside, but only a few successfully made it home.

In the early days of Marlag, escapers frequently tried wire cutting or tunnelling to break out. Determined escapers also scraped out three tunnels – one in September 1941 at Sandbostel and two at Westertimke in September 1942 and 1943. Starting at Hut 6 in "O," which was near the fence, the first tunnel went below the wire and was supposed to come up in a small wood outside; but somehow it emerged in a grassy area between the outer wire and the woods.

As an aid to their efforts they rigged up a life-size dummy with detachable limbs, and just before the big getaway, the men smuggled it in pieces to the bathhouse and assembled it. Then, holding the "man" upright in the middle of the group, they marched back to the camp with what looked like the same number of prisoners.

Two officers did escape, but the guards, assisted by their dogs, discovered the tunnel and closed it. To prevent more underground passages from being excavated, the Germans dug a trench fifteen feet deep and fifteen feet wide around three sides of Marlag. Though the trench definitely made escaping more difficult, tunnellers dug another very long passage starting at the mess building near the fence and reopened the previous one from Hut 6. A fake badminton court had been set up beside the mess hut, and prisoners whacked away at the shuttlecock, yelling and whooping to interfere with the sound detectors that were attached to posts on the wire fence.

During construction of the long tunnel, the guards found it, and to thwart any future breakouts, they put the men in Marlag "O" into Marlag "M" and vice-versa. During the exchange, Lieutenant Wells and Lieutenant Pryor walked out of the camp dressed as German workers and stayed free for thirty-six hours. "Escape from Marlag 'O' was considered very difficult, in view of the extreme vigilance of the German authorities, who, though not concerned if ratings got out, were determined to prevent any Naval officers from escaping," explained a Swiss Legation report. "The camp possessed elaborate precautions in the form of microphones, sound detectors and police dogs, and the flat, sandy area surrounding the compound afforded very little natural cover."[16]

Lister and Johnson, *Seal* ratings, with Hammond of the submarine *Shark* and eleven others, including Lt. Trevor Beet, participated in a tunnel escape from Marlag at Sandbostel. Once they were on the outside, everybody split up, but they did not get very far before they were nabbed by guards. Donald ("Tubby") Lister actually stayed out for a week and even made it to Hamburg but was captured there; when the guards escorted him back into camp, everybody loudly cheered. Shortly thereafter, the Germans sent Lister and Hammond to Colditz prison, an "escape proof" fortress for hardened getaway artists. Trevor Beet followed them to Colditz sometime later. Three other ratings pedalled out of Marlag "M" on bicycles but were recaptured after two days.

"After Tubby Lister and his pal Johnson got caught," commented Mickey Reynolds, "there was hell to pay, but we didn't mind, as we knew we were doing our little bit to keep Jerry occupied." Usually, the escapers and helpers were put in solitary confinement with bread and water for a few days, following the Geneva Convention. During the first year, Reynolds and the rest of the ratings in Marlag "M" were not forced to work, but in June 1942 Hitler ordered five hundred seamen to Silesia for factory building. Marlag naval officers strongly protested to camp officials, who replied that they were forced to follow orders: the Führer had spoken.[17]

Notes

1. Yale University, "Convention," INTERNET.
2. Truman interview, 22 September 2000; NA, WO 208/3270.
3. Truman interview, 22 September 2000.
4. Eckersall interview, 1 May 2000.
5. Ibid.
6. Ibid.
7. Truman interview, 22 September 2000.
8. Eckersall interview, 1 May 2000.
9. Ernie Truman collection.
10. Warren and Benson, *Will Not We Fear*, 189.
11. Reynolds, "HMS *Seal*."
12. Truman interview, 22 September 2000.
13. NA, WO 208/3270.

14. Ibid.
15. Ibid.
16. Ibid.
17. Reynolds, "HMS *Seal*."

CHAPTER X

Battle of Wits

In mid-1942 Hitler had his plate full, warring with American, Russian, and British foes; and after a year, the tide started to turn against him. Fleets of RAF bombers were making heavy raids over western German industrial cities, especially in the factory and railroad sections. Despite Geneva Convention stipulations that no prisoner could be sent into a region where he might be exposed to combat fire and that POW labour could have no direct relation with war operations, Hitler shipped prisoners into eastern Germany to construct and to work in war-related factories, knowing that these installations would eventually become bomb targets. Two months previously, on 21 March 1942, the Führer had signed a decree: "In order to secure manpower requisite for the war industries as a whole, and particularly for armaments, it is necessary that the utilisation of all available manpower, including workers recruited abroad and of prisoners of war, should be subject to a uniform control. ..." It was not the first time that Hitler had disregarded the rules of war, nor would it be the last.[1]

"We went to a camp at Lamsdorf [now Lambinowice, Poland], then they took us to a place, Blechammer, in upper Silesia," said Happy Eckersall. Work camps had been set up in various parts of the area, and some of the *Seal* crew were forced to work in a gasoline plant. "There the owners ran things, and they were responsible, so nobody could say boo to a goose over them – they was all right. It was a benzene distillery, and the camp was on the banks of the Adolf Hitler Canal. We was there for about two years, I think." The plant officials allowed craftsmen to enter the camp and repair the prisoners' shoes and clothing and clean up the toilets: these services would give the men more work time for the Germans.[2]

Mickey Reynolds, Eckersall's shipmate, also had to leave Marlag for Lamsdorf: he believed that the German guards at Marlag-Milag were punishing him for escape attempts by other prisoners, but he was wrong: Hitler had ordered it. Mickey described Lamsdorf, used in World War I, as "colossal," and said that his compound was located on the periphery. First used in 1870 and 1871 during the Franco-Prussian War, the enormous camp had again been activated in World War I, when the Germans had imprisoned 90,000 French POWs there. As one of the largest POW camps run by the Wehrmacht, Lamsdorf consisted of Stalag VIII B, Stalag 318/VII, and Stalag 344. During the course of World War II, about 300,000 inmates lived there; and most of them served as slave labour for the German Reich. Bleak and drab in appearance, the endless rows of shabby dormitories resembled a mass of big grey grave markers.[3]

"Initially, some of the [navy] officers who had tried to escape were here before us," said Reynolds, "and we tried to get one of them into our compound. The Jerries said we [navy men] caused more trouble for them in the short time we were there than the soldiers had all the time they had been there. Then we split up for working parties." Reynolds was sent to Cosel to help build a railway line, working at night to avoid bombing raids. "I was in trouble the first night: on arrival I ran afoul of one of the guards, and it was not long until I got a knock on the head by a dump truck and had a short spell in the sick bay."

From there Mickey went to a forestry job where he chopped down trees and sawed them into pieces. "I enjoyed this work, as you were always able to get a bit of extra grub, but then another accident caused me four stitches in my foot and into dock for another spell. Then I got a job on another railway." One morning Reynolds felt fatigued and did not work as fast as the guards expected, so they punished him by keeping him at it longer than usual. "At last, I could not stand it and hit him with the shovel. I really thought I was going to get it then and there, when he rammed me from behind and told me to march. As he was marching me away at the point of the gun, he tried to trip me by tapping my heels." Mickey told himself that he had better keep quiet and obey the guard, and his submission helped him survive. Apparently the Germans wanted him alive and working, so they yelled ugly insults at him, held a court martial, and gave him twenty-eight days in jail. "When I came out, I was lousy [full of lice] and had to report sick, saying to myself, 'it is time you were out of here.' So after spending some time in the sick bay, I was transferred to the main British Military Hospital at Cosel." During his stay, Reynolds became friendly with the camp commander, Captain Webster, who remarked to him, "Reynolds, you don't like working for the Germans, do you?" Mickey replied, "No sir," and Webster asked him if he would like to work in the hospital. To this heaven-sent offer, Mickey gave a quick "Yes, sir," and shortly thereafter became a medical orderly with a ward to look after. "I enjoyed it, as I was helping our own boys, not the Germans."[4]

While Happy and Mickey were making gasoline and chopping down trees, Taff Harper found himself in another Silesian camp with huge marquee tents, similar to those at Thorn. "We slept out in the open, with our clothes and coats on," Harper recalled. "Fitzgerald was there at the time, and I said to Fitz, 'What the hell, I'm itching all over!'" Fitz replied, "So am I." As soon as they set to work that day, they asked a fellow prisoner if he knew what to do, and he told them to take off their trousers and draw their fingernails down the inside seams, squeezing out the irritating lice. "Of course all our hair had to be shaved off: it was absolutely riddled with the bugs. Sometimes we used to burn them with candles. You could never get rid of them, so the only thing possible was to do without the straw bedding altogether – just sleep on the ground, which we did. Of course, the ground was infested with them, as well."

Finally, the prisoners revolted. When it came time to march off to work one morning, they all sat down and announced to the guards, "We're not coming until you change the tents to another location." Taff said that fortunately the German commander was a decent fellow. "Very understanding." Harper and the others told him about their agonising lice situation, and the commander shuddered and backed away. "Yes," the prisoners responded, "you have a good right to back away, but what do you expect us to do? Don't forget, we'll mix among your people and spread the disease on to them." With that, the commander ordered a big crew of guards to move the tents.[5]

In 1942 German radio broadcasts announced that beginning 6 April, all food rations would be cut, attributing the action to "the increased number of heavy workers in war industries, longer working hours, the incorporation of 1,000,000 German nationals from other countries, the requirements of foreign workmen, and millions of war prisoners." Additionally, they said that the harvests of 1940 and 1941 had been only of average size because of bad weather and that the Reich was counting on increasing food production in Russia and other occupied countries. Bread allowance would go from five pounds a week to a little over four per adult; fats from nine-and-a-half ounces to seven-and-a-fourth ounces; and meat from fourteen to ten-and-a-quarter ounces. On such meagre rations people could hardly exist, and prisoners of war felt the pinch even more.[6]

POWs all over Germany testified that the Red Cross packages reached them barely in time to keep them from starving. Parcel handout time brought delight and relief to everybody. Average boxes contained a bar of chocolate, tea, cookies, tins of pineapple and peaches, milk, and other delectables. "Of course, we looked forward to the thing, because a few of us used to make schnapps out of the currants and raisins. When the raisins and currants started coming, that's when the stills started. Oh, it was amazing the stills they used to have in those prison camps," explained Taff Harper.

"We used to get a Red Cross parcel about once a month, if we were lucky, and we collected all the fruit into one bin. We had these big metal oil drums for water storage, so we put the fruit in there and let it soak; then we'd stir it up and stir it up." After a while, the fruit started to smell ghastly, but the stirring had to be done every day. Then the distillers would throw in two slices of bread – thick black bread – and a layer of yeast. "We used to swap things to get the yeast when we was out on working parties – a package of cigarettes for a package of yeast. There always seemed to be plenty of yeast in Germany."

"Anyway, we put the yeast and two slices of bread in this great tub of liquid, with all the fruit floating there, and stirred it for three weeks. When you'd sip it, it was very, very cloudy, of course. But it did taste really good." Next, the distilling process: they strained the fruit out, put in some sugar (from the parcels), and placed a wooden lid on the drum with a stone on top to keep it from boiling over. Next, they lit a fire under the drum and ran in a copper or tin tube, then coiled the tube over and through another drum of cold water. The fruity liquid would run through the coil, evaporate when it hit the cold water, and drip down into a container. "It was pure liquor, pure spirits. Of course it was colourless, just like gin. Ha! You'd take a sip of that and AAHHHH!" Everybody drank it raw. For fun they lit a match to the brew one day, and it flamed beautifully. To make sure that the German guards remained ignorant of their handiwork, the artisans hid their still under the hut floorboards.

Along with the currants and raisins, the men received their most prized item: cigarettes. Sometimes the German guards confiscated whole Red Cross boxes or took what they wanted out of them, primarily the cigarettes. "Of course, they were short of smokes as well as we were," remarked Harper. "Smoking was a way of life in those days. I was always so desperate for a smoke – we all were – that I boiled and crushed various things for tobacco and used Bible paper for making cigarettes. Oh, gosh, yes." Any Bible would do, Taff explained. It could be pocket size or church size, no matter: the thin paper worked well. "But with a church Bible you'd be better off, because it had bigger pages. That was part of prisoner of war life."

Taff's twenty-six working party mates were Scotsmen. "I was the only Englishman amongst them, and they were a hard crowd. They used to stand up to a Jerry – it didn't matter. I've seen them being beat on the head with a rifle butt because they stood up to them. They all came from the slums of Glasgow, considered a tough town during the war days, and the only way they'd work was in the army. Of course, they all depended on each other then." Taff found out from the start that he liked the Scottish boys and got along well with them. "It was a fine crowd of lads. It was all for one and one for all."

"There was always a bloke in charge, and he was an army sergeant. What the sergeant said, got done." The men had to keep their bunks tidy and behave as though they were still in the army, following routine procedures. "Everything had to be clean – spotless. As prisoners of war, you had your own discipline to abide by, besides being under the eyes of the Jerries."[7]

While many of the navy ratings slaved away in Silesia, the lucky ones remained in Marlag-Milag for the duration of the war – all except three:

Tubby Lister, Wally Hammond, and Trevor Beet. The trio had made so many efforts to get back to England that they finally infuriated the camp authorities, who shipped them off to Oflag IV C at Colditz, about forty miles west of Dresden. Enormous and forbidding in aspect, the castle served as a punishment place for officers who had made repeated escape attempts. The *Seal* men arrived there in late autumn of 1942.

First used for British prisoners of war in November 1940, the high-walled prison gradually filled with French, Poles, Belgians, and Dutch. Later, the Germans kept only British officers there. "The castle itself was very dark," said a Swiss Legation report, "as the windows were small, and electric light had to be used continually." Due to an inadequate power supply in town, the lights at Colditz were always dim. Other facilities appeared satisfactory to the Swiss inspectors.

The guards often burst into the various sections of the citadel to try and discover forbidden activities like tunnel digging, use of radios, writing in diaries, and a multitude of other industries. They looked for items such as radios, tools, cameras, and other outlawed objects. Whenever guards arrived in prisoner dormitories late at night, they ordered the men to march into the main courtyard for roll call, then they ransacked the rooms in hopes of finding "hides" for escape articles.

At Colditz, the most accomplished and experienced escapees in the German POW system lived together, sharing ideas, experiences, and plans. None of them had any great concern that at Colditz there were eighteen sentry towers with searchlights and machine gunners; patrolling guards everywhere; strong arc lamps that lit the courtyard at night; and thick barbed wire covering the roof and periphery of the castle. After every escape attempt the Germans would increase the amount of barbed wire around the camp and the number of guards, so that finally the guards outnumbered the POWs two to one.

As in all POW camps, any plans to get out had to go through the Escape Committee, headed by a Senior British officer; but it was understood that any prisoner who was sent to another camp could make a getaway during the transfer if he had a chance. The officer heading the Escape Committee also had charge of security matters and gave lectures to the men about measures they could take. Committee activities included giving warnings when searches were about to take place; providing watchers to warn of approaching German guards where forbidden activities were going on (like escape preparations or listening to radios); the hiding of outlawed material; and covering up the absence of personnel who had escaped.

At the end of 1941 the men set up a roster system for observing the Germans' schedules on a twenty-four-hour basis, and they continued their vigilance until the end of the war. For about the first two years, the watchdogs were stationed at strategic points in the building, and by using runners, they passed warning messages to the ones engaged in illegal activities. As this method took too many men, the prisoners improved their strategy in July 1943. "A brilliant scheme was devised which overcame these factors," said the Swiss report. "It was discovered that the Germans switched off all lights in the P/W quarters at 22.00 hours by means of a master switch in the guardroom. ... The P/Ws modified the whole of the electric wiring in the building without the Germans being aware of the fact." They did it by concealing switches inside the walls – using a knitting needle to poke a small hole in the woodwork, inserting a wire, passing it through a switch, connecting a water pipe to it, and connecting the water pipe to the building wiring, thus grounding it.

Further, the officers completed the system by fitting all the lamps that were to be used in the system with lamp socket adapters and connecting them to the places where secret projects were being carried out. With the new wiring system, watchers could turn lights on and off as warnings to escape workers. Concealment of forbidden goods created an incessant battle of wits between the Escape Committee and the Abwehr Department (German Military Intelligence). In some instances the prisoners hacked holes in the floors and walls or hollowed out window ledges, beams, and furniture parts to stash their goods. The schemers even painted camouflage on things and in one instance hid escape materials in the bellows of the chapel organ.

As part of their plan to secrete a radio in the attic, the prisoners built a false wall, put the radio behind it, and made a trap door for the operator's access. Though they suspected its existence, the camp overseers could never locate the radio. After Lister and Hammond escaped from Colditz, some of their prison mates actually constructed a two-man glider in a secret attic area above the chapel, but the war ended before anyone could fly away in it.

As for clothing for breakouts, the Escape Committee left that to the individuals. Prisoners could easily obtain clothes from the prison store, and they found that naval jackets were very easy to convert into German uniforms. Other military items could be obtained by bribing guards or stealing; and the Polish, Dutch, and French prisoners sometimes contributed their uniforms, which could readily be redesigned into German ones. Artisans carved epaulettes and regimental numbers from linoleum and painted them with gold or silver paint from the canteen. They created insignia and buttons from the lead paper that encased cheeses, and they received dyes from IS9.

Lt. Airey Neave fabricated a superb German uniform before he escaped in January 1942, using a Dutch army greatcoat. He painted the buttons grey; covered the collar with dark green fabric; carved and painted the epaulettes from linoleum; and created a cap by covering a regular military dress cap with dark green material. He made a peak for the cap with varnished black paper and whittled the cap badges out of linoleum. All this effort took six weeks.

Various departments worked under the Escape Committee and included three Forgery men. One of them, Lt. Trevor A. Beet of HMS *Seal*, never did manage to make his way out of the castle. He and his fellow forgers manufactured fake identity papers through various means including bribery, obtaining some from French and Polish prisoners and IS9. But they did most of their work by hand, using paintbrushes and pens and sometimes the jelly reproduction method. A brilliant French forger named Jacques Huart arrived at Colditz in the summer of 1943. He could produce perfect documents by placing a sheet of glass over the paper to be copied and making a tracing on the glass with white paint. Then he turned the glass over, and using the white design as a guide, went over it with slow-drying black ink or water colour and then used it to make a print. A paper specialist created the correct type paper by gluing two pieces of dyed paper together and smashing it in a tennis press.

Under the Forgery Department, the Photograph men cut out individual pictures from group prisoner photos taken by the Germans to use on identity papers, as nobody owned a camera. They managed to get one from the Poles, but the guards found it and confiscated it. But never mind, two officers made a camera with a pair of field glasses and cigar boxes, and they claimed that it was better than the original. For official stamps on the documents, the Forgery Department men carved them out of rubber boot heels and linoleum.

The Escape Committee kept on hand a stock of food in case of emergency in the castle, but escape-minded souls had to scrounge up their own supplies, which they could do by sneaking tidbits out of the messes. The Escape Committee concocted a recipe for a food concentrate made of Bemax (a dry, flaky, flavourless nutritional additive), margarine, sugar, ground biscuits, and chocolate. It seems, however, that no one ever used it.

From the beginning of their confinement at Colditz the men collected maps, and before long they had a comprehensive set covering all of Germany. The rule said that escapers had to make their own copies, because it was thought that in doing so they would get to know their routes better. However, for security reasons, they could only look at and memorise detailed maps of frontiers. Two officers had charge of the maps. When they heard that the British POWs were about to be moved to another prison in June 1943, the custodians traced complete sets of maps of Germany for them.

The officer in charge of escape intelligence had an easy job, for almost every prisoner in Colditz had made at least one escape attempt. The different nationalities in the prison had their own Escape Committees, and the groups passed information to each other about their countries, frontiers, and people who could be relied upon to give shelter and assistance, as well as their own escape experiences. Many of the prisoners used bribes of chocolate, food, or cigarettes from the Escape Committee to get useful knowledge from civilian workmen who came into Colditz and from German guards. Some of the information they gained had to do with travel conditions in Germany; positions of the guards at certain times; information about the vicinity; and warnings of impending searches.

It was not long before the Abwehr Department learned that prisoners had collected a great deal of vital intelligence, so they gave search orders only a few minutes before searches were to take place. This did not deter the prisoners, who made arrangements with a German guard to hang a pair of socks in a window of the German quarters as a warning that a search was imminent. The scheme ended in the summer of 1944, when the German pal was transferred away. Some higher official must have noticed the socks.

Everyone spent a great deal of time manufacturing items like dummy rifles made of bed boards, floorboards, or furniture; tools and keys from iron bedsteads; ropes from blankets; tunnel lighting from electric cables and fittings; and many other useful items. Sometimes the prisoners simply stole things from under the Germans' noses; and these included clothing, portable lamps, bags of cement, tools (including spikes, chisels, pickaxes, and iron bars), a car jack, and Christmas tree lights for tunnel lighting. In the sick quarters they stole plaster of paris and made moulds for the production of lead buttons, buckles, and insignia. They used boots to make pistol holders and leather belts, or when no leather could be found, they took cardboard and painted it with boot polish until it looked like leather. A prisoner named Parker became the key-making expert, and eventually he provided the Escape Committee with access to any part of the castle.

In addition to everyday escape tools, the men created some remarkable gadgets. They took a tin can, filled it with margarine, inserted a pyjama string for a wick, and burned it for a short while for tunnel illumination. Two men used a gramophone motor to create a lathe, with one man turning the handle, and they forged dummy rifle barrels. Remarkably, a Major Anderson put together a sort of typewriter with bits of wood, metal, and letters obtained through a "contact." It never worked very well, so the Forgery Section rejected it.

From November 1940 to the war's end, the prisoners dug fifteen tunnels, but very few men made complete getaways. Other methods proved more or less successful, and Lt. Dominic Bruce almost made it home. When the guards ordered some of the British officers to put clothing items in wooden Red Cross boxes (measuring two feet, six inches square) Bruce, a small man, curled up inside one. Cohorts nailed the lid shut, and he was carried to a storage room in the German quarters, where helpers soon let him out. With a rope he had taken with him in the box, he scaled down a sixty-foot wall and ran off. After making it to Danzig, he tried to board a ship but was halted by a suspicious Swedish sailor, who turned him in.

Four brave souls, including Escape Officer Patrick Reid, obtained freedom by carrying attaché cases filled with civilian clothing, food, and identity papers. They had loosened the bars on a kitchen window the previous night, and the next night they made their way through the kitchen, climbed over roofs, squeezed through an eleven-inch flue, descended terraces using a sheet, woke up the guard dogs (which barked furiously), sneaked past the German married guards quarters, and climbed over the barbed wire fence to the outside. They and others who returned to England gave detailed stories of their escapes to Military Intelligence, who continued sending helpful items to the POWs all over Germany.[8]

Apparently, Tubby Lister and Wally Hammond realised immediately that the usual methods of getting out would not work for them, so they devised a clever scheme. As Colditz was an "Offizierlager," or permanent camp for officers, and as they were not officers, the two complained to the Kommandant, Col. Edgar Glaesche. They persuaded him that the officers did not like living with noncommissioned men, and that made the two feel uncomfortable, so they asked to be placed with other ratings in another camp. Two weeks later they got their wish and were shipped off to Lamsdorf. Prior to departure, the two Engine Room Artificers acquired fake papers as Flemish Engineer Collaborators, some money, and information about how to sneak across the Swiss border.

When they walked into Stalag 344 at Lamsdorf, the German guards were tying the hands of all prisoners behind their backs with Red Cross string, an act forbidden by war rules. Wally and Tubby were forced to comply along with the others; however, within a week they wangled their way into a work party in the Breslau gasworks. More than one hundred British POWs were working there, but none were known to have escaped.

Sergeant Brown, who was in charge of the workers, agreed to help the two new arrivals, and as he gathered clothing and equipment, Lister and Hammond began their dreary work – shifting piles of coal from one location to another so that it could be loaded onto rail cars. By surreptitiously giving some free coal to an elderly German couple, they acquired a pack of German cigarettes, a valuable item for their escape. The time came for their getaway one week after they had started work: 12 December 1942. Before departure, they built an oblong, low mound resembling a grave in an area of coal dust and rubbish. On one end of it they installed a crude wooden cross with large black letters: "ADOLF, R.I.P."

"For a Colditz incumbent," remarked Wally, "the getaway was a cake-walk: the filing of a few bars, the cutting of a few wires, the timing of a few patrols, obtaining some civilian attire, and we were ready." Sergeant Brown provided them with worn, rather ratty clothing; Wally would tote a large briefcase, and Tubby had a small suitcase. "We both smoked pipes, of German meerschaum design. Our pouches were filled with Bulwark

Strong underneath and covered with a layer of mixed French and German tobacco. We also flaunted the German cigarettes."

They hid their clothing in the wash room, changed while they were doing some laundry, walked through the manager's garden, proceeded to the train station, bought tickets, and rode to Dresden without a hitch. From there they travelled to Nuremberg, then Ulm. Without a place to spend the night in Ulm, the daring duo brazenly registered at the Bahnhof Hotel and enjoyed a luxurious sleep on real beds. The next day they took a train to Tuttlingen, visited a pub there, then walked into the countryside and eventually made their way across the border into Switzerland, arriving in Bern on 19 December.[9]

Of the hundreds of thousands of POWs in World War II, only a very few made complete escapes. Three hundred and fifty men tried to break out of Colditz, but only thirty-five managed to make a "home run." Lister and Hammond had beaten the odds but were not even interrogated by the Royal Navy or listed as escapers.

Notes

1. A Teacher's Guide to the Holocaust: "Use of Slave Labor in German War Industries" (Part 1 of 2) available at *http://www.fcit.coedu.usf.edu/holocaust/resource/document/DOCSLA11.htm* on INTERNET.
2. Eckersall interview, 1 May 2000.
3. Reynolds, "HMS *Seal*"; History of Lamsdorf, "Spis-1," available at *http://www.uni.opole.pl/cmjw/ecmjwobie.html* on INTERNET.
4. Reynolds, "HMS *Seal*."
5. Harper interview, 2 February 2002.
6. *New York Times*, 20 March 1942, 3.
7. Harper interview, 2 February 2002.
8. Previous sections from NA, WO 208/3288.
9. Reid, *Men of Colditz*, 158–76.

CHAPTER XI

Blitz and Pieces Krieg

In January 1943 German and Soviet troops blasted away at each other, and fierce battles continued in North Africa. The tenth anniversary of Hitler's rule fell on the 30th, and to commemorate the event, Göbbels and Göring were to deliver two hours of rhetoric praising the Führer and proclaiming German superiority. When the British military learned of the broadcast, they decided to participate by sending their own message to the German people: the RAF arranged for a group of Mosquitoes, the fastest bombers in the world, to take off at the exact time that would bring them to their targets when the speeches were to begin.

In the Air Ministry Hall of Honour, Chief of Gestapo and Black Shirts Heinrich Himmler gave a short welcome talk, and the radio announcer proclaimed that Field Marshal Hermann Göring would be the next speaker. In London, audiences who had tuned in to the German wireless heard confused shouts (probably commands) and sounds of muffled explosions. The announcer popped back on and told everyone that Göring's speech would be delayed for a few moments. More confused noises ensued, then a military march. During the next forty-five minutes the announcer continued to reassure audiences that the speech would be coming shortly. At noon the bombers turned back to London, and finally Herr Göring's voice boomed out. British radio audiences cherished the thought that the German high officials had been forced to run into air raid shelters in the midst of the ceremonies.

Later that afternoon the Mosquitoes returned for another visit to the Sportspalast and dropped another load just as Dr. Joseph Göbbels was about to speak. This time there was no interruption in the broadcast, and Britishers heard none of the thuds and confusion. Göring and Göbbels exhorted the German people to fight on in spite of "severe blows," to keep faith in their "beloved leader" Hitler and the German cause. "You all know the law," intoned Göring, "that you must die for Germany if Germany's life requires it. This is not only a duty for our soldiers. It is a duty for every German." He announced that the Führer had ordered the mobilisation of all German men and women to fight until victory, and woe unto anyone who refused.[1]

A few days before the commemoration in Germany, President Franklin D. Roosevelt, Prime Minister Winston Churchill, and the top French, U.S., and British military brass met to plan war strategy. During the conference at the Anfa Hotel in Casablanca, Morocco, French General Henri Giraud (who had made a fabulous escape from Königstein Castle) told Churchill and Roosevelt that his men in North Africa were fighting with "farcical equipment" and that his troops had suffered heavy casualties. The French forces, he explained, needed "so many airplanes that are real airplanes, so many guns that fire, and so many anti-tank weapons, so many supplies." In the field, Giraud had seen that British and American equipment was far superior to the French, and that "they [the French] have got to be helped in every action by the British or American troops for the very reason of this equipment. What will happen to their morale if they have to wait too long?"

Roosevelt listened attentively and just before he left the conference, he consented to give Giraud American assistance. The next day Giraud sent a telegram to Roosevelt expressing his gratitude for "the decisive help of the United States. France now can accomplish the mission that is hers and free Metropolitan France." In Morocco Giraud gave the same message by radio broadcast.[2]

By June 1944 the Allied air raids were increasing to the extent that in the Netherlands and Belgium, the governments warned citizens by radio that those working in factories serving the Germans should not go to work. Major targets would be aircraft assembly plants, locomotive or vehicle factories, and submarine parts industries. Radio warnings said that if people were forced to work, their families should evacuate and get to places of safety.[3]

Göring's bombers, meanwhile, began a second heavy assault on England, unleashing the heaviest raid on London since the beginning of the war. Waves of bombers targeted, among other places, Newcastle-upon-Tyne, a major shipbuilding centre in northern England. Irene Arthur, a young woman who worked at Backwith Collieries, recalled that the constant bombing caused local people to lose many working hours. "This was the whole German idea," she concluded. Each time the sirens wailed, all the workers had to run down many flights of stairs to the basement, and the electricity was cut off; as soon as they had climbed up again, the sirens would sound once more. "On each floor of the building where I worked, there was a large bucket with sand in it and a long-handled shovel with a scoop on the end, and you were supposed to scoop up any stray incendiary bomb with the shovel and drop it into the bucket, where the sand would smother it."

The Arthurs' home had an Anderson build-it-yourself air raid shelter with bunk beds, candles, teatime supplies, food, a bucket for sanitation, and a few other items. "It was just outside the dining room door in the backyard, and everybody just hopped into the shelter; that was where we spent the time when there was an air raid, and there were many." With the Germans' on-again, off-again bombing tactics, the British started calling the whole affair "The Blitz and Pieces Krieg."

"After a while we became very aware of the fact that this was for the birds, and we weren't going to do this all the time. The British government, being very proper, announced that people should not put their heads out the windows to watch dogfights, which is, of course, what we did. It was really terrific – you could see the Spitfires coming and the Germans coming." Irene's father served as a fire warden, whose duties were to warn people of air raids and to be sure that every home was totally blacked out. "There were lots of elderly ladies on my father's beat, and he would ask them if they were all right, and they'd say, 'Of course we're all right. We're not going to worry about things like that.' And they didn't. Anyway, a cup of tea solves all kinds of problems."[4]

As the war grew more intense in 1943, the number of Allied prisoners mushroomed in Germany, increasing the need for help from the U.S. and British Red Cross organisations, who stepped up their campaigns for funds and blood donors. Dr. Marc Peter of the International Red Cross Committee of Geneva arrived in New York to arrange for chartering of a fleet of "mercy ships." Sailing under Red Cross and Portuguese flags, the vessels would transport food, medical supplies, and other items to POWs and civilian internees in Europe. A few months later, the British Red Cross chartered eight ships for the same purpose, plying mainly between Lisbon and Marseille. Some of the ships sailed to the U.S., picked up parcels packed in Canada for British prisoners, and travelled to the southern French port. All eight vessels could hold a total of 1,750,000 standard, eleven-pound Red Cross food boxes that were vital for the survival of POWs who had been starving for two years. Sad to say, one of the ships, the *Padua*, was sunk in October after she hit a mine while entering Marseille Harbour. Six men, including three officers, were killed, but sixteen other people, including the Swiss delegate of the Red Cross, landed safely. Eleven thousand bags of precious mail for Allied soldiers in Germany went down with the ship.[5]

The International Red Cross sent four Swiss specialists to Germany to measure 430 severely maimed prisoners of war for artificial legs and then to provide the limbs for them. Various hospitals existed throughout Germany for prisoners of war, providing fairly decent medical treatment, but supplies were barely adequate, and as the war progressed, the hospitals became terribly overcrowded and poorly run. At some of them, captured British or American doctors ran the facilities, giving very good care.

In many cases, the prisoners who were in such bad physical or mental shape that they could no longer benefit from German medical treatment and were considered hors de combat, were allowed to be repatriated. An agreement existed between the German government and Great Britain and with the U.S. that provided for mutual repatriation by both sides "regardless of the ranks and numbers of all seriously sick and wounded prisoners of war who have been recommended [for repatriation] by medical authorities." In March 1943 seven hundred and eighty-seven British sailors and soldiers arrived back in England, showing the victory "V" to photographers. A bevy of Wrens (Women's Royal Naval Service) greeted them with cups of hot tea.[6]

Mid-1943 brought the initial tipping of the war scales in the Allies' favour. At sea, the large German supply submarines had all been sent to the ocean depths, and U.S. planes were sinking great numbers of U-boats. The Red Army was pushing back the German invaders, and in North Africa General Patton brought strong leadership and moral support to the front. A lifelong believer that military leaders should participate in live action, the noted general rode in a military automobile through heavy artillery fire in southern Tunisia to congratulate his soldiers for holding the line. "The general was forced to dismount from his command car as shells landed on a road bend ahead," said the *New York Times*. "He finished the journey on foot." As Patton climbed a steep hill to the outpost, soldiers' heads popped up from foxholes so that they could get a glimpse of "Old Blood and Guts." One corporal remarked, "It sure is good to see him on the front line."[7]

With the surrender of Italy on 3 September 1943, the German commander in chief in northern Italy announced that all prisoners of war in Italian camps must report to the Germans. The commander's proclamation also stated that "all Anglo-American prisoners found in possession of arms or resisting arrest would be treated 'according to martial law.'" The British government quickly rebutted the orders, warning the Germans that any authorities who treated POWs improperly would be held personally accountable and that free prisoners were protected under the Geneva Convention. The BBC carried the announcement in Italy and Germany, trying to get word to prisoners that they did not have to report to Germans.[8]

One of those captured by the Italians, Lt. Stewart Campbell, an airman in the Royal Navy, gave an account of his experience after he had successfully escaped and made it to England. He testified that on 11 November 1941 he and a gunner had taken off in a Swordfish aircraft to bomb three ships on the Italian coast. "We were unable to locate the ships, and owing to lack of fuel, were unable to reach our base. We crash-landed in the sea near Cefalu [Italy]. After about four hours we were forced to abandon our dinghy, as we were being fired at from the shore." Shortly thereafter, the two airmen jumped out of their craft, swam to the beach, and wandered around looking for something to eat. A search party of two Italian soldiers found them and marched them to the local police station, where the airmen found three other Swordfish crews who had flown on the same mission. The next day the soldiers took them to aeronautical headquarters in Palermo, where they were given fresh clothing and interrogated. "We gave only our numbers, ranks and names."

Campbell and friends stayed in a hotel that had been taken over by the air force, and after four days they were transferred to a quarantine camp near Rome and placed in separate rooms. "A man claiming to be a member of the Red Cross (we believed him to be a stool pigeon) visited us each day," Campbell explained. "He always carried out his interrogations in the form of friendly conversations and asked us where we had come from, what mission we were engaged in, and the type of aircraft we were flying." The visitor invariably brought a notebook containing extensive information about Malta, names of squadrons, personnel, and other things, and told Campbell that he had obtained it from a dead airman. "Our treatment during the 16 days we were here was reasonable and the food good."

About the 2nd of December the Italians sent Campbell to Campo 41 at Montalbo, where he remained until January. "During this time I took part in several tunnel schemes. We suspected a stool pigeon in the camp, as our tunnels were always discovered – one of them being found the day it was completed." Campbell submitted another getaway scheme to the Escape Committee, who accepted it. "There was a cinema in the camp grounds to which the Italians used to take their wives, and although it meant getting past a sentry, I intended to try and mingle with the crowd as they were leaving a performance, and get out." Unfortunately, the camp authorities transferred Campbell to Padula before he could expedite his plans. "I did not make any attempted escapes from this camp, as most of the time I was suffering from stomach trouble."

At the end of July he found himself in Campo 19 at Bologna. (It should be noted here that the American troops had pushed northward in Italy to a point slightly above Naples, and Bologna was far away in the northern part of the country, where German troops had no opposition.) Italy had surrendered on 3 September, and on the 9th, a bugle sounded, then an announcement blared out on the speakers that the Germans were approaching. "There was a mass attempt by the P/Ws to escape, both from the front and back entrances." Campbell said that the Germans had already surrounded three sides of the camp, and they suddenly opened fire on the fleeing men. "All those escaping from the front entrance were pushed back. One Australian Army officer … was killed and two people were wounded." German soldiers pursued and rounded up those who escaped from the back, and at dawn the next day they told the POWs that they were free within the camp. "They apologised for firing at us, but said that they had been informed that we were armed. During the next three days we were well treated."

However, bad news came with the false announcement that the prisoners would be moved away from the battle area, but *not* to Germany. "On 12 or 13 Sep. we were moved by trucks to the station. We were put on cattle carriages [railway freight cars] – 36 men in each – taking with us only what we could carry." As the train slowly moved northward, Campbell twice attempted to flee. "On one occasion, I tried, unsuccessfully, to cut a hole in the carriage. On another occasion I broke away after having filled up my water bottle at a station. I had only gone about the length of the train before I was recaptured."

Several of the men did manage to escape, but an SS officer appeared in the carriage and told the men that if anyone else tried to escape, he would shoot one man in each car. "Captain J. Johnston, who acted as our interpreter, said that if he did, we would shoot at least ten Germans for each P/W killed." Then about twenty-two prisoners dashed away from another car, and the same SS officer ordered the remaining ten men out of the car and lined them up as if he were going to shoot them. "Captain Johnston again intervened. At Bolzano station this officer was taken off under arrest."

As the journey continued, guards moved men from full cars into cars that had become half empty due to prisoners escaping. "We had about forty-three in ours before we arrived at our destination. In addition to this we all had our luggage with us." The men were allowed to take two small Red Cross parcels and to fill their water bottles when the train stopped. "At one time we were in the carriage for twenty-four hours at a stretch." After five days the train reached its destination, Stalag VII A at Moosburg, Germany. By surreptitiously moving the POWs northward, Hitler had successfully prevented the Americans from freeing them.

Campbell was sent to three more prison camps, including one used for punishment, and he ended up in Marlag-Milag at the beginning of November 1943. As an officer he would have been placed in Marlag, and there could well have met some of the *Seal* crew members.[9]

At the same time that Campbell was being transferred to various German POW camps, six French air force officers made a daring escape from a German camp. "The Germans had us repairing this Messerschmitt," they explained, "and we took our time. On September 29 we all jumped into the plane, got away safely and off to England." Two hours and fifteen minutes into the flight they ran into heavy British flak over Croydon, so they frantically radioed, "Don't fire: we are six French officers." Firing ceased, and an entire squadron of British fighters arrived to escort the Messerschmitt to a base. After landing, the six French pilots told their escape story to the British airmen, who could scarcely believe what they were hearing. After a brief stay in England, the pilots went on to Algiers to join French forces under General Giraud.[10]

Seaman Fred Salisbury, another lucky escaper who reached England, reported that the German people who had lost homes in bombing raids were throwing stones at British prisoner working groups. "German morale is falling fast," he said. Salisbury described one German soldier who started to cry because he had been told he would be going to Russia. "They dread Russians." Other repatriated British soldiers told similar stories: they firmly believed that civilian morale was cracking under the stress of heavy Allied bombings of German cities and suburban areas. In Scotland, Thomas Johnston, Secretary of State, commented to the press, "It is the profound conviction of the great majority of them [repatriated POWs] that if our bombers can continue until Christmas, the war is over."[11]

So sure were they that victory was in sight that British prisoners of war in Germany started taunting their captors. At one camp, the German Labour Minister was making a speech to the POWs, and every few minutes the guards would shout, "Heil Hitler!" After a few times, the prisoners began to yell, "Heil Churchill!" causing ire amongst the camp authorities. After that the men began to holler, "Heil Churchill!" so often that the Germans believed it was a common salute in Britain. The POWs further rebelled by slacking off in any work projects that they knew were helping the German cause.[12]

The 9th of November, on the twentieth anniversary of the founding of National Socialism, Hitler's voice once again hit the airwaves. From the Löwenbrau beer cellar in Munich he broadcast a forty-five-minute harangue that Germany would fight on, come what may. His own nerves, he claimed, were strong and steady, and his confidence in the German masses unshaken. He would allow no quarter to "defeatists" at home, and that anyone who forecast an Allied victory would be promptly executed. "Internal criminals" would not be tolerated. "If the German people despair," he warned, "they will deserve no better than they get."[13]

Speeches from the Führer made almost as much noise as the hail of explosives on Berlin, Dusseldorf, Frankfurt, Kassel, Bremen, and many other cities. RAF bombers delivered 14,500 tons of bombs in various raids; and American heavy bombers let loose 6,300 tons over Germany and Norway. The attack on Bremen by the Americans on 26 November was the heaviest yet.[14]

A few miles outside Bremen in Marlag-Milag camp, Ernie Truman and friends were busy presenting *The Gondoliers*. "At that one, we entertained the German staff," explained Truman, "and the next morning after the Kommandant had seen the show, he told me how much he enjoyed it. He said that in peacetime he was the manager of the Bremen opera house, and he asked me to let him know when we were going to do the next production – that he might be able to help us with the costumes." When the time came for the next operetta to get under way, the Kommandant asked Ernie, "How is the show going?" Ernie told him everything was coming along nicely, and the officer responded, "Well, when you're about two weeks before production, let me know, and I'll get you to come down to the opera house and see what costumes we can help you with."

"We got to the stage where we were about one week away from opening night, and I went down to see him and asked, 'Could we make a visit to the opera house?'" The Kommandant replied, "Yes, tomorrow"; but the next morning at roll call he said to Truman, "I'm sorry – I can't take you to Bremen today because they bombed the opera house last night."[15]

Notes

1. *New York Times*, 31 January 1943, 39.
2. Ibid., 32; 1 February 1943, 1. Note: for further details of General Giraud's escape, see his book, *Mes Évasions*.
3. *New York Times*, 24 June 1943, 3.
4. Irene Rice Johnson, interview with author, Galveston, Texas, 13 July 1990.
5. *New York Times*, 3 March 1943, 42; 6 July 1943, 7; 31 October 1943, 13.
6. *New York Times*, 26 March 1943, 3.
7. Ibid.
8. *New York Times*, 2 October 1943, 4.
9. NA, WO 208/3270, "Accounts of Escapes of Lieut. James, R.N.V.R.; Lieut. Kelleher, R.N.V.R.; and Lieut. Campbell. R.N.V.R.," Appendix C.
10. *New York Times*, 16 October 1943, 2.
11. Ibid., 28 October 1943, 5.
12. Ibid., 7 November 1943, 47.
13. Ibid., 9 November 1943, 1.
14. Sommerville, *World War II Day by Day*, 201.
15. Truman interview, 22 September 2000.

CHAPTER XII

1944

Events in Russia at the beginning of 1944 would cause horrifying consequences for Russian POWs in 1945, when the war turned in the Allies' favour. German troops, after twenty-nine months of laying siege to Leningrad (now St. Petersburg), gave up the fight and began to straggle back to their home country. In their wake they left devastation and 20,000 civilian casualties – 5,000 killed by shelling and bombing, and thousands more dead from starvation. On 27 January, General Govorov announced that the Leningrad blockade had been completely lifted, and Peter Popkoff, President of the Leningrad Soviet, told Allied war correspondents that his people had survived their ordeal without electricity, heat, or water – existing on a daily 125-gramme food ration.

When Hitler invaded the Soviet Union, many citizens had been evacuated from Leningrad to the east of the country, leaving behind those essential for industrial work, civil operations, and defence services. One of the most heroic efforts during the siege occurred at the Hermitage Museum, where employees remained night and day, working ceaselessly to protect the building and its huge collection of priceless artworks. Employees barely survived by eating glue. Beginning in late summer of 1941 the Germans began a horrific siege of Leningrad: in one day they delivered 500 tons of bombs and thousands of artillery shells. Eighty percent of the people who died were killed by artillery shells on days when the attacks were lighter: thinking they were safe, people had come out of bomb shelters and were walking along the streets.

War correspondents interviewed some of the workers at a huge arms factory in an outlying district of Leningrad, just four miles from the German lines. With only 250 grammes of bread and a plate of soup each day, the men had barely been able to do their jobs, they said. One factory director told the reporters that it was impossible to get much work from his men because they were so weak.

A 17-year-old girl, in pointing out some of the horrors and hardships of the blockade, said that her own father had died of hunger. Often she would go to work on a day when no shells had fallen, confident that all her comrades at the factory were fine. Sometimes she would see one sitting in a chair by a small stove, go over and talk to him, then realise that he was a corpse.[1]

Meanwhile, in Germany the Russian POWs were suffering horribly, as well. In September 1944, during the confusion after the armistice, five managed to escape from a camp in Italy. They spent twenty-eight days hiding in the mountains and were at last discovered by some Americans, who gave them food, clothing, and cigarettes. The half-starved men said that in Germany, Russian POWs were getting brutal treatment from the Germans and that Russian prisoners were being herded like cattle all over occupied Europe and forced to perform monstrous slave labour jobs. "They are clothed in rags, infested with lice, and are fed bread that can't be eaten and a watery soup," explained the escapees. "Even though the Russian POWs were weakened and ill, they were nonetheless forced to work eleven to fifteen hours a day in war factories, mines, and on roads." With no Red Cross representatives to check on conditions, the Germans did whatever they wanted with their Russian captives, and thousands died.[2]

It seemed that as the war worsened, the Geneva Convention faded into the background: neither the Allies nor the Axis paid much attention to war regulations when it came to bombing civilian areas of big cities. The former Archbishop of Canterbury and fifteen American clergymen decried the Allied policy of "blotting out whole German cities" and mass killings of civilians. Countering the criticism, President Roosevelt's wife Eleanor told the press, "They are not very realistic about the fact that if you want to bring the war to an end quickly, you have to use methods which seem very cruel. But you do have to use them." In London many citizens were dying as Luftwaffe planes unremittingly bombarded the city, trying to set it afire. Churchill marched out to inspect the damage about noon after the last day of a raid and attracted such a big crowd that traffic became jammed in all directions. As throngs loudly cheered, he smiled and raised two fingers in the "V" for victory sign, then called to workers clearing away rubble, "It's like old times again."[3]

The day after Churchill's inspection, Lt. Stewart Campbell, the navy airman who had been sent to Marlag-Milag at the beginning of November 1943, finally made a successful breakout. When he had arrived at Marlag, he wasted no time in joining the tunnel-digging teams, but none of his efforts succeeded. "About January 1944," he explained, "I sent in a plan of escape to the Escape Committee which was accepted. I intended to leave the camp as a naval officer in the company of a rating, with orders to join our ship, the SS *Waal* in Rostock." Campbell invited Lt. Dennis Kelleher to join him, and Kelleher agreed. Kelleher had also spent time in Italian prison camps and had tried to escape from a transport truck by cutting a hole in it.

To initiate their plot, the two forged an Ausweis (travel and work permit) for each, stating that Campbell was a Steuermann (third officer) and Kelleher a ship's engineer. "We also had a letter purporting to come from the Arbeitsamt at Wilhelmshaven to the Harbour Master at Rostock stating that we were reporting to join the 'S.S. *Waal*.'" Although the letter appeared to be typewritten, it was in fact hand printed. "If we were caught, we intended to say that we were taking the place of an officer and seaman who had been wounded in an air raid."

Before departure, the two officers took six German lessons from Sublieutenant Jackson, who instructed them in how to ask for railway tickets, enquire about trains, platforms, and so on. Everything was ready, but the two men had to come up with a way to leave the camp, and for this purpose they submitted five ideas to the Escape Committee, who turned down four and approved the last one.

As he walked around the grounds one evening trying to see a feasible way to exit, Campbell noticed that one of the perimeter lights had gone out, leaving about thirty yards of wire fence in shadow. "I mentioned this to Sublieutenant McLister and Lieutenant Taylor, who told me that they had already noticed it, but that we could join them by trying to get out of this place. It was some time before the Escape Committee allowed us to go ahead with our plan, because the Germans had become much stricter in their dealings with P/Ws owing to recent escapes." A new order had come down that all prisoners were to be in their barracks by 6:00 P.M., and anyone who attempted to escape would be shot by the guards. If any prisoners did make it out, the guard responsible for that area likely would be shot, as well. "In the end, it was agreed that McLister and Taylor should cut the wire and go out first. If we were given the word, we were to follow immediately after."

On the side where Campbell and Kelleher intended to break out, the wire was about two hundred yards long and patrolled by a sentry; at each end of the wire were a searchlight and machine-gunner. The darkened lamp stood about seventy yards from one machine gun and 130 from the other. "We had arranged that the guard who turned the officers into their barracks about 1800 hours should be engaged in conversation, thus preventing him from completing his rounds. We also had someone watching one of the guards at the machine-gun post, and we planned that about the time the sentry on patrol duty was approaching the guard manning the other machine gun, one or two P/Ws should … start an argument, bartering some of their goods." By a stroke of fortune, many of the guards were removed from Marlag the night before the escape, one of them being the sentry who patrolled the perimeter wire. Everything was falling into place.

At about 6:30 on 22 February, McLister quickly cut the outer wire, and in about seven long minutes, he and Taylor scrambled under, intending to make for Holland. "Just after that, the searchlight did a beat round the camp, and we were then given the word that we could follow on. It took Kelleher and me about one minute to get through. As soon as we were on the other side of the wire, the searchlight flashed along the wire." The two lay flat on the ground, scarcely breathing; they could see sentries inside the camp and hear dogs barking. Between searchlight flashes they crawled about a hundred yards into a cart track that ran parallel to the perimeter fence for about two hundred yards. "Beyond this was open country." Several hundred yards along the track, the two officers jumped into a stable, straightened themselves up, and set out for Tarmstedt station.

Campbell and Kelleher had outfitted themselves in what appeared to be German merchant marine uniforms. Campbell had cut short the gold bars on his jacket cuff so that they did not encircle the sleeve and had taken a merchant seaman's cap and removed the badge, leaving only the leaf. Over this apparel he wore a naval overcoat. Kelleher had no officer's stripes on his sleeve and wore nothing on his head. They carried fifty marks apiece, along with four "escape cakes" that the Escape Committee had concocted out of porridge, margarine, sugar, and cocoa. "We had a shaving kit, a towel, and a bar of soap between us. Before we left, I had copied a map showing the railways and roads from Westertimke to Bremen and another showing Hamburg, Lübeck, Wismar, and Rostock. In addition to these, we had a map of the harbour area at Rostock and a large-scale map of the route from Rostock to Danzig."

At Tarmstedt they had hoped to catch the last train to Bremen, which left at 8:00, but when they reached the station, they found that they had missed it. Fearing that the alarm would go off before they could get away, the two men decided to walk to Bremen and catch the 2:28 A.M. train for Hamburg. After walking for five hours, Campbell and Kelleher reached Bremen station and were told that the train was late and would not be leaving until 4:00. "After buying a glass of beer, we spent the night in a waiting room in the station."

Finally, the escapees boarded the train for Hamburg, and to their great relief, no security guards questioned them during the journey. Upon arrival at Hamburg, they noticed that a train was about to depart for Lübeck and decided to jump on it, even though they had purchased tickets to Rostock. "On that train we were asked to produce our Ausweise. The official did not seem very impressed with them and had started to take us off, when I produced the letter that had been forged for us." Satisfied, the guard let them go, and they made it into Lübeck at about nine in the morning. From there, the two escapees walked straight to the docks.

After looking around for a few minutes, they noticed an unguarded area and headed for it; there they spotted a small Spanish collier but could not board it, as a sentry was walking back and forth in front. "We decided to return and try to board her at night. We then went back to the station and caught a train to Wismar, where we hoped to catch a train on the single track to Rostock. On arrival at Wismar at 1030 hours, we found that there were no trains for Rostock." Campbell and Kelleher wandered around the town, then returned to the station and caught a train to Lübeck, where they walked from the station directly to the harbour. Their determination to sneak onto the same Spanish ship they had seen earlier dissolved when they discovered that she had already departed.

"By this time, our feet were very sore, and we went to a café near a tram stop. There we were asked by a German what train we were waiting for. We mentioned a local one, and were told that it did not run at that hour and that we should not sit around where we were." They searched the area for an air raid shelter, found one, and spent the night in it. Policemen awakened them once to inspect their Ausweise passes but noticed nothing amiss. Now they had insufficient money to get back to Rostock, so Campbell tore up the forged letter to the harbour master.

Next morning at eight o'clock (24 February), the escapees trudged once more to the docks and there found a Swedish coal ship of about 2,000 tons. "By this time, we were both feeling very desperate, and we decided to try and board her right away. We walked up the gangway, passed a sentry, and were met by a ship's officer. We asked him, half in English and half in German, if we could come aboard. He said, 'No,' and we left the ship."

Every two hours the two returned to the Swedish vessel to see whether it had departed; meanwhile, they spent the day trying to find something to eat and a place to rest their weary feet. After obtaining a "couponless" (no ration ticket) meal that was completely tasteless, they managed to drink a little beer, and had nothing more for the rest of the day. As the two famished travellers searched for food and watched the ship, air raid sirens wailed three times, forcing them to rush into nearby shelters.

Back at the harbour, they discovered that the Swedish collier had moved to a heavily guarded, wired-off area. As dark was setting in, they decided to try to sneak into the enclosure, so they walked up to the main gate and showed their Ausweise. "We told the sentry that we wanted to join our ship, the 'S.S. *Waal*.' He said we must have a letter from the harbour control officer and started to take us off to his office. Fortunately, someone distracted his attention, and we managed to get away." The two, after trying to convince several sailors to row them across to the ship and being told that it was "verboten," boarded a ferry that crossed to a shipbuilding section on the other side of the harbour. There, they thought they could reach the ship from the other side, but they found the plan impossible and returned on the ferry.

At the foot of a bridge where a guardhouse stood, they saw a concrete platform with a barbed wire-covered board across it. When dark set in, the two escapers tried to climb onto the platform but could not make it through the coiled wire. No one saw them, even though there was a German minesweeper about fifty yards away. "We climbed up some steps onto a wharf and there made for some coal trucks. Keeping in their shadow, we reached the Swedish ship. At the last truck we heard a sentry cough." They waited for about five minutes, then heard the sentry walk away and "nipped up the gangway onto the boat."

Jumping into the first door they saw, they found themselves in the kitchen quarters of the officers' mess, where two women stared at them in surprise – they were the matron and the stewardess. Campbell and Kelleher quickly explained to them that they were British naval officers and asked if the ladies could please help, but the Swedish women could not understand what they were saying. One of them left to get a ship's officer – one of the ones who could speak some English – and when he appeared, the officer said that the crew dared not provide aid, for if they were caught, they would be shot by the Germans.

"He tried to persuade us to leave the ship. One of the women spoke to him, and he told us to wait. He went off and returned with the cook, who also spoke English." The cook explained that even though the risk was high, he would be willing to help the escapees, as the (British) navy had saved his life when his ship had been sunk. On this day, the vessel was still being loaded with coal and would not depart for five days, so for two days Campbell and Kelleher hid in the cook's cabin; and for three nights they slept in the matron's room, while she and the stewardess slept in a double bunk. "We were then told that they were expecting a search on board, as it had been discovered that some of the coal had been stolen."

At about four in the afternoon on 27 February the friendly cook escorted his friends to the engine room and instructed the engineer to hide them. "We had to lie on the floor in one-and-a-half inches of water under a boiler, the clearance from the boiler being sixteen inches. We remained in this position for 70 hours, and during that time we were fed twice." On the 29th at 7:00 in the morning, German guards quickly inspected the Swedish vessel just before her departure at 7:30. "We remained under the boiler for fourteen hours after the ship had sailed, and during that time the water had dried up and the heat became unbearable."

At ten that night Kelleher and Campbell went up on deck to stretch and get some fresh air, then they hastened to the crew's quarters, where the cook had laid in some food and hot water for sponging off. He told them that they would not be talking to the captain until 1:00 P.M. the next day, and even then they were not to mention that they had seen anyone on board or been helped in any way. "He told us to tell the captain that we had boarded the ship and had gone straight to a small chart room that was never used." When they met the captain the next afternoon, they still looked terrible, with black faces, arms, and clothing. He offered them a bath, which they gladly accepted. "After that, we told him who we were, but he said he did not want to know anything about us, as it was better he should know nothing when he returned to Germany. He gave us some dry clothes and fixed us up in a cabin. He told us that we might have to disembark at Kalmar [Sweden], but that if possible, he would take us to Stockholm."

Campbell and Kelleher made it to Stockholm on 2 March, and there they were taken to the police and kept for five hours; the police handed them over to representatives of the British Legation, and from there they landed back in England.[4]

Although POWs who had escaped and made it home had orders to tell no one except Military Intelligence of their adventures, the two officers apparently obtained permission to talk to the press. The *New York Times* announced that two "audacious British naval officers" had succeeded in getting out of a prisoner of war camp with "no other aid than nerve and a six-week course in German." The article said that the men had not even bothered to disguise themselves, wearing their Royal Navy uniforms for twenty-two days in enemy country, a statement that fudged a little on the truth to make the story more exciting.

"They set out along the thirty-mile road to Bremen, posing as merchant marine officers, and completed their trip to the city by morning," the article explained. "Lieutenant Kelleher said it was there that the two met what was to prove their greatest snag during the entire trip – inability to get food. Ration points were needed." With train tickets in hand, the two "were speeding to their next destination." From there they made it to freedom.[5]

War records of Marlag-Milag say that although forty-two men managed to get out of the camp, only three arrived safely back in Britain, and those three were 22-year-old Campbell, 25-year-old Kelleher, and a Lieutenant James. Apparently, officers McLister and Taylor, who had cut the fence wire at Marlag and headed for Holland, never made it.[6]

By now, escaping prisoners of war were becoming a serious aggravation to Hitler, who went to extremes to punish a big group of them who got out of his "escape proof" camp at Sagan, in Silesia. A repatriated airman, who arrived in Liverpool from Stalag Luft III (camp for air force prisoners), brought with him shocking news of Hitler's fury. The pilot told British officials that seventy-six RAF and Allied air officers had made a mass breakout through a 450-foot-long tunnel: they had spent fifteen months digging with improvised tools, working in relays, and hiding the dirt by different means. "Just after dark," the airman said, "the first man shook hands with Smith [the leader] and dropped into the dark mouth of the tunnel. The rest followed at intervals, and all of them managed to make it into the trees some distance away."

But the escapers had used the tunnel for too long. At 5 A.M. the German guards noticed the last of the men emerging from the exit and fired several wild shots at them as they raced towards the woods, hitting none. The guards then sounded an alarm.

"The entire province of Silesia became a madhouse," the airman continued. "Battalions of military were turned out. Police dogs, bloodhounds, the whole civilian population over a wide area were mobilised to join in a manhunt."

At the end, according to an eyewitness, the Germans rounded up about fifty of the escapees, drove them to nearby Görlitz, and put them in jail. After several days, forty-seven men were herded into trucks and driven away into the countryside: there, the guards forced them out of the trucks and into a large field. Then they shot them all dead. To the world, the German authorities explained that the guards had fired at the men as they were attempting to flee from Stalag Luft.[7]

At first, the British government could not believe the story of the executions, but prisoners' accounts proved that such an event actually happened. Foreign Secretary Anthony Eden promised the House of Commons that the murderers of the fifty Royal Air Force prisoners of war would be brought to "exemplary justice" after the war. The death toll had risen to fifty in an official German report, and the U.S. State Department declared that the killings were a crime and that the American Government fully agreed with Mr. Eden's condemnation of the executions.[8]

According to the Germans, the guards had shot only prisoners who were resisting arrest, and furthermore, Berlin radio announced that German police would now "refrain from interfering with German mobs who attempt to lynch American aviators who bail out and land in Germany." They said that the German people welcomed Propaganda Minister Josef Göbbels' new policy. An editorial in the *New York Times* rebutted the news by calling Göbbels' order an incitement to German civilians to murder Allied aviators parachuting into Germany. "If United Nations aviators are killed in contravention of the laws of war, there will be an answer to it," commented the editor. "It will not be the shooting of an equal number of Nazi aviators. It will be an air assault of renewed fury on the German Army and every railroad, highway, ammunition dump, landing field, factory and city that supplies or aids it."[9]

On a cheerier note, some American POWs captured at Anzio reported that they had invented a rhyme about conditions in Germany:

"The game is up,
The bolt is shot:
First goes Hitler,
Then the lot."[10]

Attempting to guess the date of an enormous Allied invasion, Hitler and his cronies decided that the enemy would be first attacking the Balkans, then sweeping from England into Europe on 22 June 1944. They calculated that on that date there would be a new moon and extremely high tides on the French invasion coast. Berlin circles believed that Allied preparations had been fully completed and that an amphibious attack would be the fourth and final phase of their conquest.

Even in May, Hitler and Admiral Dönitz were convinced that an invasion by sea would be coming, and to help deter it the admiral ordered twenty U-boats to stand guard near Norway. After patrolling from the 2nd to the 14th of May with no sign of the enemy, the boats were ordered to resume their searches for convoys.[11]

While rumours of the approaching crisis circulated in Germany, Red Cross representatives warned senior officers in prison camps to prevent their POWs from trying to escape to English Channel ports or to try to contact invasion armies in the coming chaos. Travellers in Silesia revealed that two camps there had already agreed to stop escape attempts and that the Red Cross was storing two or three months of food supplies to use after the big assault.[12]

When the invasion rumour story hit the New York papers on 3 June 1944, little did anyone dream that the very next day, the great Normandy Invasion would roar into France. So successful was the Allied onslaught that twelve days later, King George VI made a trip to the Normandy beachhead. As his vessel *Arethusa* and escort destroyers approached the French coast and Spitfires circled above, the crew hoisted the royal standard. The cruiser *Hawkins* fired salvos overhead while His Majesty disembarked, climbed into a "duck," and rode to shore. Escorted by British and American military police, the King was then driven to General Bernard Montgomery's advanced headquarters at Courselles, just six miles behind the front lines. After a half-hour of visiting and lunching with the general, His Majesty decorated seven officers and men, then began his journey back to the ship.

By this time, word of his visit had flashed through Courselles, and local citizens were waving French tricolors, Union Jacks, and Stars and Stripes from doors and windows. An old French woman dressed in black stood at her front door waving a handkerchief and calling, "Vive le roi" ("Long live the king") and "Vive l'Angleterre" ("Long live England"), as tears ran down her cheeks. The King noticed her and saluted.[13]

The immense Normandy invasion, together with the King's appearance in France, heightened Hitler's rage; but ten days after His Majesty had returned to England, German troops captured the King's 21-year-old nephew Viscount George Henry Lascelles. Berlin radio blared out the news on 26 June. On the 27th the King sent a coded message through the Foreign Office to Bern saying that he would be grateful for any information they could obtain from Swiss authorities about Lieutenant Lascelles – how badly he was wounded and where he had been sent. After a couple of return messages giving very little information, another response from the Swiss Legation on 21 August offered a clearer picture of the situation. The Swiss said that according to a witness, Lord Lascelles had been captured at Perugia, Italy, on 19 June. The young officer had been shot in both thighs, but the bullets had not hit the bone. "He was taken to Forli hospital until June 29th and then by ambulance to Bologna hospital until July 5th, when he was removed to Mantua military hospital, where he remained until July 17th. He was transferred to Stalag VII A [Moosburg], where he remained about twelve days before removal by train to Upper Camp Oflag IX A/H [Spangenberg]. He is treated in exactly the same way as all the other British officers," the report said, "and shares a room with several companions." The lieutenant's wounds, they stated, had healed nicely, and he would have no after-effects. And last of all, the young man had been well treated and could write letters home.

On 22 August a top secret telegram flashed into the War Office announcing that sources believed that Lord Lascelles was still in the Mantua Hospital. "We are endeavouring to ascertain state of health and possible rescue but will take no rash action." At this point the King and Military Intelligence feared that Lascelles would be held as a valuable hostage and possibly mistreated. Military Intelligence the next day received a phone call asking, "Shall we try any action either positive or for information? Reply urgently." The following day, 13 September, the War Office instructed Military Intelligence not to take any action – that Lord Lascelles was reported recovered from his wounds and was now in Oflag IX A/H.

On 18 October the Swiss Legation in Bern sent information to His Majesty's Legation in the city, listing names of British prisoners at Colditz. The list included Captain Lord Hopetoun, Lieutenant Alexander, Mr. Romilly, Lieutenant Sutherland, Colonel Duke, and Brigadier General Davies. There was no mention of Lascelles. The letter went on to say that a representative of the Swiss Legation had discussed the prisoners' situation with the Commander of Prisoners of War in Berlin and asked why these people were being subjected to "special treatment." During the day the ones listed could mingle with the other prisoners, but guards constantly checked on their whereabouts and locked them up at night in a separate area, from 9:00 P.M. until 8:30 the next morning.

Responding to the question of "special treatment," the German authorities replied that they thought these high-ranking British people "might be maltreated by the population or the Gestapo if they were recognised during an attempted escape." Also, they went on, "Because certain of these prisoners of war are suspected of preparing further plans to escape."

Then at last the looked-for message arrived from Captain Gilliat at Colditz. On 19 December he told Military Intelligence: "This week 4 so-called very important prisoners have arrived. John Elphinstone; Lascelles; Haig, and an obscure 2nd cousin of Winston Churchill, called de Hamel. They occupy a special suite and are subject to the same local rules as Charles H[opetoun]. No comment is advisable. ..." He went on to report that "as Adjutant I have had a lot of fun getting them settled in. ..."

Two days later Viscount Lascelles sent a message to Her Royal Highness The Princess Royal, Harewood House, Leeds, Yorkshire. He wrote: "As you will see from the address [Oflag IV C, or Colditz] I am now at a different camp from the last time I wrote." (Records show no letter arriving in England from the young prisoner.) "Probably the Red Cross will know something of the facts about this camp. I will not describe it in this letter." He said he was sharing a room with Lord John Elphinstone, Lord Haig, and a distant relative of the Prime Minister's (Max de Hamel). Life was "orderly," he went on, "quite different from the last camp I was at, where one came and went as one chose. … Here the atmosphere is rather different. …"[14]

When POWs wrote letters home, they had no way to accurately describe their condition and environment, lest the censors black it out. All letters to and from the prison camps sounded bland and innocuous, and the facts came out only occasionally when Swiss Legation or Red Cross emissaries made inspections and wrote reports. Messages to Mickey Reynolds from his relatives, for example, were written on a special fold-up paper called "Prisoner of War Post" that went by air mail and had a warning at the top, "Important. For a prisoner of war in German hands the prisoner of war No. must be clearly shown. It must not be confused with his British service No." Handwriting had to be neat and legible so that the censors could read every word.

Reynolds' Aunt Ina wrote on 1 June 1944 from Belfast asking if Mickey had received the cigarettes and commenting that she could tell him "a lot of things, but then you would not get my letter, so they will keep till you come home." She said she supposed that he had received many letters from all his fans "and, of course, your girlfriends, of which you have a lot. When you come home there will be a bit of fighting for you, who can get a date with you. Keep smiling. Love, Ina."[15]

Letters from family and friends reached Mickey at the Cosel hospital in Silesia, where he was working as an orderly, tending to the British, French, and Russian wounded. In the year and a half he was there, Mickey met many men from different working parties and took a great interest in hearing their stories; in his off-hours he kept fit by running and playing soccer. After eighteen months at the hospital, his former working party requested that he return, but "the surgeon said he would give me a small operation, and then I could go back to the main camp, Stalag VIII B." Mickey's operation for an epigastric hernia turned out well, and after a short convalescence he was sent back to Stalag VIII B. "I did not stay there too long, as I volunteered for a small working party forestry job, and I met up with some of the boys I had looked after in hospital. Here I helped the medical orderly with the sick and did some forestry work."[16]

If Mickey Reynolds and his fellow prisoners had been able to hear news of the events in Berlin on 20 July 1944, they would have yelled with joy.

Colonel Count von Stauffenberg, a high-ranking German military officer, had carried a bomb hidden in a briefcase into Hitler's conference room and had detonated it. But just before the blast, someone moved the case slightly from where it had been positioned under the conference table, and the impact failed to kill the Führer. Immediately afterwards, Hitler executed von Stauffenberg and many thousands of others he suspected of participating in the conspiracy.[17]

Notes

1. *New York Times*, 14 February 1944, 3.
2. Ibid.
3. Ibid., 23 February 1944, 5.
4. Previous sections from NA, FO 208/3270, Appendix "C."
5. *New York Times*, 4 April 1944, 6.
6. NA, FO 208/3270, Appendix "C."
7. *New York Times*, 29 May 1944, 2; 31 May 1944, 3.
8. Ibid., 24 June 1944, 4.
9. Ibid., 29 May 1944, 5; 1 June 1944, 18.
10. Ibid., 24 April 1944, 8.
11. Wiggins, *U-Boat Adventures*, 175.
12. *New York Times*, 3 June 1944, 3.
13. Ibid., 17 June 1944, 3.
14. Previous messages concerning Lascelles from NA, FO 954/28 A.
15. Letter to Hugh ("Mickey") Reynolds, 1 June 1944, Lawrence Reynolds collection.
16. Reynolds, "HMS *Seal*."
17. *New York Times*, 25 July 1944, 1.

CHAPTER XIII

The Allies Advance

Enthusiasm for the plot against Hitler inspired three German POWs in England to speak out on a BBC broadcast to the Reich, urging their fighting comrades to overthrow the Führer's regime and eliminate the madman himself. The three, an army officer, a Berlin civilian, and an engineer from the Rhineland, said that "highly placed generals at last have decided to get rid of these criminals so that the German people can be spared further senseless sacrifices and bloodshed."[1]

Removing Hitler from power proved an impossible task: his forces were executing suspects and instilling more fear than ever in the country's starving population. In the year to come, many thousands more Allied and German troops would have to die before the Third Reich disintegrated into smoking ruins. Hitler refused to give up, even though Germany was being destroyed in front of his eyes.

To bolster his crumbling defences, the Führer rushed tens of thousands of slave labourers and prisoners of war to southern Germany and northern Italy to work on a new line of defence that ran from Bolzano, Italy, near Austria, northward to the eastern edge of Lake Constance, then northeastward to upper Salzburg, near Munich. Having fallen back from their previous "Gothic Line" north of Rome, the German troops needed a second strong wall of defence against the British Eighth Army, surging up through Italy. Meanwhile, American forces marched towards Germany from France, and the Russians began to close in from the east. The trap relentlessly closed.

During the desperate days of autumn 1944, Taff Harper had been transferred to an Austrian string factory. "It was up in the mountains, and I can't even remember the name." Oddly enough, the factory was producing heavy twine made from paper. "We worked with great big rolls of paper, five and six hundred-weight a roll. You put this on a machine, and there was a cutting bar across the top with all these blades, and you cut strips off the roll, turning all the time." After the strips were made, the workers twisted them into string. "It was great until it got wet. Dry, it was as strong as any type of twine would be."

Everyone in the local village worked in the string factory, and the jobs were handed down from father to son, mother to daughter. "And, of course, most of the German women were married, but their husbands were all up at the Russian front. The German women were forced labour, and they had a lot of Polish women, too."

Before the war, the factory had been privately owned, but the Germans took it over for the war effort. A large number of young girls who had been imported as workers lived in the owners' grand mansion, and piles of paper rolls were stored in warehouses around the mansion grounds. "We lived in one of the old warehouses that had been converted, a barn kind of thing with outside toilets," explained Taff. "We dug a hole and put a bar across: that was our toilet. We used to have very heavy snowfalls up there, too."

If anyone missed a shift at the factory, they were interrogated about the reason. "You'd say you didn't feel too good, or what have you. And they'd send a German doctor to examine you; they wouldn't take your word that you were 'krank.'" With pitiful food rations, the workers had to struggle to maintain their work schedule. "Each day we got one potato, a small portion of horsemeat, and a bit of cabbage. We mostly ate what we could steal. We called the cabbage 'grass': it tasted more like grass than cabbage. We ate what we could pinch, mostly."

Fortunately, Taff's group of ten POWs had the freedom of the compound, and they soon discovered a big cache of potatoes. "Underneath the mansion there was this great cellar, stacked chock-a-block with potatoes, and we used to break into it at night. We used to sneak out after dark when we were supposed to be locked in. For ten of us there were five guards with a sergeant in charge, but we'd get out and pinch as many potatoes as we could, then come back in again."

Without any kitchen facilities in their barn, Taff and his friends used their heating stove for cooking. They sliced the potatoes and roasted them on top of the fire, turning the slices once. "We was too far away to get the Red Cross parcels in those days, so we had to depend on what we could find to feed ourselves." Amazingly, Taff's sojourn at the string factory could have been worse. "It wasn't too bad at all," he said.

As winter set in, the stream that ran through the factory grounds froze up. With its swiftly flowing current, the ice formed at the bottom and worked towards the surface, causing a problem for the pumps that forced the water into the boilers. "Everything worked on steam. They didn't do nothing to prevent the stream from freezing over, so we had to break up the ice. We had these great big poles with a sharp metal point on the end, and we used to stand at the edge of the stream and break the ice from underneath the water." Every winter the string factory had traditionally employed extra workers to break the ice, and the Germans kept the old system going.

As for thoughts of breaking out, Taff recalled that "there was no place to escape to. It was too far inland, and you got a passenger train maybe once every three days. Often the freight trains brought in coal for the boilers and the rolls of paper, but there were no buses – nothing at all, and nobody was allowed cars." In fact, everyone's cars were now sitting up on blocks, if they had not been commandeered by the German army. No BBC news reached the prisoners in their high mountain village, so they were denied the joy of hearing reports of Allied successes.[2]

While Taff struggled to exist in northern Austria, six American aviators in a German POW camp wrote a postcard on 8 June 1944 to the Pasadena Tournament of Roses Association requesting twelve tickets to the Rose Bowl game. Their message said that "due to the heartening news of the past few weeks we, the undersigned Californians, feel extremely confident that this New Year's Eve will find us at home." D-Day news had spread throughout the German prison camps like a grassfire, bringing enormous hopes to the inmates; but the six flyers would have to miss the 1944 Rose Bowl game and instead go to the one in 1946.[3]

Sadly, after the Normandy Invasion and Allied victories in France, the internees' initial jubilation soon dwindled to despair: the war continued, their hunger grew more acute when Red Cross and family food packages stopped coming, and mail deliveries of letters and cigarettes became almost nonexistent. In England military experts studied POW letters, and realising that the writers had to make light of their travails, concluded that during the last half of 1944, prisoner morale and treatment of prisoners was growing decidedly worse. At Stalag VIII B, Lamsdorf, a prisoner wrote home that the guards were shooting first and not asking any questions; from Stalag XVII B one mentioned "trigger happy guards"; and a third at Stalag XXB said, "Our boys get shot very often." At Colditz the prisoners were being forced to do labour and were shot if they refused; at Lamsdorf a POW said that he had been stabbed by a guard with a bayonet on a working party, once in the leg and once in his face, along with being beaten with the rifle butt – "for no reason at all."[4]

POWs were being put on trial for trumped-up charges such as treason and being jailed; others were sent to punishment camps, where they were kept in isolation and almost starved; and in general, the treatment of prisoners of war drastically deteriorated. Even civilians carried guns and made threatening remarks to the prisoners in working parties. One prisoner wrote from Stalag 398 C that, "I am well, but only just, as some of the civvies have firearms, and they aren't safe with them, as I well know. I have been threatened. I don't know what to make of it, but something must be done and quickly." Another told his family: "There have been a spate of check roll calls, and last week we were kept outside for 9½ hours in a temp. below zero without rations. I never thought that such human endurance were possible, but it left its mark in the form of colds and 'flu.'"

Adding to the prisoners' discomfort, the German army's lack of food, clothing, and medical supplies meant shorter rations and health maintenance for the prisoners. German Food Minister Herbert Backe announced on 20 November that Germany would now have to depend upon her own food supplies and that there was a widespread passive resistance to Hitler's appeals for increased farm production. He explained that for the last five years Germany had imported foods from nearby occupied countries, but that this was no longer possible. "We can do nothing about lack of faith and confidence among German farmers by general measures of coercion and compulsion," he droned. "But we can punish individual culprits who present a stumbling block in the path of duty."[5]

About the same time, November 1944, the Parisians, who had been freed in August, flocked into the Place de la Concorde and celebrated the liberation of Strasbourg in Alsace-Lorraine. The statues surrounding the Place represented principal French cities, and the one for Strasbourg had been draped in crape since the Franco-Prussian war in 1870 to remind the people of their "lost provinces." In 1918 the crape had been removed and a tablet put on the pedestal in honour of the liberation of the city. At noon Paris officials placed wreaths at the foot of the statue and led the vast crowds in singing the "Marseillaise."[6]

In Metz, France, General George S. Patton had succeeded in capturing the city and was presented with a medal by General Dwight D. Eisenhower. At Allied Advanced Supreme Headquarters, Patton received a distinguished visitor – General Henri Giraud, who had once been governor of Metz. After a pleasant chat, Giraud went on to his old city and reviewed the American troops stationed there. Conditions in Metz were improving, with civilians returning to their homes, but one night a German plane flew low over a nearby prisoner of war camp and dropped packages attached to small parachutes. An American lieutenant observed the descending objects and notified his guards. Inside the bundles they found hand grenades, dynamite, and pamphlets for the POWs. The pamphlets viciously attacked Patton's character and incited the men to make a prison break using the explosives. The absurd plot was foiled, and no uprising occurred.[7]

Around Christmastime the POWs' letters to their families grew more depressed: "I am not getting any parcels, therefore, no smokes. ... We have a couple of issues of food parcels but nothing for Xmas yet. Jerry has cut our rations again." He noted that there would not be many of them left to return to England at the rate they were going and that no one was the least bit interested in Christmas. "No one talks about it, and there are no decorations up in the hut ..."

Another prisoner remarked that he was "browned off to tears" and that the only thing the men could do these days to forget their hunger was to sleep. Sergeant Harold Dryhurst at Stalag Luft III wrote: "Our Canadian friends have up till present received five special parcels from their government through Relatives Associations, namely special clothing, 2 parcels of utensils, i.e. cups, knives, saucepans etc., and last Xmas a special bumper food parcel. On top of that they have the privilege of having food sent in their personal parcels. Will you enquire into this, asking the people at home who the hell they think Englishmen are, a nonentity per usual?" He explained that the situation was causing great tension, but thanked goodness that "our country tends to its people."[8]

In England, confidence steadily rose that the war would soon be over. As a sign of the coming victory, King George VI brought his royal horses out of their paddocks at the Windsor Royal Farm, where they had been kept since the war began in 1939. The head coachman and two cockaded postillions rode the four bays – "Rodney," "Chesterfield," "Baldwin," and "Felix" – through London, practising for their postwar duty of pulling the King's coach. Until that time, the royal steeds would serve as messengers in order to help conserve petrol.[9]

Germany had begun to crumble under incessant, massive raids by American and British bombers: industrial zones, communications, railway lines, bridges, factories, and many other targets vital to German war efforts were being turned into smoking ruins. In a desperate attempt to hammer down German morale and force Hitler's surrender, Allied planes were blasting even suburban sections of cities. On one mission, fourteen hundred heavy bombers returned to home bases without a single plane loss.

As horrific air assaults blew Germany to bits, the critical need arose for aviators to be apprised of prisoner of war camp locations. American and British families were worried that their captured relatives could be killed by bombs or mistreated in the camps; but the American Red Cross consoled everyone by announcing that Allied bomber pilots were being given daily information about the exact location of prison camps. Perhaps this was so, but pilots high in the air could not see through clouds, nor could they avoid hitting POW facilities if the camps were near a military target: for these and other reasons, American and British planes sometimes bombed POW installations, killing hundreds of their own countrymen.

In London, Foreign Office strategists discussed the matter and decided that "the marking of prisoner of war and civilian camps in Germany with special signs is unlikely materially to assist aircraft of the Strategic Air Forces to distinguish them. This is because during the course of an attack, bomb aimers are not normally concerned with visual identification of the aiming point. That duty is assigned to special crews who mark the aiming point or otherwise indicate the main force where their bombs are to fall." In other words, Pathfinder crews normally flew ahead of the bombers and dropped flares or gave other indications of the targets, so that camp markings would not affect the heavy bombers in daytime, and there would be no way to illuminate the camps at night. "On the other hand," they continued, "the marking of camps with special signs would undoubtedly assist both the fighter and bomber aircraft of the Tactical Air Forces, particularly during the final stages of the war ..." Lastly, they concluded that the Germans were unlikely to agree to such a proposal and made none.[10]

A monthly list was being compiled of American and British prisoner of war camps for all air commands, but the problems of monitoring the movement of prisoners became more and more difficult. In November 1944 the Germans began transferring their captives from various camps towards the interior, and Red Cross representatives desperately tried to ascertain which prisoners were where so they could notify Allied military authorities.

The Red Cross reported that "A substantial number of base camps, work detachments, or hospitals are now situated in close proximity to airfields, railway stations, war industries, or other objectives. Prisoners being killed by Allied raids." Upon receiving the news, the British pressed the German authorities to remove all prisoners being held near military objectives and told them to provide adequate air raid shelters. When the Swiss Legation requested that the Germans move POW camps in dangerous areas to safer places, they retorted that transfer of POW camps would be "impossible," as the Reich lacked the manpower and material to build new camps. "POWs must take the same risks as civilians," they said.[11]

At the benzene distillery in Silesia, Happy Eckersall and his mates were forced to endure nerve-wracking bomb attacks. When the heavy raids began, plant owners would tell the POWs, "Any time there's an air raid, you are allowed to go out [of camp], but don't go too far away. You've got to be back as soon as the air raid finishes."

"We made shelters in the camp for air raids, because when you had flak coming down, there was no protection from it: it used to go through the buildings and wooden roofs." At first the prisoners jumped into narrow trenches covered with branches, twigs, and layers of flimsy material; but as conditions grew worse, the distillery owners constructed a concrete bomb shelter. However, in a heavy bomb attack on 4 December 1944, Happy remembered that about thirty-five died, and about thirty-two were badly injured and sent back to Lamsdorf. "That was the worst Christmas there was. Everything went down. Everybody was so sick and weary."

At times the Allies dropped delayed reaction bombs on the benzene works, creating a confusing situation for the workers, who were taken off guard and often killed. Small groups of Jewish people made dangerous trips from the town to the factory carrying food for the Germans. "If they got there and back, they got a little drop of soup and a little bit of bread for their effort. A lot of them used to make it. Finally, they started hanging around us, thinking we knew when they was going to bomb: they felt they was quite safe being with us, and even the guards did the same."[12]

About two days before Christmas, Hitler, in a fit of desperation, sent expert spy Erich Gimpel over to the United States in a submarine (U-1230) to try to ferret out U.S. atomic bomb secrets. The mission failed when Gimpel's accomplice, an American turncoat, revealed the whole plan to the FBI, and the two landed in Leavenworth prison under sentence of death. Just before his departure, Gimpel described the scene in Germany: "I looked … into the street where women, weary from the strain of air raids, weeping and waiting, were going about the day's affairs. They would now be on their way to get their few ounces of cheese on Coupon VII/3, or their half-pound of apples on Special Points II/I."[13]

January 1945 rolled around without the traditional German cheering and toasting of the New Year. Hitler did two things: he launched his last offensive in the Forest of Ardennes in southern Belgium, and he moved into the Reichschancellery, where the windows had already been boarded up. In the Ardennes, the Germans almost completely surrounded Bastogne and demanded that the Americans surrender. General McAuliffe gave a short retort: "Nuts." Meanwhile, the enormous Soviet army relentlessly drove towards Germany from the east. As they came nearer, Hitler moved into the vast underground complex fifty-five feet below the Reichschancellery, where he hoped to survive and achieve ultimate victory. But by this time the Führer was plagued with what seemed to be Parkinson's disease and addiction to drugs: his hands shook and he was physically deteriorating, but he kept functioning, issuing orders from his cement submarine. Air force chief Göring, a hopeless morphine addict, departed Berlin for his house in southern Germany, where he felt safer; and propagandist Josef Göbbels, accompanied by his family, loyally remained with Germany's master in the Berlin bunker.[14]

As Allied forces gained more and more ground, Hitler decided that prisoners of war might be captured by their own countrymen and possibly used against him; therefore, he ordered all POW camp inmates transferred towards central Germany. His reasoning was so warped by paranoia by this time that he believed the weak, starving prisoners could actually fight. Additionally, he put the SS in charge of prisoners of war, a highly ominous change for the camps: SS troops were known to have little regard for human life, and many regular German soldiers feared them. Since the POW transferring had begun in a small way the previous November, the Allies began to get seriously concerned for the captives' welfare, and rightly so.

General Eisenhower suggested to the British War Cabinet that to obviate the great hardship of moving POWs from eastern Germany during the current chaos, the U.K. and U.S. governments should make a proposal to the German government through the Swiss Legation. The idea would be that in cases where it was more hazardous to move the prisoners than to leave them where they were, the prisoners should be released as soon as German forces withdrew. The Allied Chiefs of Staff put under consideration Eisenhower's proposal, along with another from the International Red Cross that trucks be made available for taking supplies to Allied prisoners: most of the railway system had been bombed and wrecked.

It was known at the War Office in London that seven prominent prisoners were being closely held at Germany's highest security prison, Colditz, near Munich. At the OSS (Office of Strategic Services, predecessor of the CIA) in Washington, word came in that the leading Nazis planned to take prominent foreign political and military POWs to the redoubt and use them as bargaining chips to obtain safe passage for themselves to Switzerland. Rescue of the "Prominents" was now becoming critical.

Meanwhile, P. R. Reid, former Escape Officer at Colditz, had remained in Switzerland after his escape and was now an assistant military attaché in Bern. His job entailed escape planning for POWs from Colditz, and on 29 January 1945 he wrote the following letter to Military Intelligence:

Dear Colonel:

On my return from Kreuzlingen this weekend ... I saw for the first time a telegram about getting a certain Lt. [Mickey] Wynn to England quickly. I put Wynn on the train – he comes from Colditz. I feel now that the request may have come from your end; and I am sure that both the M.A. [Military Attaché] and myself would have done something about it had we known. [Wynn had faked a severe back injury.]. ...

I had a long talk with Wynn and hope you will see him very shortly. This brings me to the point of my letter. There is no doubt in my mind that the officers (including the Prominents) of Colditz and for that matter of other officers camps will be held as hostages. The SS already control Colditz though they do not actually guard it. The war may be over sooner than we expect – but it may go on for some months. The POWs will at a specified moment be moved from Colditz to the centre of the Nazi ring wherever that may be (this redoubt).

I feel that something should be done for them just before they are shifted. This should be the optimum time, because they will be moved only when they have to be moved – i.e. when Germany is beginning to crumble. This will give the POWs a chance for their lives – if they are freed. As for freeing them I have only the one suggestion – and that for Colditz as I know it: Blow the Garrison Courtyard and the Guardhouse to bits by very low accurate bombing – drop arms in the inner Courtyard and give the officers a chance for their lives. I know they will react. Simply warn them to be ready – saying the above may happen any time. They will do the rest. I am not a brave man but I know that if I was offered a last chance [to be] free, preferably with a weapon, to becoming a Nazi hostage, I would choose the former course any time. The men in Colditz already feel that they are going to be hostages.

This is written in a great hurry, as we are terribly busy these days, but seeing Wynn seemed to crystallise a few things in my mind, and I felt I had to write to you personally, as obviously this is all I can do. … I may be completely on the wrong track … but, anyway, I had to write it.

> With kindest regards
> Yours sincerely
> P. R. Reid[15]

Nothing came of Reid's bombing idea, but at the end of January a Major Miles Reid arrived in England as a repatriated POW from Colditz. Upon Major Reid's return to England, he visited E. C. Gepp, Director of Prisoners of War and explained to him that the "Prominents," namely Lord Lascelles, Lord Haig, Giles Romilly (news reporter and nephew of Clementine Churchill), and Lord Hopetoun were not being treated in accordance with Wehrmacht tradition, but under SS supervision. Reid told them that the Germans had given no clue as to their intentions regarding the officers but looked upon them as "political prisoners" and "officers they might use when they were in a tight place."

Reid explained that Giles Romilly, a civilian, had been sent to Norway earlier by the *Daily Express* and captured; the Germans had treated him as an officer after ascertaining his relationship to the prime minister's wife. Romilly asked Reid if he had come up with any scheme to help the officers, saying that he hoped that if possible, the prisoners could be brought out with the help of parachute or ground forces. The young civilian also suggested that "we might approach captured [German] Generals such as von Thoma, tell them the situation, and ask whether they would make a personal approach to Ribbentrop or Rundstedt to persuade them to let the Prominents have the same privileges as were given the rest of Colditz prisoners."[16]

Gepp made notes of the conversation and sent them to Supreme Headquarters Allied Expeditionary Force and Military Intelligence, asking for their opinion about talking to Ribbentrop or Rundstedt. "Perhaps you would think well to discuss it with von Thoma. It may be that such a communication would do more harm than good since I imagine that the influence on the German official opinion of your charges is probably at rather a discount. …" MI agreed that they should avoid making inferences about the officers' treatment, since they were "of doubtful value and merely serve to indicate to the enemy those of his actions which cause uneasiness." MI put forth other arguments against communication with Germans, arguing that the Wehrmacht were already highly suspect in the eyes of the Nazis; that it was a part of the present propaganda policy to discredit the German General Staff lest an attempt be made to set them up as an alternative government in Germany; and that it would be very difficult to make a convincing case, because all that could be said was that the officers were being held in a special camp. "I have not heard that their treatment has yet given any cause for complaint," wrote Gepp.[17]

Supreme Headquarters responded to the situation by noting that "As Oflag IVC is in the Russian sphere it is not considered that any action can be taken at present. The matter has, however, been referred to the Operations Division, Supreme Headquarters … for consideration."

Mr. Gepp left London, and his replacement, R. Elwes, typed a note to Supreme Headquarters saying that he was enclosing a photograph and sketch map of the camp (Colditz) given to Giles Romilly's mother by a French officer who had been repatriated from there. "These may be of some assistance in the preparation of any plans that you may be examining for the evacuation of the prisoners who are receiving special treatment. I should be glad to know as a matter of urgency how this matter stands." Lastly, Elwes requested that the photo and sketch promptly be given back to Mrs. Romilly.

Responding to the sketch and photo, Supreme Headquarters replied: "The photograph and sketch are of great interest, and we are therefore having copies made of them. We will return the originals to you as soon as this has been done."

On 7 March, three days later, they sent another message to the Director of Prisoners of War saying that "the whole question of what can be done with regard to this camp is being carefully examined in conjunction with G-3 Division and the Air Staff at this Headquarters. The fact that this camp is in the area of eventual Russian responsibility imposes additional difficulties, but all possible steps that can be taken will be carefully examined."[18]

From the time Major P. R. Reid wrote his letter urging quick action to save the "Prominents" in Colditz to 7 March, five weeks passed with nothing but bureaucratic quibbling. Without outside assistance, the prisoners would now have to await their fate.

Notes

1. *New York Times*, 25 July 1944, 5.
2. Harper interview, 3 February 2002.
3. *New York Times*, 9 September 1944, 9.

4. NA, AIR 40/2361.
5. *New York Times*, 20 November 1944, 3.
6. Ibid., 25 November 1944, 7.
7. Ibid.
8. NA, AIR 40/2361.
9. *New York Times*, 25 November 1944, 7.
10. NA, FO 916/889.
11. NA, FO 916/1184.
12. Eckersall interview, 1 May 2000.
13. Gimpel, *Spy for Germany*, 59.
14. Kershaw, *Hitler*, 775, 777, 780, 783.
15. NA, FO 954/28A.
16. Ibid.
17. Ibid.
18. Ibid.

CHAPTER XIV

Exodus

While the British "Prominents" and other high-ranking prisoners remained hidden in castles, the "not-so-Prominents" faced a different fate. At Stalag VIII B in south-west Poland on 22 January 1945, Mickey Reynolds and his fellow inmates received orders to begin a transfer on foot: no one had any idea where they would be going or that the journey would last for three wretched months. "On the march, it was so grim at times we had to house the sick with the cattle at night, if we were lucky. We carried our medical kit in a portable gramophone with the innards taken out, but which was a godsend at times. It was hell making sleighs to pull the unfortunate and trying to do something for those who were not as lucky as yourself." Sometimes twelve men had to share one loaf of bread; and Reynolds remembered halting one night and taking out his portion to eat, but the bread was so hard that "it was like trying to cut through a piece of frozen meat, even though the bread had been next to my body, inside my battle dress tunic." In some areas, the men could not find any water to drink, so they resorted to sucking on balls of snow.

From Teschen, in southern Poland, they trudged over the Alps, through Prague, and ended up on 9 April at Glemitz, Austria, where the American Eighth Army freed them on 24 April. "They brought us white bread, fresh eggs, and some of their own rations. We certainly tucked it in."[1]

By now, Swiss observers estimated that there were 65,000 British prisoners and 27,000 Americans on the march; many suffered from sicknesses such as dysentery or bad colds; some had frozen toes; and most were weak and underfed. With almost no food or medicines, they were forced to keep going, even though their journey was frequently interrupted by heavy Allied bombing and strafing.[2]

Conditions at Marlag-Milag had worsened – no more decent living with adequate food, sports, and theatre productions. A Swiss report said, "The men are living on one cup of water a day, and there is a shortage of [heating] fuel." One of the prisoners explained, "We are making quilts out of paper to keep warm in bed and are receiving 1/5 loaf of bread a day." Rations had been severely cut, and there were now shortages of clothing and boots.[3]

So concerned was the American Legation at Bern that on 28 February they sent an urgent secret message to the U.S. Department of State describing the terrible situation concerning prisoners of war in Germany. The report said that there were three main movements of prisoners throughout the country: the southern, central, and northern. It was estimated that 80,000 POWs, including 25,000 Americans, were marching through Sudetenland to Toplitz Schonau, where they were being assembled and split into groups. One half were heading towards the Munich, Stuttgart and Nuremberg area, the other half to Karlsbad and Eger. "This group has particularly suffered since they have crossed the Czech mountains in bad weather with little food and have been repeatedly strafed by Allied aircraft."

In the central marching line there were about 60,000 prisoners moving westward in an area bounded by Leipzig, Dresden, and Berlin. Conditions were still somewhat calm in the southern part, and trains were still running. "Because of the gentle climate, these prisoners of war are in relatively good condition." Food parcels from a supply depot at Luckenwalde would be delivered to them along the line of march. "Three hundred severely wounded American officers were abandoned in Camp Lazaret and overrun by Russians at Sagan (possibly Stalag Luft III)."

Three hundred and fifty seriously injured of various nationalities had been transported on coal barges from Lazaret Furstenberg on Oder (in present north-east Germany) to Werder, south-west of Berlin. "The transport took eight days, and there were no bedding, heat or light, two blankets per man, one American doctor and 15 Allied sanitators. Practically no Americans received Red Cross food parcels at Werder."

A Red Cross representative named Schirmer reported from personal observations in Pomerania that the northern line of march had approximately 100,000 POWs who were inching along the northern German coast towards the west (away from the advancing Russians). "The rear-guard is still on the roads west of Danzig between Lauenburg and Stolp, but the great bulk of prisoners of war are now between Demmin, Anklam, Swinemunde and Neu Brandenburg, where they are resting." Their trek would take them to Bremen, Hamburg, and Lübeck. "Approximately three potatoes, one quart of hot water daily, plus two hundred grammes of bread when available, once every 4 or 5 days, constitute their rations. The same rations are eaten by the accompanying German guards and officers." Eighty percent of the men were suffering from dysentery, which was thought to be contagious, and they were selling everything they possessed in attempts to get food, but with almost no success. One of the Red Cross officials had procured two 22½-ton trucks in Germany and with them had delivered 22,000 food parcels to marching prisoners. A further sixty tons of food boxes went on passenger trains to a storehouse in Brandenburg, and supplies went out from there to men along the northern march line. Additionally, storehouses had been set up in Petrow, Anklam, and Demmin and were being overseen by sick American prisoners "who have been helped by their German guards."

"At Alt Kalen [north-east Germany] 800 officers from Oflag 64 [at Schubin] have been resting for three or four days. Due to soft physical condition resulting from failure of work at camps, these prisoners of war are in the worst condition yet seen." Some had lost fifteen to twenty kilos of weight – thirty-three to forty-four pounds – and others were too weak to carry even one eleven-pound food parcel given them by the Red Cross. Schirmer had arranged with the Germans for the men to halt the march and be allowed to rest.

While in Berlin Schirmer had collected information about the southern and central marches from other Red Cross delegates. The delegates also highly praised the conduct and discipline of the American prisoners of war on the march. From the prisoners it was learned that whenever an evacuation was announced, the Volksturm (German territorial army) would appear at the camp and grab all the food boxes, then distribute the contents to civilians before the POWs could get any.

An American Red Cross delegate named Robinson, who was in Wehrkreis VI (work camp area) from 6 February to the 25th, said that many camps in that section were being strafed and bombed by Allied aviation, especially the British. "The camp that suffered most was Stalag VII D at Dortmund, which was destroyed completely on the night of 22 February. It was reported that the camp was illuminated with parachute flares and then bombed and that allegedly no bombs fell outside the camp area, and all barracks were destroyed." Robinson said that because the men took shelter in trenches, only one French prisoner and seventy Russians were killed (did the Russians have trenches?), while approximately 200 were wounded. "On 2 February at 7:20 P.M. Stalag XII A was bombed again. While there were no American casualties, one French enlisted man and 77 French officers were killed. Three hundred French officers were wounded and 17 missing." Another camp on a hillside at Bonn was totally destroyed, as well.

Robinson finished the report by announcing that a new International Red Cross Headquarters had been established at Uffing, about fifty kilometres south-west of Munich. The building – an old, crenellated, square brick structure with a single tower – sat on the crest of a hill at the northern end of a small lake called Staffel. To those who saw it, this funny-looking old building probably represented Allied victory and hopes for a return to a peaceful life.[4]

The RAF received many letters from men who had survived air raids in POW camps, on trains, and on marches: Bomber Command Headquarters was well aware of the problems and continued to try to gather information about camp locations, but exact information was scarce. One report came in from a Swedish YMCA representative on 24 February explaining that the prisoners of Stalag VIII A at Görlitz in Silesia had marched past him, and that they told him they had spent nine days on the road. The POWs had foreseen the move and had constructed handcarts and collected some baby carriages to tote their belongings. At night, the prisoners told him, the Germans were quartering them in barns, and food had often been scarce but they had an adequate supply of Red Cross parcels. "They were in quite good shape and splendid spirits."[5]

At Work Camp 21 (the benzene distillery) at Blechammer, Silesia, Happy Eckersall heard the news that they would be leaving soon and marching to an unknown destination that had a church with a double spire. "I said I would supply the handcart from the camp so we could take all the injured, wounded, or people suffering from sickness. We put them on there, got some medical parcels, and this, that, and the other, and off we all went."

To their surprise, that night they were ordered to return to camp. "The Russians were only a couple of miles away, so we went back to the camp and spent another night – not much sleep – and then the next morning we was off early, and we eventually carried on until we got near Czechoslovakia, the bottom part." As they tramped along, the column passed a line of Jewish men and women, and the German guards made the Jews stand aside so that the prisoners could pass. "The snow at this time was about two foot deep, and I saw with my own eyes this Jew who must have known he was going to die: he stood and stripped off all his clothing and threw it to his comrades. He was standing naked – what an act of charity."

When they arrived in Prague, the local citizens standing along the roadside appeared to be somewhat fearful of the German guards and walked off, but they returned shortly with bits of food for the prisoners, who gratefully accepted them. "We was marching in fives. I wouldn't have said marching – we was ambling along. We lost a lot of men on that march, and any bodies, we left behind: we took the [identification] disc from the body, broke it in half to give the Red Cross and left the other half so they would know who they were."

One night the POWs found shelter in a brick works. "It was quite warm in there, with brick dust everywhere, and at three A.M. soup was served up in a factory in the village." The next day Happy and friends found a dead horse along the road, so they dragged it back to the factory and cooked it in one of the copper boilers. "We had horsemeat that day."

Desperate for materials to protect themselves from the cold, Happy and friends discovered a fifty-foot-long drive belt at the brick factory and removed it with the idea of fashioning footwear. "I took a piece about two foot long and about ten inches wide. I thought I might be able to get my shoes repaired, because I had no bottoms in my shoes." But that day while marching, the guards announced that someone had stolen a belt from the factory, and Happy was forced to surreptitiously drop his leather scrap and stomp it into the two-foot-deep snow.

At one point in the endless journey to nowhere, a young soldier came up to Happy, who was pushing the cart, and told him, "I feel ever so sick. Can I get on the cart?" Eckersall replied, "All right, but what's the matter?" "Nothing," responded the boy, "I've got the radio with me." Ernie let him ride on the cart for a while, then told the soldier to get off. Before the young soldier walked away, he left his pack in the cart. Happy then called Davis, the sergeant major, who marched up, swiftly took the boy's pack out of the cart and placed his own in it. "So the next time they searched the hand cart, we had the sergeant major's pack, and we passed it back that night when we got settled in."

As they headed west towards Germany, the weeks wore on, and the weather grew steadily milder. "We slept in barns, cow sheds, pig sties, hedges – anywhere. We used to go around the farms trying to get potatoes and that." When they arrived at Bayreuth, north-east of Nuremberg, they were greeted by big white Red Cross trucks rumbling down the road. "One of the chaps got out and came over to us and spoke to me in German. He said, 'Where are you from?' I explained where we'd come from, and at first he wouldn't believe it, then he says, 'All right. Are there any more of you?'" Happy told him there were many more coming up the road, so the German informed him that the marchers would remain in the present location for that day and the next. He gave out Red Cross parcels, one for two men at first, and later one for four men, and "that lasted us until we got to the end of the march."

Eckersall told the German that the Yanks were on the way, that it wouldn't be long before they were there, but his words fell on disbelieving ears. "I showed him on the map how they was cutting in to cut off Berlin, and he said, 'Oh my God, oh my God!'" From Bayreuth the prisoners plodded on, finally reaching Regensburg. Just outside a German POW camp, the German Kommandant informed them that the Yanks were bombing the town and that they would have to sleep in a tent where the Americans had been. Disgusted with the idea, the British submariners replied, "No thank you, we'll clean it out first." As they entered the POW confinement area, they saw throngs of prisoners inside the barbed wire fence, and "they was all crying when they saw us come in, because, you know, we must have looked such a terrible mess."

To clean up the Americans' tent, Happy and others chopped up their handcart, made a fire, and used a big drum to boil some water for washing out their new quarters. "Then the next day [12 April], President Roosevelt died, and the Yanks arrived at the gate."[6]

The food trucks that Happy's team had encountered were the result of a desperate effort by the International Red Cross to supply provisions for the hordes of prisoners marching towards central Germany. Beginning in mid-December of 1944, the German transportation system had been so thoroughly disrupted by bombing that the Red Cross had lost the means to transport vital foodstuffs to prisoners by train. To expedite an emergency plan, the Supreme Allied Headquarters and the German Government made an agreement to get supplies through to the POWs. On 8 March the Red Cross painted twenty-five large Allied Army trucks white with red crosses on the roofs and sides, loaded them with food boxes, and drove them across the Swiss border into Germany. Fifty-five more trucks were soon to follow, rushing provisions to starving prisoners like Happy Eckersall and many others. German authorities had agreed to give the convoys safe conduct; hence the German soldier who rode along with the trucks that aided Eckersall's group. Another part of the emergency agreement allowed a trainload of food for 100,000 POWs to travel from Switzerland into Germany.[7]

Switzerland, the protecting power, succeeded in getting the Germans to agree to transport sick prisoners by train or truck; however, as later testimony revealed, Hitler refused to do it. The Germans disagreed with a Swiss idea to parachute supplies in, saying that it would not be practical, and they were right: the situation was too chaotic.[8]

By the first week of March (1945), the Allies were advancing into Germany from the east and the west, and the food crisis was a long way from being solved. POW camps were gruesomely overcrowded, and men of all nationalities were jammed together with scarcely a bite to eat. Before the emergency agreement, thousands of tons of food parcels from various nations had been sitting in Switzerland, and the U.S. had stockpiled 100,000 tons of food boxes in Sweden, Switzerland, and Spain.

It was thought that in Germany there were around 100,000 American prisoners of war, 150,000 British, 720,000 French, 60,000 Poles, 70,000 Belgians, 13,000 Yugoslavs, 1,150 Norwegians and 1,250 Greeks. No one knew how many Russian prisoners there were, but it was thought that there were several million. Now that all of these unfortunates were either existing in camps or marching through the countryside, the old German system of feeding them became impossible; and the prisoners' only hope for survival lay in the Red Cross parcels.[9]

Formerly, camps were segregated according to nationalities: the Americans received four packages a month; the French and most other nationalities got one package monthly; the Russians had nothing; and the British Red Cross sent its own supply boxes. In early 1945, when prisoners from various nations lived together, this situation was to change, saving the lives of thousands of Russian prisoners: under new rules, all nationalities would receive Red Cross boxes on an equal basis – including Russians – even though the Soviet Union had never signed the Geneva Conventions.

The German Government had little interest in the POWs except for keeping them – dead or alive – out of Allied control. Hitler, who was violating every rule of war, probably would have let the prisoners starve to death if the Red Cross had not intervened; and his harsh policies were affecting his own officers and countrymen, as well. Just days before General Patton's Third Army stormed across the Rhine on the 22nd of March, American Military Intelligence picked up a secret message from the Germans saying: "The Commander ... Battalion 212 reports that the Demolition Detachment ordered to blow up the [Rhine] bridge at Trittenheim were offered by civilians, allegedly at the request of the community, 'as much money as they wish, 5 large measures of wine, their pick of the women and civilian clothing, if they did not blow up the bridge.' Investigation is in progress."[10]

That same day a return message from Fieldmarshal Kesselring stated that "an important Rhine bridge, in spite of thorough technical preparatory measures for demolition, has fallen undamaged into the enemy's hands, because responsible commanders, through their indecisive, irresponsible and cowardly behaviour, gave up the head of the bridge, and issued the demolition order too late." (General Patton's troops would march across that bridge one week later.) The message went on to say that the five guilty officers had been sentenced by court martial to death and that the arrest and detention of the officers' relatives had been carried out. "The above mentioned is to be made known at once by the quickest means to all troops, and is to serve as a warning to all." Kesselring, C in C West, ordered that "any failure to be checked out and dealt with by the shortest method," and "I expect from the Courts Martial the most drastic action and the most severe sentences."[11]

Shortly before the bridge incident, Hitler had ordered a scorched earth command for all fronts: he wanted the total destruction of industrial plants, buildings, bridges, and food storage facilities before the Allies could make use of them; however, many of his army leaders tried to prevent the decree from being expedited. At the same time, the agitated Führer hurriedly began to fortify his southern Alpine redoubt, including his mountain retreat at Berchtesgaden. The Allies believed that in this region of high mountains, limited roads, and deep snows, Hitler and his SS guards would make their last stand. They also thought that the Germans had blasted out caves in mountainsides and had hidden food and ammunition in them.[12]

In reality, Hitler never built supply caves but had earlier constructed air raid bunkers on his Obersalzburg fortress: the supply problem may be one of the reasons that he later refused to leave his underground lair at the Reichschancellery and move to Berchtesgaden.[13]

Hitler's preparations did nothing to daunt Winston Churchill, who by now was so confident of Allied victory that he travelled to western Germany to inspect British and American bridgeheads. With a pleased expression on his face, the doughty Prime Minister walked on ground that the Germans had vacated only thirty-six hours before. He had desperately wanted to accompany the Normandy Invasion but had been vigorously restrained by Parliament; and instead, the King had made on 16 June a triumphant visit to France. Now Winnie could at last show his presence in Germany and feel the glory. But German gunfire could be heard not far from the PM's observation point. Undeterred, he boarded a landing boat and proceeded to make a short cruise on the Rhine; then he climbed up on a bridge. As he stood there peering through his binoculars, a German shell exploded about fifty yards away. A rain of enemy fire landed in the river as American troops forged across the Rhine in landing craft and Allied planes buzzed overhead. Churchill thoroughly enjoyed the whole experience, especially his close call from a German shell. He told reporters that it had been impossible for Hitler to defend such a long river, the same way that it was difficult to protect a lengthy (French) coastline from invasion. After a lunch of fried chicken the PM mused, "The last time I was on the Rhine was at Cologne during the last war. We cruised fifty miles upstream in a British gunboat."[14]

Because of the worsening war situation and Hitler's refusal to surrender, the Swiss feared for the ultimate safety of the fifteen million Allied POWs and foreign workers throughout Germany. The International Red Cross had lost track of hundreds of thousands of prisoners and labourers because of long marches and changes of camps. On 31 March the Allies deciphered a top secret message to a senior SS official and police commander, Dr. Martin, from Gottlob Berger, Waffen SS general, saying that Berger had consulted with the Führer about prisoners of war problems. "The Führer stressed most emphatically that the American and English P.W. Officers and N.C.O.'s should under no circumstances fall into the hands of the enemy. They will be transported away to the South. Camps are for the time being not available, therefore, above all, every measure should be taken to ensure that the tents available in Langwasser are transported away." The message explained that sick prisoners who were unable to march could be left behind in case of a surprise enemy attack, because the enemy would not be able to use them for about a year. "Please confirm arrival of this letter, Heil Hitler!"[15]

Two days before Berger's radiogram went out, a dramatic scene began to play out at Limburg when the Germans herded a thousand British and American prisoners of war into railway freight carriages, intending to transport them to Berlin. No markings on the outside of the train indicated that it held POWs. For thirty-six hours the men were left inside the cars without food, and on Wednesday night, as the train chugged eastward, American planes spotted it and dived in for an attack. As they approached, the engineer had just reached a tunnel and sped the train into it. Once inside, he halted. After sitting there a day and a half, the men started to sicken from lack of food, water, and the terrible stench.

On Friday the train started off once more, but on Sunday, American planes found it a second time, swooped down and made a direct bomb hit, killing eight men in one car and wounding eight more. As soon as the prisoners saw that the German guards were running away, some of them managed to break out of the carriages and slide open the doors of the other cars. As machine-gun bullets popped everywhere, one of the American officers ordered all thousand prisoners to run into a nearby field and form the letters "P O W." Then he commanded them to strip to the waist and bend over, so that the pilots could see their oversized human sign.

The attacking P-47 pilots fortunately spotted the P O W letters, ceased firing, then slowly circled to study the situation, trying to decide whether or not it was a German trick. On the ground, officers continually yelled at the soldiers, telling them to keep the formation. As the sun relentlessly burned the prisoners' backs, two more groups of P-47s dived in and let loose with machineguns. Out of a thousand prisoners, only one man broke and ran. The attacks continued, and a few of the soldiers did get killed. Two chaplains, seeing them fall, walked over to where they lay dying and gave them last rites. As the afternoon wore on and the heat became unbearable, many of the prisoners fervently prayed that they would survive. For six hours they held the P O W formation, until finally it appeared that the American pilots had passed the word to the air force to leave them alone.

That night the German guards returned, assembled the men, and forced them to march eastward. When they had walked about twenty miles, they saw American tanks on a nearby highway, and at that instant, the guards took off like sprinters at the starting gun. Fortunately for the POWs, the American tank men accompanied them to safety.[16]

Good news at last for war prisoners. On 3 April came the announcement that the American Eleventh Armored Division had overrun a hospital at Grimmenthal and liberated seventy Americans and 450 Britons. Most of the POWs had been hospitalised after a forced march across Germany to a location near the Russian front, then back – during which more than a thousand died. Food was so scarce in Germany that civilians were fighting over ration scraps left behind by their retreating soldiers. Violent, heavy fighting continued everywhere as the Allied armies approached. On the day of the Grimmenthal rescue, the prisoners at Stalag IX B at Bad Orb awaited help as all 6,500, confined in a 400-square-foot enclosure, neared death by starvation. A war correspondent who accompanied the 106th U.S. Cavalry when they captured Bad Orb and the prison camp, interviewed the French, British, American, Serb, and Russian prisoners. Some of the British prisoners had come from camps at Lamsdorf (Stalag 344) and Sagan (Stalag Luft III) after a 500-mile march that lasted eight weeks.[17]

A reporter described the men's stories of being forced, sixty at a time, into freight carriages that should have held forty. They had no food, heat, or light during the journey, and no way to sit or lie down, as they were too tightly crowded. To make matters worse, the guards ordered them during the journey to get out into the bitter cold and repair bomb damage on the tracks. Under such intolerable conditions, many of the prisoners died from exposure, illness, or starvation, or were shot by guards when they could no longer perform the gruelling labour. One group explained that they spent Christmas Eve inside a carriage, taking turns attempting to rest on the filthy floor, using helmets as toilets, and singing Christmas carols.[18]

Another war correspondent accompanying the Americans wrote about the liberation of Camp 326 at Eselheide, eleven miles south-east of Bielefeld, where men were as close to starvation as humans could get. Twelve to fifteen had been dying daily, and the others seemed to be staying alive only by effort of will. One prisoner told the reporter, "I don't suppose you could say they mistreated us. I guess you could call it neglect."[19]

When the Russians saw American tanks approaching, they had but one thought: food. Ignoring the 200 German guards with machine guns in watch towers, they surged towards the camp provision warehouses as the POW leaders tried to quell the riot by firing rifles that the German guards had given them to keep order. With their sheer body weight the Russian crowd smashed down the walls of the two warehouses and plunged into them.

An American officer who witnessed the scene remarked, "I never saw such a fight. One man would grab a loaf of bread and try to wolf it down. Others would fight him for it until finally there would be nothing but crumbs on the ground." He added that the German guards were afraid to come down from their towers and did not budge when the American troops fired machine guns over their heads. "Our men had to go up and haul them down."[20]

Along with the several million suffering Allied war prisoners, seven million displaced Europeans walked along the jam-packed roads with their families, trying to escape from the Russian army. Obtaining shelter and food for the refugees increased the Allies' enormous problems at the war's end, and solving them became the top priority of the United Nations Relief and Rehabilitation Administration. However, there was little they could do: it was too overwhelming.

In a heroic effort to assist the fleeing East Europeans, the German navy, under orders from Admiral Dönitz, utilised every possible vessel to transport refugees from eastern to western Germany. Under heavy air and sea attack by the Allies, German warships, minesweepers, torpedo boats, and submarines plied the Baltic with their precious human cargoes for five months – from January to May 1945 – and many sailors and civilians were killed. The German Navy performed a memorable feat by helping more than two million European refugees reach safety and freedom.[21]

Notes

1. Reynolds, "HMS *Seal.*"
2. NA, FO 916/1156.
3. NA, AIR 40/2361.
4. Previous sections from NA, AIR 14/1239, 75A.
5. NA, AIR 14/1239.
6. Eckersall interview, 1 May 2000.
7. *New York Times*, 9 March 1945, 8.
8. Ibid., 1 March 1945, 5.
9. Ibid., 7 March 1945, 6.
10. NA, HW 5/706.
11. Ibid.
12. *New York Times*, 24 March 1945, 1.
13. Beierl, *History of the Eagle's Nest*, 135.
14. *New York Times*, 26 March 1945, 5.
15. NA, HW 5/706.
16. *New York Times*, 29 March 1945, 5.
17. Ibid., 3 April 1945, 5.
18. Ibid., 4 April 1945, 1.
19. Ibid.
20. Ibid.
21. Dönitz, *Memoirs*, 433.

CHAPTER XV

Marlag-Milag Takes to the Road

By the end of March 1945 the war seemed to be grinding down, and the Allies grew more and more concerned that prisoners of war might be subjected to "massacre or violence by the enemy upon or immediately before the cessation of German resistance." They formulated a plan to charge the General First Allied Airborne Army with despatching airborne troops for protection of prisoner of war camps; ground forces would then relieve them when they could get there. Somehow, this scheme never went into effect, and the fear of reprisal remained, as SS men were now in charge of prison camps.[1]

As later events proved, many of the German guards merely abandoned the camps when the American and British armies were at their doorsteps. Few instances of shootings occurred, and starvation became the greatest threat – to POWs and the German population as well. So intense was their hunger that a mob of civilians stormed the Wehrmacht headquarters at Gotha on 9 April and grabbed all the clothing and food they could carry. Others ransacked railroad cars abandoned by the Third Army.[2]

At Hannover, American forces rolled into town and started their mopping up operations; at the same time the inmates at Marlag-Milag, including those from HMS *Seal*, received word from Camp Kommandant Schmidt that all prisoners were to evacuate on foot to Lübeck. Schmidt ordered prisoners to be prepared to set out that evening, 9 April. "I protested strongly," said Senior British Officer Graham Wilson, "owing to the danger of the roads through action by the Tactical Air Force." Schmidt told Wilson that he totally agreed with him, but that he had received orders that morning from the general in charge of all prison camps that all personnel were to depart, including himself. "Finally," Wilson went on, "he agreed to leave behind those officers and men considered … to be unfit to march."

As quickly as they could, the German doctor and Wilson sorted out about seventy-two older officers and men in weakened physical condition and allowed them to stay behind. Nine more were already in the camp hospital, and they would be transferred to the Milag sick bay that evening.

"At Milag," Wilson continued, "I found that out of 670 ratings detailed for march, only 187 had actually left; the remainder having been hidden up by the Merchant Navy in their big camp." Korvettenkapitän Rogge told Wilson that he (Rogge), along with two officers and a hundred guards, had been placed in command of Marlag; he also had orders to surrender to the British when they arrived. "For this reason, he said he had no intention of sending anyone else on the march and agreed to allow escapers from the column to enter Milag without hindrance."[3]

By now the British were only seven miles from Bremen, and around 7 April, just before the great exodus, POWs had seen a V-2 being fired one evening from northwest of the camp. "It took off in a northerly direction … accompanied by a prolonged roar and a flash of white flame," wrote Robert Buckham, Flight Lieutenant, Royal Canadian Air Force. "An hour later the camp was surrounded by a ring of parachute flares over a circumference of several miles, a performance which lasted from about 8:30 till 10 pm, creating rumours of a paratroop landing in the vicinity."

"At 11:15 a more distant curtain of flares identified a raid on Hamburg. Over a period of forty-five minutes we watched the most spectacular raid of our imprisonment, huge sheet-like explosions of flame illuminating towering columns of smoke, which rose from beyond the brilliantly-lit horizon. … It was as though we were the audience to a film without the sound track."[4]

Buckham noted that on 8 April "a second V-2 was fired last night, and rumour has its source as being an experimental station about two miles north of the camp." (At the time, V-2s were being shot off from camouflaged portable launchers in various locations, with the main production of rockets at a secret location in the Hartz Mountains, to the south.) "There has been no light in the camp for over 48 hours and water is available only one hour a day in three twenty-minute periods. We have been advised to fill every available container with water, as there may be no further supply after 6 pm."[5]

The next day, 9 April, Buckham recorded in his diary that "A number of us broke into the kitchen supply shed in order to obtain some white soap powder, which we spread over the sand of the parade ground, forming POW and RAF in huge letters and indicating our likely route with a large arrow."[6]

Graham Wilson, Senior British Officer, had previously ordered all Marlag-Milag prisoners not to attempt escapes from the camp; but now that the exodus was imminent, he rescinded the order and told all personnel that men were free to break away if they wanted to. Wilson said that he would give permission for no more than fifteen men to hide in the camp when the column moved out: he presumed that the Germans would conduct a muster before they departed, and more than fifteen would be hard to conceal.

Wilson realised that he could not flatly refuse to leave Marlag-Milag, but he decided that he would use delaying tactics, but not to such extremes that the guards would open fire. RAF Group Captain Wray agreed that he would do the same. When the announcement came on 9 April to make marching preparations and to leave at 6:00 P.M., the two officers fiddled around as much as they could and lengthened the departure time by two hours.

With RAF prisoners leading, the inmates walked out of Marlag-Milag between 8:00 and 8:30 P.M. After they had trudged a short distance in thick fog, the German officers ordered them to return to camp: they had decided to postpone the move until early the next day. Finally, on the afternoon of 10 April, 1,950 RAF officers and other ranks led the way, followed by 546 Marlag "O" officers and ratings, then 200 from Marlag "M," with Capt. E. H. B. Baker as Senior British Officer. Kapitän Schmidt, Kommandant of Marlag-Milag Nord, had charge of the enormous column. "Throughout the march, he was entirely ineffective, rarely to be seen or got ahold of, and it was evident to all that the whole undertaking was far beyond his control," reported Captain Baker. Schmidt's own officers repeatedly complained about his ineffectiveness, refusal to accept responsibility, and being inaccessible.

Each group had a commander: Oberleutnant Schoof, Chief Abwehr Officer of Marlag-Milag, led Marlag "O," and throughout the march he proved to be totally inefficient. "When pressed to improve conditions, he either fell back on excuses and saying he was sorry that things were so bad, but we must make the best of it, or he lost his temper and shouted," said Baker. "In his favour, it must be said that he did not use threats about escaping etc., and seemed to restrain any guards who might be inclined to take extreme measures or forcing anyone to keep up with the column on the march."

Oberleutnant Holz, in charge of the Marlag "M" column, proved to be "reasonably efficient and considerate." Baker observed that Holz not only did his best for his own column, he helped the Marlag "O" men, in spite of the obviously strained relations between him and Schoof. "He always slept in the same field or barn as his column, rather than sleep in a moderately comfortable house, as did all the other German officers and guards."

Baker noted that the guards that had been provided for the march were mostly from the Marine Artillery and Luftwaffe personnel who had been on duty at Marlag-Milag. Another hundred field police had been added until the columns reached the Elbe river. "The vast majority of the guards were reasonable and easy going, while many of them stood up to the conditions on the march much less well than the prisoners," Baker observed.

Group Captain L. E. Wray, Senior Allied Officer, commanded the RAF column; Baker had charge of the Marlag "O" group; and Petty Officer Parsons was Man of Confidence for the Marlag "M" contingent. "The

RAF column was highly organised from the start, in view of the large numbers, and as a result of their experiences when marching from Sagan. The Marlag 'O' column started out in a somewhat haphazard manner, as the German orders and control of the start were so chaotic."

During the journey eastward, the order of the navy column was maintained, with an advance party headed by Baker and two other officers, and their conveyances bringing up the rear. The Germans had provided no transportation for the prisoners; however, some of them had managed to build a large wagon for provisions that was pulled by ratings and a small cart for the supply and medical officers. Some of the more enterprising POWs had constructed makeshift wheelbarrows and small wagons, but the majority of prisoners had to carry whatever they could in improvised rucksacks and makeshift containers. The German guards had a horse-drawn wagon to haul their gear.

Captain L. MacLean of the British Medical Corps loaded as much medical equipment as he thought necessary for the trip into a small cart and ordered five medical orderlies to accompany him. "Lack of transport prevented me from including many things, but the German Stabsarzt [doctor] promised me he would help us from his own supplies along the route when necessary." For identification from the air, the orderlies had covered the cart with a sheet and painted the rough shape of the Red Cross on it, "a not very distinguishing mark." MacLean said that camp officials supplied no vehicles for anyone who might fall sick on the route, and for the first two days, the ill and exhausted had to be accommodated on top of a German baggage wagon. "On day three, Senior British Officer Baker procured from the Germans a wagon for the sick. This was a great boon, and for most of the time it was filled to capacity."[7]

As for their destination, the Germans said very little, leading Baker to understand that they were to march to Buchholz and there get on trains for Lübeck, which was probably their final destination. Baker and his officers did manage, however, to keep up with the progress of the war by listening to the BBC or News to Europe on one hidden radio and various secret crystal sets that they carried.[8]

At the outset of the journey, the RAF contingent deliberately kept a slow pace, hoping that Allied troops would rescue them. That first day, "the marchers had a taste of things to come," remarked Ernie Truman. "A couple of RAF Spitfires came over and strafed the road astern of the column, and one and all, guards included, took to the ditches. Again, after leaving Kirchtimke, we had another dose, and we began to realise what we were really up against. ..." Baker noted that when they saw the Allied fighters, they got the impression that the pilots had seen them and identified them as POWs. "As a result of this, when fighters flew over, the general policy was to stay on the road and wave rather than take cover as if expecting to be attacked."[9]

On that day and the next, twelve officers and nine ratings broke out of the Marlag "M" column and ran off, as they had previously been given permission to do by Captain Wilson. "That night," reported Baker, "we arrived [at Heeslingen] in the dark – hungry, tired, and with our nerves strung up like violin strings, having covered 14 kilometres in our first day."[10]

They were forced to stay overnight in a small, damp, marshy field outside Heeslingen with no shelter, causing many of them to suffer from chills. "While establishing our campsite," wrote Flight Lieutenant Buckham, "we spotted two haystacks in an adjoining barnyard, and with thoughts of a straw mattress under our bedrolls, a half-dozen of us jumped the fence to gather hay. Suddenly a guard appeared, stepping from behind a stack, and levelled his rifle, shouted, and immediately fired into the midst of our group. Scattering for the fence, we turned back to see Matheson and Barker attempting to crawl after us, writhing in pain. We got them over the fence while the guard continued to scream hysterically, his rifle held at the ready." Fortunately, tourniquets stopped the bleeding, and "an ambulance eventually arrived to carry them off to a Zeven hospital." [11]

Next day, 11 April, at about 3:30 in the afternoon, the column had halted for a brief rest. "We sat down on the roadside to eat … and after about half an hour we were preparing to move on when the RAF planes came over," recalled Ernie Truman. "They circled around us and then suddenly, to our great surprise, came down on the tail-end of the column in a beam attack. Everybody scattered for ditches and houses, and to the tune of machine-gun and cannon fire sought what cover they could."[12]

"I had been about halfway up the column at the time of the attack," said Captain Baker, "and as soon as the attack had taken place, I went to the head of the column to inform Oberleutnant Schoof that the rear had been attacked and that he must stop the column and make them take cover." Schoof insisted that the prisoners keep moving, but Baker refused and walked to the rear of the line to see about the wounded, with Schoof following. "It was obvious that he was much shaken. I insisted that the column remain where it was until the wounded could be got away to Hospital. An ambulance was ordered from Zeven, but as none was available there, one had to be obtained from Bremervurd."

In the air assault, Sourfield, Linton, Bogie, and Faerber were severely wounded, and King was killed. Bogie died two hours later, and Sourfield died at the Zeven hospital. Both horses on the medical wagon were so badly injured that they had to be shot. The medical officer, Captain MacLean, immediately tried to assist the wounded men as they lay along the roadside: he administered morphine to each and had them carried on improvised stretchers to a nearby barn. "The German authorities [were] asked to call for an ambulance as soon as possible," said MacLean. "This, however, did not arrive until more than two hours after the accident, by which time Bogie had succumbed to his injury, and the condition of Commander Sourfield, on whom it was necessary to perform an emergency amputation of his left leg above the knee, was grave."[13]

Three days after the strafing, word reached Marlag-Milag that four prisoners who were marching to Lübeck had been wounded on the 11th and that they were in a hospital at Zeven. One of the German lieutenants volunteered to drive a British commander to the hospital, and they took off with clothes, blankets, and a few other things necessary for bringing back the injured men. The two returned safely but reported that although the officers were being well cared for, they were in no condition to travel.

After the ambulance had picked up Sourfield, Linton, and Faerber, Schoof tried to order the column to continue, but "I refused to move any more that day, as evening was coming on, and the nerves of many in the column had been badly shaken," explained Baker. "After some blustering and trying to force us to move, he finally agreed to stay in the village, and camp was made in a small wood at the East end of the village in which the column was now resting." As Ernie Truman remembered it, "That night was very uncomfortable, as flares were dropping all around us, and the roads in the vicinity were constantly being strafed."[14]

"From this point on, we were able to obtain from the Germans some sort of shelter for the sick each night," said MacLean. As for the escaping situation, Captain Baker called the whole company together on the night of the 11th and told them that he would allow no further attempts to break away. His reasons were these: "I considered it my first duty to get the column to its destination and finally home to England without further casualties, and I could only do this by giving my personal assurances to the Germans that no one would escape when taking cover in the woods when our aircraft were carrying out road strafing in the vicinity. ..." Secondly, Baker did not think that anyone attempting to escape from that point on had a chance to make it: he had been informed that the Germans were combing the woods for their own deserters and POW escapers, and that the farther they got away from Marlag-Milag, the less chance they had of anyone getting back. From that time on, the British prisoners could take adequate cover in woods or houses without the guards' interference when aircraft attacks hit them.[15]

After the deadly strafing on 11 April, Baker thought it was obvious that the German officers had lost whatever control they had originally possessed, so he decided to immediately take complete command of the march. With no objections from the Germans, he did so. "No orders were issued by the Germans on any subject ... without obtaining my sanctions, and the Field Police fell into line as regards this."

When the great mass of prisoners reached Harsefeld on 12 April, RAF Group Captain Wray informed Baker that he had taken towels and placed ground signs forming the letters "RAF" and "POW" in two fields where they were resting. "I ordered the sign POW to be laid out," said Baker, "in our field, made up with sheets which we had brought with us. Thereafter, this sign was laid out at each campsite and also in fields along the road when we halted for any lengthy period."

At the beginning of the journey, two Red Cross parcels had been allotted to each man, as well as what was left of the mess supplies, making the amount of food available for the trip more than was possible to carry; and a good deal of it had to be left behind. Along the journey, Red Cross representative Monsieur de Bloumet doled out one parcel per man each week – hardly enough for survival. In addition to the food boxes, the Germans provided bits of bread, tinned meat, and fish. "The arrangements for the supply of hot water," said Baker, "were either non-existent or grossly inefficient, and it was only after I had insisted on sending two officers ahead of the column so that they arrived at the stopping place about an hour before the main body arrived, that any semblance of organisation was possible." In some locations, water could only be obtained more than a kilometre away from the camp site; and in several instances the local German people did their best to provide hot water and other provisions. "Along the march through the villages, people put buckets of water at their gates for us to drink or fill our water bottles. They were for the most part very sick of the war and were looking forward to the British or the Americans arriving. They had, however, a horror at the thought of being taken over by the Russians."[16]

After the terrifying air attack on the 11th, Baker designated 13 April as a day of rest – an enormous relief for the men. "A German issue of canned meat provided a surprisingly tasteful dinner when mixed with an onion and some potatoes," said F/Lt. Robert Buckham. "While boiling water for coffee we threw in our last two eggs and hardboiled them for a future lunch. A wood-gathering party has just been fired on by a guard. No injuries are reported."[17]

Gravely disturbed about the constant bombing and strafing of the column, Baker and Wray went to confer with the Kommandant at Harsefeld and tried to persuade him to let the marchers return to Westertimke. However, the Kommandant pointed out that he had received his orders and would be shot if he did not carry them out. "He had been told that he would be held responsible for the casualties that had occurred and any that might occur in the future," recalled Baker, "since to us he represented the German Government. He appeared to be a most unhappy man."[18]

Some of the marchers asked for food from nearby farm people, who gladly traded what they could in the way of eggs, bread, apples, powdered coffee, and other edibles for cigarettes, chocolates, and items from the Red Cross boxes. "Getting food on that march was part of the problem," explained Ernie Truman, "and during the course of our stay in Germany [Marlag], we had collected a few American sailors, and they were real bucks of boys, no doubt about that." Ernie remembered that as they were plodding along on the march, they came to a farmyard, and some chickens ran across the road in front of them. "One of these [American] lads grabbed a chicken and with two fingers – one on each side of its neck – flipped it over his wrist, broke its neck, and straight into his battle dress jumper. That was the neatest thing I've ever seen. We had a good supper that night." Ernie said the young sailor was a cowboy in real life and had not even broken step when he nabbed the fowl.[19]

When the marchers reached Hadendorf on 14 April, they spent the night in a dry field surrounded by farms. By the 15th, they had made it to the Elbe river and there camped on the grassy banks. Next day the columns were ferried across the Elbe, landing at Blankenese, just north of Hamburg, where smoke lingered from an Allied raid the previous night.

The ragged stream of marchers trudged over the cobblestone streets while locals gazed at them from hotel balconies. Without stopping, the haggard POWs marched on to Sulldorf and there camped in a dry field near a farmyard that had a nice large water pump. Some of the more desperate men took a shocking, ice-cold bath under the pump.

Back at Marlag-Milag, tension rose as British troops neared the camp on 16 April. "It became clear that the German control of the camp was fading out due to the complete indifference of the guards to their orders or duties," reported Wilson. "The situation was somewhat serious, as the surrounding country was occupied by SS and 1st line troops, who would have welcomed an excuse to clean up the camp. A Royal Marine guard was therefore called up, and they maintained a continuous patrol, unarmed, inside the wire to prevent anyone from leaving the camp." At the main gate a British naval officer and two quartermasters stood guard as well. Wilson conferred with the American officer in charge of Marlag "O" and the British officer at "Dulag," telling them to start inner patrols there; the same for Marlag "M." That night two bombs were dropped on Marlag "M" after a Polish prisoner lit a flare in the toilet area. Six men were killed and four wounded.

Because 4,000 new prisoners had been brought in from Sandbostel, the feeding of the camp caused major concern; but, "owing to the brave action of Captain Simssen of the Danish Red Cross and Dr. Stein and Captain Foskett of the International Red Cross in risking the dangers of the road and bringing back a stock of parcels from Lübeck in their vans, this difficulty was overcome," explained Wilson.

During the next week gunfire could be heard to the south and southeast, while the RAF made continuous attacks on nearby roads and lanes. "At 1130 on 26th April, Captain Notman and I, accompanied by Kapitän Rogge, were taken to General Rodt's headquarters in Westertimke, which was about 400 yards from the camp." There the German general informed the two officers that in order to comply with the Geneva Convention, they intended to send an envoy to the British general to propose that a twenty-four-hour truce be declared at 3:00 P.M. to allow prisoners to be evacuated and marched five miles to Bahnstadt and there turned over to the British. "As this was an obvious excuse to gain time to fortify their positions and reorganise their troops, I refused to have anything to do with it and told the Staff Captain that they should evacuate Westertimke, a remark that was not well received."

A short time later, Kapitän Rogge and Oberleutnant Reuken mounted a motorcycle with sidecar and drove off towards the British lines carrying a white flag. "They did not return, and Oberleutnant Wessel assumed nominal command of the camp." On the morning of 27 April the British started a heavy bombardment of the surrounding area, and at about 4:30 that afternoon they stormed into Kirchtimke, about three kilometres from the camp. "This was followed by fierce fighting with tanks and infantry in the wood around the German guards' barracks in Westertimke, and the village was not cleared of the Germans until midnight," Wilson declared. "Some splinters and .303 bullets fell in the camp but caused no casualties."

Shortly after midnight on 28 April, Lieutenant MacGregor of the Scots Guards appeared at the main gate of Milag and told Wilson that they were free and that he was going to round up the German guards. That afternoon Wilson made a point to thank the Scottish officers for releasing them and for the protection they had given Marlag-Milag during the attack. "Oberleutnant Wessel behaved correctly during the action, and the German camp guard took no part in the fighting." After the camp was liberated, the British Marine Guard formed riot squads who watched for looting and prevented the POWs from bringing liquor and German weapons into camp. In short, they maintained order.[20]

With no idea of what was taking place at Marlag-Milag, the huge contingent of marchers straggled into Ellersbeck on 17 April, and a day's rest was announced. In a field they set up camp, and Red Cross parcels were doled out, one to each man. Captain Baker, impatient with the slow pace of the RAF group, decided to do something about it. "At the commencement of the march, the RAF columns were in the lead, carrying out the agreed delaying tactics of only marching a few kilometres per day and taking a long time about it. After crossing the Elbe, I informed the Group Captain [Wray] that I intended taking the lead and that we were going to make our own arrangement about billets, since the Germans were so inefficient about it." Wray agreed, and after leaving Ellersbeck, Baker's navy men passed through the RAF column (no doubt with a certain pride), then kept well beyond them. "This was much more satisfactory, as we found that with the RAF ahead of us, we were continually bumping and boring and having to stop every few minutes, which was most tiring for everybody."[21]

Before the POWs reached Ellersbeck, however, 147 officers and ratings headed towards Pinneburg and Ellersbeck to catch trains to Lübeck. The rest of the marchers, after travelling through several more farm towns, arrived at the Artillery Barracks at Bad Schwartau, on the Baltic coast near Lübeck. "On arrival at Bad Schwartau, confusion reigned," remarked Baker, "although our train party had arrived and had done their best to secure adequate accommodation. German soldiers, German women, and P/Ws were milling around, all trying to seize accommodation and anything they could lay their hands on."

Kapitän Schmidt was nowhere to be seen, and the German POW march organisation almost nonexistent: no orders were being given about anything. "By evening," Baker went on, "we had settled down in one of the blocks, and it was more than evident that if the 1,950 RAF personnel arrived, there would be worse chaos than ever. The Kommandant arrived late in the evening but was quite incapable of grappling with the situation." Shortly afterwards, the RAF advance party came in, but Baker sent them back to Wray with a message to hold his column outside until some decisions could be made.

The next day General Rossum, the German general in charge of all POWs in the Hamburg area, drove in, and Baker urged him to let the RAF remain in the countryside, as per Wray's desire. "He would not agree to this and appeared to be almost as helpless as our Kommandant." Baker had seen that the sanitary conditions were entirely inadequate in the block and feared that by crowding in more people, there would be the possibility of an epidemic outbreak. He suggested that Group Captain Wray be brought in to see the conditions before allowing his column to advance, and this was agreed to.

On 27 April Wray and a German army doctor who was also a Red Cross representative, arrived – three days after the navy had trekked into Bad Schwartau. "The latter was most helpful and insisted that the Kommandant get through to General Rossum and tell him that it was iniquitous that the RAF should be brought in, and from the medical point of view, most undesirable. This was done, and an order given by the General that the RAF should remain outside in the country."

After the new arrangement, the navy was given the whole block, except for four rooms on the ground floor, and all Marlag personnel could exist in moderate comfort. The 147 RAF people who had arrived by train occupied a floor of another block, giving them ample room.

Baker concluded his report of the massive prisoner transfer by saying that "All German officers and men viewed the order to move [from Marlag-Milag to Lübeck] with astonishment and all repeatedly said that it was a most unnecessary thing, and that none of them held with it, but having received orders from the higher authority, they had to carry it out." Baker asked General Rossum point blank why he had ordered the march

– that it had been useless and had endangered the lives of the whole column from the moment of leaving camp. "He said that he had been ordered by Berlin to issue the orders to move and had no option but to carry them out. This has been typical all along of German authority. All blame the next above."[22]

The remaining RAF contingent, after spending nights in places like pig sties, deserted factories, and barns, straggled into the Bad Schwartau Artillery Barracks and settled into a five-storey concrete building across the square from the Marlag "M" group. With thousands of prisoners of many nationalities, they made do with little heat but with sufficient food until the magic day of 2 May. "The morning brought rumours that the 11th division of Montgomery's 2nd Army was in Lübeck," recalled F/Lt. Buckham. "Artillery could be heard in the distance. The parapet overlooking the city was constantly crowded as we watched the aircraft fly over the city, to the accompaniment of the sounds of mixed gun-fire on the ground. The spasmodic firing continued all day as the city's silhouette gradually dimmed under a thickening pall of smoke."

"At 5:20 an armoured tank appeared on the road, clattering out of the smoke as it approached the camp. Others followed behind. ... The lead tank stopped opposite the camp, the turret flew open, and a khaki-clad figure popped out and waved in our direction."

Buckham's diary describes the following moments: "A roar of cheers; crudely-made flags waving; laughter and tears mingling; the guards running off, weaponless; men climbing the wire to run to the tanks; men embracing each other, shouting incoherently; men kneeling to pray; men staring vacantly, bewildered; thousands of men in a state of hysterical, blessed release. It continued for minutes."[23]

Notes

1. NA, WO 32/11110.
2. *New York Times*, 10 April 1945, 7.
3. NA, WO 208/3270.
4. Buckham, *Forced March to Freedom*, 57.
5. Ibid., 58.
6. Ibid., 59.
7. Previous sections from NA, WO 208/3270.
8. Ibid.
9. Warren and Benson, *Will Not We Fear*, 212.
10. NA, WO 208/3270.
11. Buckham, *Forced March to Freedom*, 60, 61.

12. Warren and Bensen, *Will Not We Fear*, 212.
13. NA, WO 208/3270.
14. NA, WO 208/3270; Warren and Benson, *Will Not We Fear*, 213.
15. NA, WO 208/3270.
16. Ibid.
17. Buckham, *Forced March to Freedom*, 66.
18. NA, WO 208/3270.
19. Truman interview, 24 August 2001.
20. NA, WO 208/3270.
21. Ibid.
22. Ibid.
23. Buckham, *Forced March to Freedom*, 91, 92.

CHAPTER XVI

The Third Reich Bites the Dust

During the two months that Marlag-Milag prisoners were tramping towards Lübeck, Hitler's edicts became more and more vicious. On 16 April a directive went out to the SS central office telling them that Flossenburg concentration camp had fallen into the enemy's hands and that in other places "The enemy has turned part of the prisoners (many of them armed) loose on the civilian population. Please take the necessary measures from your end and on your responsibility." Obviously, this false statement gave the SS guards an excuse to shoot internees at camps that were about to be liberated. And lastly were the words, "The Jewish prisoners must at all costs be transferred to Concentration Camp Dachau [chief extermination facility]."[1]

Three days later a message flashed from the SS main office to the Commander of Prisoners of War Wehrkreis 4 saying, "In complete forgetfulness of your duty, you have abandoned 30,000 Prisoners of War of every nationality who are in area Meissen and marching northwards. Get in touch with Red Cross immediately and ensure Prisoners of War are supplied with Red Cross parcels. Billet English and American Prisoners of War in Luckenwalde Z70, other nationalities in vicinity." As the Allies closed in, the SS apparently were trying to make a show of following war rules so as to save their hides.[2]

One can imagine the interest and worry with which the American code breakers listened to the desperate words of the Germans. General Fieldmarshal Kesselring gave the Commander in Chief Eleventh Army a shocking directive on 17 April, telling him that "In spite of the fact that there exists a strict order against transports of prisoners marching with white flags as protection against fighter bombers, to-day [sic] I again met such a transport. I affirm that the escort ... completely failed in their duty." Kesselring demanded that every Wehrkreis (work camp sector) and commander scrupulously carry out all orders and told them he was making them responsible for taking extremely severe measures against officers who were disobedient.[3]

As Kesselring issued his commands in late April, the British captured Bremen and Patton's Third Army took Regensburg, while other units of the Third Army marched into Austria. Former Vichy Prime Minister Marshal Pétain attempted to get back to France from Switzerland and was arrested for treason and collaboration; later he would be tried and condemned to death, but de Gaulle would commute his sentence to life imprisonment.

A massive Red Army advanced from the east, and on 16 April they stormed towards Berlin with two million men, six thousand tanks, fleets of aircraft, and sixteen thousand guns. Holed up in his huge bunker under the Reichschancellery garden, Hitler refused to surrender and continued to give out mad edicts, while Göbbels pleaded with the German people to keep faith that their Führer would lead them to victory.

At Halle, tenth largest German city, the Americans arrived on the scene and went into fierce combat with fanatical local defenders, whose commander had been ordered to hold the town. The citizens, aware of the total destruction of population centres throughout Germany, pleaded with German Maj. Gen. Fritz De Witt to peacefully surrender and save the still-intact city; but he flatly refused. On the morning of 15 April, after the Americans had captured 800 prisoners, they flew a couple of planes over the town and dropped 100,000 leaflets warning the people of Halle that unless they gave up, their city would be quickly demolished. A day passed, and no surrender: the fighting continued – house to house, street to street. Gestapo and SS officers followed General De Witt around with drawn pistols to be sure that he did not raise a white flag.

Al Newman, a reporter from *Newsweek,* and C. K. Hodenfield of the Army *Stars and Stripes,* who had ridden into Halle in one of the Task Force Clark tanks, suddenly had an idea. Outside town they had come upon a clay pit where twenty-one Russian prisoners were working with their local German overseer; the two stopped to talk to the German and decided that they could depend on him. Newman remembered that one of the most colourful figures of World War I lived in Halle, and he asked their friend to go and fetch Count Felix von Luckner, although he doubted that the count would actually show up for an interview.

After waiting a short while, the reporters spotted a grey vehicle with red crosses painted on the sides coming towards them; a soldier was sitting on the hood waving a white flag. The count had arrived. Von Luckner, known as the "Sea Devil" in World War I, had sunk twenty-five Allied ships; however, he took immense pride in extending to the crews and passengers the utmost hospitality. He would bring the "guests" aboard his magnificent sailing ship *Seeadler* (*Sea Eagle*) and serve them champagne and excellent food. Everyone had a grand time on the voyages, and a few hardy souls even climbed to the crow's nest to help von Luckner spot ships. When the war ended, the courtly count toured the United States as a goodwill ambassador and made a big hit everywhere. When Hitler came to power, the Nazi party jailed him for a short time because he refused to give up his honorary citizenship in the State of California. But because he was so popular with the German people, the Nazis released von Luckner, and he returned to Halle.

Newman described the encounter: "A tall, burly, somewhat stooped figure in a grey knicker suit erupted from the back seat and ran over and embraced me. 'By Joe,' he choked, 'I'm glad to see you. I haven't been so happy since I broke through the British blockade in 1916.'" Here was von Luckner, as chipper as ever. With mortar shells exploding nearby, the men hurried to get under an overpass. Once under cover, the count took from his pocket a photograph of himself and wrote: "Never say die, my dear Al Newman, the first American I have seen in my native town." Hodenfield and Newman took some fast photos, then marched to the headquarters of General Terry Allen, with von Luckner and friends bringing up the rear.

In a lengthy conference, the count pleaded for the Americans to discuss surrender plans and to set up neutral zones where citizens and prisoners could safely remain. Allen handed him a message and ultimatum for the German general to surrender unconditionally. Newman and Hodenfield then delivered von Luckner to the spot where they had met him in no-man's-land, and the count took the message to De Witt. Fearing for the safety of his family, De Witt refused to surrender, but he did agree to withdraw his men to the southern one-third of the city and to keep fighting, saving many people's lives and keeping Halle intact. However, the Americans quickly won the battle.[4]

In Berlin on 20 April, Hermann Göring, second in command to the Führer, celebrated Hitler's birthday in the Berlin bunker, then drove to his lavish home, Carinhall, west of the city. There, he loaded the best pieces of his priceless, looted art collection onto two trains for Berchtesgaden and then blew up the house. After the demolition, he scurried southward and settled into a second, more modest dwelling on Obersalzburg near the Eagle's Nest, within the so-called redoubt.[5]

One of the first things he did there was to send a message to his boss:

> To the Führer:
> My Führer. I beg you most fervently in the interest of the Reich and the nation to come here into the South German area. I have been able to assure myself sufficiently on my journey that, by making the fullest use of every possibility, much can still be achieved for the struggle, and that, with the old energy [word or two illegible], resistance can still be offered here successfully.My distress at knowing that you are at this hour in Berlin has no limits.
> Hail my Führer!
> Your faithful
> Hermann Göring[6]

A couple of days after Göring's unheeded plea, Allied planes began dropping leaflets over German-held areas of the country, warning all Kommandants, guards and other prison camp officials that any individual who mistreated an Allied prisoner, internee, or deported citizen would be "ruthlessly pursued and brought to punishment." This included the German High Command, as well. Prime Minister Churchill, President Truman, and Premier Stalin all signed the message.

Eight days passed; then on 30 April Adolf Hitler committed suicide. Papers around the world heralded the news on 1 May, and U.S. Army decoders picked up a message from Admiral Karl Dönitz to C in C Naval Command West: "I have received following order: in place of the former Reichsmarschal Göring, the Führer appoints you, Herr Grossadmiral, as his successor. Written authority follows. With immediate effect, all measures are to be decreed by you."[7]

That same day, 1 May, SS General Berger sent a message to all commands that "Most signs of disintegration can now only be held in check by issuing ... clear political instructions for the final struggle. Among many other signs, reminiscent of 1918, is the fact that SS officers, still severely wounded, are being turned out of Armed Forces' hospitals because they are an encumbrance." The next paragraph stated that it was "urgently necessary" that all forces be concentrated in the South under one supreme command. Finally, he said that "The measures at Dachau which ran counter to the Reichsführer's order [probably to demolish it] have had disastrous consequences. An SS Officer from Dachau and an Officer of the security service whose names, unfortunately, are not known, reported to the International Red Cross and the Swiss Legation and unsolicited, made the most monstrous statements."[8]

Patton's Third Army had liberated Dachau two days earlier, and two of the German officers there apparently informed the Americans about the gruesome activities at the death camp: the gassing and cremation of many thousands of Jewish people; but the American soldiers could see the evidence for themselves.

After Berger's command to ensure that no American or British officers fall into Allied hands, a directive went out to transfer the "Prominente," or socially prominent POWs at Colditz castle. This was the beginning of an almost comic opera manoeuvre by the top Nazis to keep their hostages under control.

The British high-ranking prisoners incarcerated at Colditz were Lt. Viscount George Lascelles, the King's nephew; Capt. Lord John Elphinstone (nephew of Queen Elizabeth); Capt. Charles William (Earl of Hopetoun); Lt. Michael Alexander; Giles Romilly (news reporter and Clementine Churchill's nephew); Lt. Max de Hamel; Capt. Dawyck Haig; and Lt. John Winant, son of the American ambassador to Britain. On 12 April, as the Americans approached, Heinrich Himmler ordered the Prominents, plus about twelve Polish officers (including Lieutenant General Tadeusz Komorowsky, who had led the Warsaw Uprising), to be transferred without delay. Late that night the group were ordered to climb into two buses and were driven under heavy guard to Königstein Castle. When they arrived, senior British officer John Elphinstone made arrangements with the Kommandant for Lord Hopetoun and Lord Haig, who were ill, to stay at the castle; but the rest of the party had to move by truck to Oflag VII C (Laufen fortress), now a civilian internment camp. Elphinstone, realising the danger of being out of Wermacht protection, strongly protested the placement of high-ranking officers in a civilian camp, and as a result, the Germans moved the Prominents that same day to a medieval castle prison for Dutch officers at Tittmonig, east of Munich on the Austrian border.

After three days at Tittmonig one of the Dutch officers heard from the guards that Göbbels and Himmler had been seen in a vehicle speeding through the town towards Berchtesgaden; later that day Lascelles and friends were told that they would be moved back to the civilian camp. They discussed their fears with Elphinstone, asking him to approach Dutch officer Capt. Machiel van den Heuvel, an escape genius, about finding them a hiding place. The captain and his friends had already dug out a space inside one of the castle walls, and it was in this tiny room that the five British prisoners hid. Two other Dutch officers and Giles Romilly carried out a diversionary escape over the castle parapet using a rope, but once the SS guards discovered that they had fled, they searched the castle twice, and after two-and-a-half days discovered the Brits in their cubbyhole. When Hitler heard about the three men who had escaped, he sentenced to death the camp Kommandant and Security Officer.

The same day that the SS found Lascelles and friends, they transferred them by truck with several armed escorts back to Oflag VII C, the civilian prison at Laufen. For one week they stayed at VII C, where they were kept within barbed-wire barricades inside the barracks and guarded around the clock. Seeing no way for the Allies to rescue them, Winston Churchill contacted the Swiss and the International Red Cross to get their help in locating the missing prisoners. The Swiss representative, Dr Feldscher, ascertained their whereabouts, drove to the internment camp, and warned General Gusselmann to protect the Prominents. In spite of Feldscher's efforts to keep the prisoners there, Gusselmann had the frightened group loaded into trucks and driven under SS guard to Markt Pongau, a large international camp for non-officers. Here the inmates were housed in a separate barracks, away from all other prisoners. After about five days at Markt Pongau, one of Feldscher's aides, who had followed the Prominents' convoy, prevailed upon General Berger to hand the party over to the Swiss and to grant them safe conduct through the German lines. The war was essentially over, and Berger's agreement came just in time: Hitler had ordered the execution of the Prominents. On 5 May the beleaguered prisoners rode into an American command post at Innsbruck and there celebrated their liberation.[9]

At headquarters the newly-freed British and Polish prisoners encountered a group of jubilant, high-ranking French prisoners, who had just been rescued from Itter Castle at Wörgel, thirty-five miles north of Innsbruck.

On the day after the rescue at Itter Castle, Wilhelm Keitel, Chief of OKW (High Command of German Armed Forces) sent out a short message to all services that in agreement with the Reichsführer SS, all prisoners of war, foreign workers and people in concentration camps were to be handed over to the enemy under a small guard when areas were evacuated. "They may no longer be brought back nor may camps be moved." It seemed that finally, the terrible marches had ended, but only at the moment of German surrender.[10]

On Obersalzburg Mountain in southern Germany, site of Hitler's second command post, nine anti-aircraft guns had been stationed on high peaks in surrounding mountains early in 1944. The Führer had bought a house on the mountain in 1933, which became known as the Berghof; and Hermann Göring and Martin Bormann, Hitler's deputy chief of staff, also purchased residences. Bormann bought out all fifty local house owners, demolished the dwellings, and supervised a massive construction project on the mountain to fortify Hitler's retreat. He built permanent SS barracks buildings; a steep, winding road with tunnels; the "Tea House" (a meeting place atop the Kehlstein with direct phone line to Berlin); a subterranean elevator; a hospital; work camps; an electrical power plant; telephone cables; air raid bunkers, and an underground control centre. Deep inside the mountain of Göringhügel, members of the Obersalzburg SS staffed the centre, and there they recorded the enemy's movements on enormous glass walls. They sent air raid warnings, all-clear signals, and weather reports to the Luftwaffe.[11]

For some time, the Americans had known that Hitler's base at Obersalzburg would be of great importance to Germany and that its destruction would accelerate the war's end. To get detailed information about the place, they contacted the British Secret Service, but the Brits could not get a spy in to check the layout because of strong fencing and guards; Service agents could supply only coordinates, old photos, and general descriptions of the terrain. However, the Allies were not deterred: on the morning of Wednesday, 25 April 1945, they sent 318 Lancaster bombers to destroy the Alpine fortress. As six-ton earthquake bombs exploded, the defenders rushed into air raid shelters, and the anti-aircraft guns fired a few useless rounds, hitting nothing. The skilled gunners had already been sent to the front lines, leaving novices behind.[12]

British bombs severely damaged Hitler's chalet (the Berghof), as well as the SS barracks, Göring's house, and Bormann's house. The Tea House remained untouched. The next day, as clouds of smoke rose into the mountain air, hundreds of American Ninth Air Force fighter-bombers roared into the Bavarian redoubt, blasting railway lines and roads to pave the way for Patton's Third Army. RAF heavy bombers cut loose on rail yards near Salzburg, thinking it was the seat of the German Government. A nonstop blitz from the west and south continued as George Patton's columns advanced. Mustangs at the south-eastern tip of Germany shot up a thirty-truck convoy carrying ammunition and fuel for Obersalzburg. All over Germany, RAF Typhoons, Tempests, and Spitfires wreaked vengeance on the Germans.[13]

After the Americans and French occupied the town of Berchtesgaden at the base of Obersalzburg, General John O'Daniel blocked the French troops under General Jacques LeClerc, and entered Obersalzburg, where he lowered the large swastika flag from the Berghof flagpole. The next morning, when the victory ceremonies were about to begin, LeClerc then blocked the remainder of American troops from the Kehlstein Road, telling them that the area around Obersalzburg had been declared a French occupied territory. He wanted the French to claim victory first and to fly their own flag over Hitler's house; however, a discussion ensued with the Americans, ending in a decision to fly both the Stars and Stripes and the French Tricolor; but the French banner was so large and heavy that it kept sliding down the pole. Actually, there was no French Tricolor around, so the French soldiers used a Dutch flag displayed sideways, which gave the right effect. After his flag fell down, LeClerc changed his mind, allowed Old Glory to wave, and draped his immense "French" banner across the ruins of the Berghof balcony.[14]

The Allies had been liberating prisoner of war camps for a month before the war's end, but unfortunately for Taff Harper, the Germans shipped him and the rest of the POWs out of the paper factory before he could be rescued. After a difficult journey in railway freight cars, they arrived at Stalag VII A at Moosburg just as Patton's Third Army was advancing. In early April Hitler was evacuating camps throughout Germany to the vicinity of Stalag VII A, thirty-five kilometres north-east of Munich. "This influx," said a U.S. Military Intelligence Service report, "brought about a state of unbelievable overcrowding and confusion. Large tents were erected in whatever space was available; straw was provided as bedding. It was not uncommon to see men sleeping on blankets in foxholes." The population of Moosburg camp had swollen from 3,000 to about 30,000, and the Allies feared that the Germans could still move all the POWs to Hitler's redoubt and hold them as hostages. Fortunately, that never happened.

Some of the prisoners at Moosburg had heard on their hidden radios that Patton's Third Army was north-west of Munich; and when they ran to look at their secret maps, they found that Moosburg was not too far from Patton's position. Excitement prevailed as everyone prayed for deliverance.

Two Swiss representatives arrived at Stalag VII A on 27 April to arrange for the transfer of prisoners to American authority. The next day the emissaries tried to get General Berger to agree that no fighting would take place in the camp vicinity, but Berger had not received permission from German military authorities, so a 2½-hour battle ensued on Sunday, 29 April. In the camp, the guards ordered everyone to take shelter inside the barracks or some of the trenches. One shell crashed into a barracks, wounding twelve guards and killing one. Lt. Harold Gunn, crouched next to a brick wall in the kitchen building, described the scene: "Bullets are flying; the chatter of machine-gun fire and spasmodic rifle reports, punctuated by the heavy explosions of large guns makes a fitting background for our long anticipated liberation." Aside from that one incident and a few other injuries, the camp remained undamaged.

Curiosity finally overcame the prisoners, who slowly made their way to the parade grounds. One of the first sounds that greeted their ears was the purr of a Piper Cub observation plane as it flew overhead. An exuberant roar of voices greeted the little craft as it wiggled its wings at them; and the shouts grew even louder when two P 51s thundered by, performing victory rolls over the barracks and tents. When the men heard the growl of approaching tanks, they went wild with joy, and thousands of happy shouts drowned out the sound of the tanks. Then several jeeps and tanks of the Fourteenth Armored Division rumbled into the camp, and POWs swarmed over and around them, greeting their heroes.

One of the prisoners, Martin Allain, had a brilliant idea. He had formerly been incarcerated in Stalag Luft III, where he managed to smuggle into camp a large American flag, to be used for identification in case Allied planes appeared. Allain had hidden the banner by sewing it between two German blankets and later carried it with him on a forced march in January to Moosburg. When the American liberators showed up to free Stalag VII A, Martin quickly grabbed his precious flag and ran to the main gate. A fellow prisoner, Robert Hartman, described what happened next: "Allain began shinnying up the German flagpole. Everyone knew immediately what he was going to do, and there was no doubt in our minds he would make it, despite his malnourished appearance. ... The recollection of this grimy, skinny but smiling GI tearing down the ugly swastika and replacing it with the beautiful Stars and Stripes has never wavered or grown dim." Most of the prisoners cried unashamedly when they saw their country's symbol fluttering in the air, and Martin Allain carried home with him the Nazi banner, leaving Old Glory to continue waving.[15]

"When we were freed," recalled Taff Harper, "The Scots lads walked over to a pig farm about a mile away. They could hear them squealing and fighting." McGinness had already told his pals some time before that if they ever got evacuated, they would "go and strangle one of those things."

So one morning nine of the lads decided the time had come. "Great," said McGinness, "We'll away to the pig farm." When they got there, the nine ravenous men went after a very large sow they had spied in the fifty-pig herd. Taff, who later heard the story, said, "They was stabbing it all over the place; it was screaming; they were running around the pen with two men hanging on, and there was blood everywhere. And when they killed it and cut it open, it had five little piglets."

Carrying the great sow, the Scotsmen arrived back at camp, where they managed to partially roast it in a cookhouse manned by British POWs. "It was beautiful," said Taff, "and half-cooked, but OOOH, I ate it all right, by gosh, yes. We lived on pork for about a month after that. We never tried to escape – we were too busy waiting for our meals." They were free to go anywhere, but they hung around the cookhouse all day, savouring the aromas. "That's how bad it was. You were really waiting for food." After nearly starving for years, Taff's sumptuous meals caused him a touch of internal trouble. "I had it bad for about four days: I got constipated."

With nothing much to do in the camp, a crowd of ex-POWs drove into the village of Moosburg one day to see what they could find in the way of food or other prizes. "We seen this bank open and went in and found all this money scattered around and started picking up twenty-thousand, fifty-thousand mark, half a million marks and notes. I was going very carefully, looking for the big denominations to pick up so that I could carry more money: I thought I was going to be a millionaire. Of course when I got back to the camp, there was an interpreter that I knew, and he said, 'What the hell have you got there, Taff?'" Taff, in his excitement, told him he would take him to the bank where all the money was, but the friend responded, "Let's have a look at it. That money's no good – it's only Hitler money." Shocked, Taff asked him what he meant, and the friend explained that Hitler just printed currency whenever he wanted, to be used only in Germany. "I was very disappointed, because, I thought, 'Well, at least I'm going to be paid for the five years I was a prisoner of war,' but it didn't work out that way." Shortly afterwards, having endured five years of gruelling labour, loneliness, and near-starvation, Taff and friends would be going home, but that would not be the end of their problems.[16]

Notes

1. NA, HW 5/706.
2. Ibid.
3. Ibid.

4. *New York Times,* 20 April 1945, 5; "Saale River Offensive: The Seizure of Halle," available on *http://www.104infdiv.org/saale.htm* on INTERNET; "The Sea Devil," *Newsweek,* 25 April 1966, 42, 43.

5. Nicholas, *The Rape of Europa,* 319.

6. NA, HW 5/706.

7. Ibid.

8. Ibid.

9. NA, FO 954/28A; *New York Times,* 7 May 1945, 6; Chancellor, *Colditz,* 352–66.

10. NA, HW 5/706.

11. Beierl, *History of the Eagle's Nest,* 13, 135.

12. Ibid., 135.

13. Ibid., 139.

14. Ibid., 141; "Berchtesgaden," available at *http://www.warfoto.com/berchesg. htm* on INTERNET.

15. Previous sections from *http://www.moosburg.org/info/stalag/allaeng.html* on INTERNET.

16. Harper interview, 3 February 2002 and 17 December 2000.

CHAPTER XVII

Home Again and Haw-Haw

"When we got repatriated," explained Taff, "we were living at Newcastle, and my parents were living down in South Wales. We went to see my mother, and she had a little corgi dog. I don't remember this, but my wife told me about it." Shortly after they entered the house, Harper noticed that the pet pooch had left a bone under the dining table, so the ravenous sailor grabbed it and started chewing on it. "I was so hungry for meat: I'd eat anything – anything. Joan said she was really disgusted with me." When Taff arrived back in England he weighed only eighty-four pounds: he had lost seventy pounds in prison camp.

Shortly after that visit, the Admiralty sent Taff and his wife Joan to a special recuperation facility called Stanhope. "It was in a little country market town, and I was there for two months on this special diet, but I couldn't have beer at all. In the hotel there was a public bar and special food, but I was not supposed to drink." The doughty Welshman soon discovered another pub in the village, and "Joan and I used to sneak down there in the evenings for a couple of pints. I put on about a stone-and-a-half (twenty pounds) in two months, and I built up from there on."[1]

Taff's submarine comrade, Mickey Reynolds, began his homeward journey to Ireland on 1 March, when he and other prisoners were flown to Reims, France, "and we had a bird's eye view of where some of the fierce battles had been fought. On arrival, we were bathed, deloused, and fitted out in American army uniforms and treated like lords, with the Germans acting as our batmen." Two days later the prisoners boarded another plane and flew to an airfield just outside London, where Red Cross representatives met them, gave them cigarettes, and "fussed over" them. The former POWs travelled into London and boarded a train to Chatham; upon arrival at the Portsmouth Royal Navy base, they piled into some barracks, ate proper nourishing food, and had medical tests. Next morning, 4 March, the navy gave them toiletry kits and let them go on leave: Mickey caught a train to Ballymena, Northern Ireland, arriving on 5 March – five years to the day since he had departed.

"I don't remember much about it, but I think it was on a Sunday, and that afternoon my old Boy Scout Troop was having a service [meeting]. I was invited to join the parade." To celebrate VE Day on 8 May, Ballymena held a grand parade and invited everyone to join the organisations that were already included, like the British Red Cross, St. John Ambulance Brigade, Girls' and Boys' Brigades, Scouts, and Pipe and Drum bands. [2]

That night local movie fans flocked into two theatres to enjoy the latest American films. "No one who was at either cinema that night could ever forget it," recalled Bertie Templeton. "For the first time since the war had started, all the neon lights were on, and both the State ... and the Towers ... were a blaze of colour, and both were decorated with Union Jacks." During the war years, a special screen had been built around the front of the State Theatre to prevent even a small crack of light from showing when the doors opened to admit people. "The glass doors themselves were covered with a coat of black paint," said Templeton.

From 1939 to 1945 the two theatres provided the townspeople with their main entertainment. "The State seated one thousand people, and the Towers 1,200, and they were packed to capacity every night, with people also standing two deep down the two side aisles. Of course we had international audiences, with the locals being joined by the American and Belgian soldiers, and the Gibraltarians from the local camps," explained Bertie.

Tom O'Neil, a local man, walked around town advertising the films on sandwich boards hung over his shoulders. "Tom was one of the town characters," Bertie went on, "and he was a tremendous whistler. He could be heard from streets away as he paraded along with his sandwich boards featuring that night's movie." Often Tom would dress according to the film that was showing: for instance, one day he appeared as Robin Hood; another time he came out as an American Indian.

On the big VE night, movie fans crowded into the State to see Ronald Reagan and Margaret Lockwood, while others enjoyed a western featuring singing cowboy Gene Autry at the Towers. It was the perfect ending to a perfect day.[3]

In July 1945 the King and Queen with one of their daughters, Princess Elizabeth, went on a grand royal tour of Northern Ireland to celebrate Victory in Europe. Several notables, including Northern Ireland Prime Minister Sir Basil Brooke, accompanied the King, whose parties flew in two aircraft to Eglinton airfield outside Londonderry. From there they drove to Lisahally, a dock area, and boarded a patrol yacht, *Hiniesta*, which motored them over to the Royal Yacht; there they were piped aboard, and the Royal Standard was raised.

Parked a few yards away from the monarch's dock, fifty-five German U-boats awaited ultimate disposal. The King explained to his wife and daughter that the submarines had been surrendered at the end of the war, were maintained by small German crews and guarded by American sailors. Farther down the Foyle river, the Royals came upon some anchored

British warships, including a submarine, whose crews loudly cheered as the yacht passed by.

At the landing in Londonderry, Mayor Sir Basil McFarland and his wife walked onto the yacht, greeted Their Majesties, and invited them to come ashore. After the group disembarked, a series of presentations followed, introducing various personages. Then the City Marshal and Sword Bearer, the Mace Bearer, and Sergeant-at-Mace, dressed in picturesque old-world costumes, led the Royal Party from the landing stage to Guildhall Square. Lavishly decorated with Allied flags and red, white, and blue bunting, the square had been set as a great stage for the ceremonies: Royal Welsh Fusiliers; United States Navy and Marine Corps; the Ulster Special Constabulary; Fife and Drum Band; and the Colour Party all saluted the King. Then everyone sang the British national anthem.

Next, the King inspected the Guard of Honour; then, with the Queen and Princess Elizabeth, he mounted a dais to view the parade. Every imaginable group marched: Fusiliers, Home Guard, Sea Cadets, Army Cadets, various training corps, National Fire Service, and many others. Following the grand parade, the Queen presented a bouquet to Lucy Neely, employee of a shirt and collar factory who had spent the war years making shirts for His Majesty's forces. Then His Majesty walked over to congratulate a group of wounded servicemen who were seated in the square. A photo appeared in the *Ballymena Guardian* showing the King and Queen bent forward to speak to Mickey Reynolds, who was recovering from hernia surgery. Protocol required people to stand when greeting royalty, but in this remarkable instance the King stood – a supreme honour for the wounded sailors. More festivities followed at St. Columb's Cathedral, and the royal trio flew back to England.[4]

As for the remainder of *Seal*'s crew, those from Marlag-Milag, after marching to Lübeck, flew home from Lüneburg in the first few days of May, as did Happy Eckersall. By a miracle, every man from the submarine's crew had lived through the prison camp years and had come home except two – Able Seaman Smith, who had disappeared when the Germans attacked the *Seal* and Maurice Barnes, an unsuccessful escaper from POW camp.

One particular "British" citizen had not been accounted for since the latter days of April: Lord Haw-Haw. During the entire war British Intelligence had monitored and recorded his derogatory broadcasts, and they listened to the last one on 30 April, the day Adolf Hitler took cyanide and ended his life. "An interesting thing to note is that … he is far from sober and rather despondent." Another description in the *New York Times* said that "his voice broke in a choking, stuttering admission that Germany might be beaten."[5]

Things had not been going well for the loud-mouthed traitor: in September 1944, three months after the Normandy Invasion, Haw-Haw's

"Views on the News" was broadcast on the Cologne wave length by an associate named Edward Dietze; and Haw-Haw's favourite stations – Calais, Hilversum, Friesland and Luxembourg – had gone silent. British Military Intelligence believed that Dietze had been previously employed by the BBC and educated at Eton and Oxford. "He is assisted by William Joyce," read a report sent by a Stockholm agent, "who is now almost permanently in a state of intoxication and who has adopted the system of writing out his scripts wherever possible two days in advance, so that they should be available for reading should he himself be incapable of coherent thought at the time of the broadcast. … Dietze is completely powerless, as Joyce is a personal friend of Göbbels, whom he sees about three times a week."[6]

"His disintegration seems to have kept pace with that of the Wehrmacht," reported the London *Daily Express*. As probably the world's most listened-to commentator, Lord Haw-Haw seemed to be nearing his end: at first he made four daily broadcasts, then three, then two, and after D-Day, only one. At that point he used pure propaganda – no news – such as claiming that the Allies had taken horrific blood baths at Normandy; and he used mockery and threats: "You will be thrown back into the sea to drown like other rats." Gradually he became more vague, without a story line, and when the Germans started firing rockets at England, he chortled and bragged spitefully.[7]

After the 30 April broadcast, William Joyce and wife disappeared. On 5 May a British broadcaster employed by the Allied Military Government announced that Haw-Haw was mute and that the British were using his microphone. "After the capitulation news just published, I wonder what Haw-Haw's views on the news are now," he commented. "Hamburg, the city Haw-Haw made notorious, is this evening under the control of British forces. … He left rather hurriedly for a vacation – an extremely short vacation, if the British Second Army has anything to do with it." Further, the announcer told his fascinated audience that he had rummaged through Lord Haw-Haw's desk and found a "revealing" timetable that Joyce had drawn up for 10 April, 1945. On the page for that date was found a "glorious" item: "14.50 to 15.00 hours – a pause to collect my wits."

The reporter mirthfully continued, saying that the people of Hamburg now had plenty of time to collect their wits. He finished by declaring that a radio station employee had testified that the former British propagandist had left for Denmark by automobile one night after his last broadcast.[8]

The search for Haw-Haw became intense: Allied Supreme Headquarters assigned Guy Della-Cioppa and Francis McLean, chief engineer for the Prisoner of War Department, to the 21st Army Group "T" Force that was moving into surrendered German territory. The two arrived at "T" Force headquarters near Emden on Sunday afternoon, 6 May 1945, where they learned that they could not progress northward until a Canadian Division arrived. As they waited, a Polish Liaison officer handed them a note saying that his division had occupied a small town called Apen, and that in the town there was "an exciting broadcasting installation with transmitter and studios. We immediately jumped in our jeep and reached Apen at 5 p.m."

In the centre of town, inside a small inn next door to the post office, the two operatives, accompanied by the Polish officer, entered a "mock-up studio arrangement, which was entirely of an emergency nature. There was no transmitter in the town, nor was the site intended to be a permanent broadcast installation." Immediately, Della-Cioppa and McLean went to get the Bürgermeister (mayor) and brought him back to take an extensive survey of all the rooms in the inn. "He knew very little," noted Della-Cioppa, "but explained that there had been a number of editorial and announcing personnel stationed in his town, as well as the necessary technical staff." Unfortunately, Polish troops had smashed everything to bits and had thrown all documents, scripts, and files into a huge pile in one of the rooms.

"We noticed that certain key equipment was missing, notably the valuable magnetaphone recorders, and we suspected that the Polish soldiers were not clever enough to realise the value of this equipment, and in all probability had not removed it themselves. We determined to investigate this point further." The two men then went through the papers, hoping to find payment records for employees, but the files had disappeared.

With the mayor, the investigators walked to a house where some of the broadcasting employees were still living; there they met a Doctor Hartmann, who said that he had been a professor of German in England before the war, and a second man who had also been a professor. From the Germans, they learned that Lord Haw-Haw and his wife had been stationed in Apen from November 1944 to the middle of April 1945, and that Apen had been chosen as a station because from there they could reach by landline the transmitters at Norden, Hamburg, and Wilhelmshaven. If any of these transmitters were destroyed, they could continue to programme on the others without interruption. Hartmann told Della-Cioppa that Haw-Haw was very sincere in his beliefs but "was extremely nervous towards the end. Both of these men were anxious to go to work for us."

"We also talked to a man named Günther, who had been the engineer-in-charge." The Polish officer, in an attempt to get the whole story, threatened to hang him if he did not reveal the whereabouts of the valuable equipment; and with that, the engineer told them that he had hidden it in barn lofts around the countryside. Later, the men collected all the equipment and locked it up in the post office.

The ever-obliging Bürgermeister took Della-Cioppa and McLean to the small house near the studio where Haw-Haw and his wife had been living. "We went to the house, examined the room ... but found it completely bare. A small boy indicated that there were some pieces of baggage which had been left in the attic, and there we found two suitcases and an old battered trunk." In the trunk they found a pile of books and among them some diaries, which Della-Cioppa immediately confiscated. They also found some photographs and papers about Haw-Haw's days in England, particularly about his time in the National Socialist League. "I particularly looked among the papers in his trunk for any records of payments or moneys received from the German Government for his services. We found none. In the suitcases were a number of personal effects of Mrs. Joyce with a few old boots and clothing of Mr. Joyce."

Della-Cioppa's report ended by saying that the Germans told them that Joyce and wife had departed for Wilhelmshaven at the end of April 1945 to use the transmitter there. It seemed that the trail had ended.[9]

On 30 May London newspapers proclaimed the thrilling news: "Haw-Haw Captured, Seriously Wounded" – a particularly gratifying victory for the British Empire. New York and London papers (among others) gave a brief summary of the capture – all that reporters had been able to ascertain – and the fact that Joyce had been shot. Without the juicy details, British and American readers' frustrations grew intense. In Germany, word of the big capture had flashed across the country while Haw-Haw was being driven by ambulance to the military hospital at Lüneburg, 180 miles away. When they saw the medical vehicle drive up, British soldiers crowded around shouting, "Traitor! Make him walk!" They crowded around the vehicle, and one tried to take a quick picture of Joyce, but an officer grabbed his camera and handed it to the military police. At that point, the officer ordered the soldiers to leave, and meanwhile, Joyce, who lay inside wearing pyjamas, complained, "In civilised countries, wounded men are not peep shows." Photographers did manage to get some shots of the patient, with shaved head, being carried on a stretcher into the hospital.[10]

An hour earlier, the British military had brought by separate vehicle a woman who claimed to be William Joyce's wife Margaret. When photographers began to take shots of her, she put her hand on her coiffure and explained, "They didn't give me a chance to arrange my hair."[11]

At 10:45 on the morning of 31 May, Captain W. J. Skardon of the Intelligence Corps paid a visit to Haw-Haw, who was recovering nicely from the bullet removal. During the day, Skardon interviewed Joyce three times, informing him of his rights, asking questions, and getting ample opportunity to listen to him talk. "I identified his voice as the one recorded on discs taken from Radio Luxembourg … which also indicates the date upon which I found them in the material left behind by the Deutsche Europasender Service."[12]

While Haw-Haw rested, hundreds of British soldiers stood around the hospital building, hoping that they could have a chance to see him and "tell him what we think of him." London newspapers had a field day with articles like "Doctors and Nurses Disgusted," " Haw-Haw Hush Hush," and " Haw-Haw Ha Ha."

Military authorities told the press that Joyce and his wife would be held in Lüneburg under close guard until further notice, as Home Office and Scotland Yard officials would be making official interrogations. After that, the two would be secretly flown to England, and the press would be given the date. Meanwhile, when Joyce's wife went to see her husband for a few minutes, he told her he was doing fine.

A senior intelligence officer had questioned Joyce's wife, who was about 30 years old; she had been living under the name Margaret Hansen. When reporters questioned the officer, he informed them that they had found a great many incriminating documents in her house, packed in three suitcases. Along with the papers they found 150 photographs – some of German soldiers, others of casual groups on German beaches. Her diary gave further details of her association and activities with Joyce.

Before questioning Joyce's wife, the intelligence officer removed a large ring from her hand that "possibly could have contained poison," and a silver bangle bracelet "that might come in handy for a suicide attempt." The questioning took place at the British Second Army Headquarters detention house on Ulznerstrasse, an ivy-covered villa where one week earlier infamous war criminal Heinrich Himmler had died by swallowing poison. A female guard and two nurses thoroughly searched Margaret Joyce's clothing for any toxic substance but found none.[13]

A great deal of official secrecy closed in, causing reporters to write comments like, "Lord Hush Hush: Why?" Writer Selkirk Panton commented that sentries at the Lüneburg hospital had been warned not to let war correspondents or anyone else near Joyce, and to shoot if necessary. He further testified that official secrecy surrounded Joyce's supposed wife, as well, and that when he watched the detention villa, he noticed that most of the windows were open, but that the wife was probably in a corner room where the windows had been blacked out. "On the second floor, a shaving British officer stuck his lathered face out of the window when I passed." He also saw other security guards playing a game "in the red-plush front-room parlour where Himmler took poison."[14]

A new and longer version of Lord Haw-Haw's capture, as told by British Second Army war correspondents, brought fresh excitement to Londoners. In the *Yorkshire Post* the story appeared, saying that the whole adventure had begun in Flensburg, Germany, at a small house used as an officers' mess for personnel of the Number 4 Information Control Unit of Publicity and Psychological Warfare. One evening the men were discussing the disappearance of William Joyce, and one of them remarked that he had attended the same university as Joyce, and that Joyce was well educated and had a sharp mind.

The next day, Monday, 28 May, three of the Control Unit members set out to gather wood for the kitchen stove. Near the border with Denmark they came upon a large, heavy log and were struggling to drag it back when a slightly-built stranger in a well-cut tweed suit walked up and told them in French that he knew where there was some better wood. As the new arrival started to wander away, he pointed with his walking stick to an area nearby and said in English, "I, too, have to gather wood for the fire." When Captain Lickorish heard the nasal twang of the stranger's pronunciation of "gather," he thought that it sounded extremely familiar. Then Lieutenant Perry asked the man what kind of trees he was referring to and whether they were similar to those in England. To answer the questions, the stranger talked and talked for about twenty minutes, describing the deciduous and coniferous varieties and comparing the forests in Germany to those in England. As he rattled on in perfect English without a trace of a German accent, the resemblance of his voice to the broadcaster of "This is Germany Calling" became more and more obvious.

By the end of the stranger's narration, he had strolled off, keeping his right hand in his pocket. Before he got very far, Lieutenant Perry whipped out his revolver and yelled, "You don't happen to be William Joyce, do you?" Continuing his walk, the nasal-voiced man casually replied, "No, I am Fritz Hansen" and drew his hand from his pocket. At that point Perry shot him in the buttocks, and Joyce collapsed. The two men rushed over, examined him, and found that he was not seriously wounded. As they stood over the broadcaster, Joyce remarked, "I was a fool to have done it," apparently meaning that his gun-grabbing ruse had been stupid.

When the officers searched Joyce's clothing, they found a German passport in the name of "Fritz Hansen" and a Wehrpass, or identity card, made out to William Joyce.[15]

After Haw-Haw had sufficiently recovered in the Lüneburg hospital, he was driven in a jeep through Lüneburg to the airport and from there flown to Brussels. A reporter said that Joyce was limping slightly and looked very weak; his appearance had changed enough that local British soldiers did not recognise him at the airport. In Brussels, Joyce and his wife were both put into prison.[16]

After about five days, British authorities secretly transported Haw-Haw by plane to London and took him to Bow Street Police Station in a closed black police van, with one police car leading and two closely following. Once inside the station yard, Joyce emerged from the van wearing a rumpled blue suit and a handkerchief draped over his head to hide his lack of hair; he stood waiting as police officers unloaded suitcases from the second car. One woman, observing the scene from a nearby balcony, said, "He was looking pale. He stood for one moment and then followed one of the police officers into the back door of the building, while the two others followed behind. He was not handcuffed."[17]

Once inside, Joyce appeared before a magistrate, who read the charges against him: "For that he committed High Treason in that he, between September 2, 1939, and April 29, 1945, being a person owing allegiance to His Majesty the King, adhered to the King's enemies elsewhere than in the King's Realm, to wit, in the German Realm, contrary to the Treason Act of 1351." Joyce, wearing a dirty blue collarless jail suit, was assigned Cell Number 6, where the murderer Crippen had resided in 1910. Police listed his age as 39, with no occupation.

"The police are taking no chances with William ('Gairmany Calling') Joyce" said the *Daily Mirror*. "The Bow Street police station yard and cells were floodlit last night. A double guard was put on the locked doors at the station." Threats had been made on the broadcaster's life.

Crowds of curious citizens were eating their meals on the balconies of surrounding apartments, where they could keep a constant eye on the police station and possibly catch a glimpse of the renowned prisoner. Only one elderly lady had had the luck to spy the pale, hobbled man limping into the courtyard for exercise, and she told reporters that she "knew him at once." In his five by eight-foot cell, Joyce now possessed only a book of poetry by Horace. As ever talkative, he jabbered to everyone within earshot: "Will the reporters come to see me? Will I have many photographs taken?"

A search of Joyce's pockets at the jail had turned up two packages of razor blades and a copy of Vacher's Parliamentary Companion (probably for finding a friendly MP). In his two suitcases police found a jumble of clothing, personal articles, and a Smith and Wesson revolver with five rounds of ammunition – all of which they handed over to Scotland Yard.[18]

At 6:30 on the morning of 18 June, a throng of people gathered around the Bow Street Police Court and formed a long line. Forty-two extra police officers kept them under control, and a group of mounted police waited in the courtyard in case of demonstrations. The crowd wanted to have the privilege of watching the magistrate read the charges against William Joyce, but only a few made it inside, as the courtroom was packed with detectives; military officers; representatives of the Russian, French, American, and Brazilian governments; and local citizens. Joyce, dressed in wide, floppy trousers, black jacket, split brown shoes, and a pyjama-collared grey shirt, stood before the dock, keeping his hands clasped behind him and twitching his thumbs. The magistrate, Sir Bertram Watson, read the charges of high treason against the King and his Realm, and afterwards asked Joyce, "Are you legally represented?" Joyce answered, "No, sir." He told the Court that he had been informed of the proceedings and charges and that at this time he needed legal assistance. Then the magistrate announced that there would be a remand of one week for Joyce to prepare his case and for foreign witnesses to come to England. The whole procedure had taken just ten minutes.[19]

For the one-week remand period, Joyce resided in Brixton Jail. There, the prison doctor examined him, found that he had dermatitis and ordered a medicinal bath. Joyce's cell, with its steel-grilled door, allowed observers to watch him around the clock to prevent suicide attempts. Major Benke, head of the jail, told reporters that Joyce's day would begin at 7:00 (unlocking time) and that if the prisoner wished, he could work by sewing mail bags, and it would pay him about 6 pennies a day. Lunch would probably be what Brixton inmates called "C pie," or cottage pie.[20]

Without funds to hire his own legal representative, Lord Haw-Haw was assigned an imminent solicitor, Charles Head, who would help Joyce try to defend himself.[21]

On 17 September the Crown treason case against Haw-Haw opened at the Old Bailey, with L. A. Byrne as Crown prosecutor. (Byrne had gained recent fame for his success in the "Cleft Chin" murder trial; and here again he was facing a cleft-chinned evil-doer – William Joyce.) Byrne read the statement that Joyce had written just after his capture in Germany. In it Joyce claimed that he had adopted German nationality in 1940, but the Crown maintained that "a British subject could not acquire a foreign nationality during a war, and that an act of naturalisation at such a time was in itself an act of treason." For the two-day length of the trial, great crowds of people, including a group of fourteen men wearing black bow ties (probably sympathisers) came to listen. At the end, the judge pronounced William Joyce guilty of treason and sentenced him to be hung on 3 January 1946. When he heard the verdict, Haw-Haw clicked his heels, gave the Fascist salute, and walked down the dock steps. He appealed the case, was denied, went to his death as scheduled, and was quickly forgotten.[22]

As for Lady Haw-Haw, the British Military Intelligence pushed to have her prosecuted, but the government decided that she had suffered enough in prison, and they declined to put her on trial. Investigators knew that Margaret Joyce had occasionally broadcast with her husband, thereby participating in treasonable activities, but they said, "Her case is only less serious than that of William Joyce because she was less well-known and not so frequently heard in England as her husband." In any event, the British government deemed Her Ladyship a security risk and shipped her back to Germany, but she returned to London years later and died there in 1972.[23]

Notes

1. Harper interview, 3 February 2002.
2. Reynolds, "HMS *Seal.*"

3. *Ballymena Guardian*, 3 May 1995, Commemorative Supplement, "Victory in Europe."

4. *Daily Telegraph* (London), 20 July 1945, 3.

5. NA, HO 45/25780; *New York Times*, 31 May 1945, 1.

6. NA, KV 2 /245.

7. NA, HO 45/25870.

8. NA, HO 45/25870, 85, *Daily Telegraph* (London), 5 May 1945.

9. NA, HO 45/25780, 112, 113.

10. NA, HO 45/25780, 388, *Daily Mirror* (London), 30 May 1945.

11. Ibid.

12. NA, HO 45/25780, 110.

13. NA, HO 45/25780, 348, *Daily Telegraph* (London), 31 May 1945.

14. NA, HO 45/25780, 336, *Daily Express* (London), 1 June 1945.

15. NA, HO 45/25780, *Yorkshire Post*, 6 June 1945.

16. NA, HO 45/25780, *Daily Mirror* (London), 11 June 1945.

17. NA, HO 45/25780, *Sunday Chronicle* (London), 17 June 1945.

18. NA, HO, 45/25780, 216, *Daily Mirror* (London), 18 June 1945.

19. NA, HO 45/25780, 184, *Daily Telegraph* (London), 19 June 1945.

20. NA, HO 45/25780, 186, *Daily Herald* (London), 19 June 1945.

21. NA, HO 45/25780, 173, *Daily Express* (London), 22 June 1945.

22. NA, HO 45/25780, various newspaper reports.

23. BBC News, "Lady Haw-Haw spared out of pity," *http://news.bbc.co.uk/2/hi/uk_news/1016284.stm* on INTERNET.

CHAPTER XVIII
Wildly Improbable

No sooner had Rupert Lonsdale and his crew arrived in England than the Admiralty requested that Lonsdale give them a full report of the surrender of the *Seal*. Their Lordships also informed him that they had sent him two urgent messages approving his decision to save his crew – words that he never received at the time. Without verification of his actions, the commander had agonised over his surrender for the five long years he spent in prisoner of war camps. On 30 May 1945 Lonsdale submitted his written summary, along with a letter to Flag Officer Submarines Max K. Horton, briefly explaining that he had compiled a report shortly after he was captured, but that in 1941 the Germans had found it in a periodic search and had taken it. "I requested the Senior British Naval Officer to inform the German Authorities that I should require this report after the war, and they promised that it would be returned; I applied for it in 1944, and the German Authorities then told our Senior Officer that it had been lost."

Lonsdale went on to tell Horton that after so many years, he could not accurately remember such details as courses, times, and distances. "The actions which I took as circumstances arose, are, however, to the best of my belief, reported with accuracy." Lastly, the commander called attention to the fact that he had added remarks about the disappearance and presumed death of Able Seaman Smith and further comments about the behaviour of his crew.[1]

When Horton received Lonsdale's summary, he gave it to Rear Admiral G. E. Creasy, who wrote up an opinion, stating that he did not believe the commander's report gave a clear account of the proceedings, but that from conversations with Lonsdale, several officers, and a few of the ratings, he had obtained "a fairly clear narrative of events…" Included in his writings, he kindly brought to others' attention that "It must be remembered that these events occurred in the opening months of the war at a time when little consideration had been given to the action necessary to prevent a submarine falling into enemy hands. Such an event had always seemed wildly improbable." No British warship had surrendered since the War of 1812, when *Reindeer* struck her colours to the American *Wasp*.

Furthermore, Creasy wrote that the officers and crew must have been suffering from the mental after-effects of a prolonged dive "without the modern assistance of oxygen and CO_2 absorbent, which may well have clouded their judgment." The Admiralty knew full well that *Seal*'s crew had experienced terrible problems with weakness and sickness just before the surrender, as they possessed a letter that Chief Engineer Clark had written to his wife on 9 January 1941. Clark's wife had dutifully passed it on to the navy, as she considered it important, and they filed it under "Secret." "I was unhurt when captured but was suffering acutely from lack of air and carbon dioxide poisoning. The last 4 hours down below make me shudder to think of them, particularly the last 2 hours when we had all secretly given up hope." Clark said that no one could stand up, and several were unconscious. "They just fell where they were. We merely looked at them, not being able to do anything. The main thing I wished to do was sleep, and of course, I had more to do than anybody." He concluded by saying that the situation was ghastly, that his pulse was 145, and he didn't think a person's heart could work so hard."[2]

The Rear Admiral went on to suggest three courses of action: a court martial of the commanding officer, as earlier directed by the Admiralty; court martial of every surviving officer and man; or dropping the matter. Regarding the first option, Creasy said, "I am fully convinced that no charge of cowardice or of misconduct in the presence of the enemy could be laid against Lieutenant Commander Lonsdale. I consider, however, that he was guilty of a serious error of judgment in abandoning his ship when he did, though I am doubtful if the end of the story would have been very different even had he remained on board." He went on to say that it seemed improbable that evidence could be held valid five years after the event.

Creasy decided that the second option would be the best course of action, then he remarked:

> I feel very strongly that such a court martial, coming at the end of the German war and winding up the brave and gallant record of our submarines during the war, is open to serious objections. Such a court martial would inevitably attract a blaze of unfortunate publicity which would cast a shadow on the splendid achievements of our submarines in the past and might even have unhappy repercussions on the present submarine effort in the Japanese war.[3]

In conclusion, the Rear Admiral requested that Their Lordships consider rescinding the direction by letter of 28 April 1941 that Lonsdale be brought to trial and to let the matter rest. Of course, Their Lordships did not care much for Creasy's recommendations: one discussed the matter with Max Horton, then wrote, "I find myself in disagreement with the Flag Officer

(Submarines). ... The Articles of War and the K.R. and A.I. are quite clear on the action that should be taken, and I consider that the Commanding Officer should be court-martialled. ... This will give him a chance to clear himself of the stigma of surrendering his ship to the enemy ..." The writer went on to say that news of the *Seal*'s surrender was at the time broadcast by the enemy and published in the British press. "It is well known to everyone."[4]

Arguments continued between Their Lordships that lasted for almost a year: they could not decide whether to hold a Board of Enquiry or a court-martial, and finally, they opened the courts-martial against Lieutenant Trevor Beet and Lieutenant Commander Rupert Lonsdale in the spring of 1946.

The entire crew of the *Seal* had been ordered to attend the event, and the navy quartered them in the town where the trials would take place: Portsmouth. "They kept us away from submarine crews, and we had to stay in the hotels. Only some of us went to the actual trials," recalled Taff Harper. "It had never been known for a submarine to surrender, and Lonsdale had lived for five years thinking he might have done the wrong thing." Taff believed that the Admiralty should have notified Lonsdale at Marlag-Milag about the two messages that they had sent and that Lonsdale never received. "They should have told him, 'You've done the right thing.' I think the navy treated him very shabby – the submarine service, especially."[5]

Mickey Reynolds felt surprised by the court-martial and thought that "it was a hard blow for our Captain. But it cleared up a whole lot of uncertainties. I personally thought the Skipper done everything possible for his ship and his command."[6]

At the Royal Naval Barracks in Portsmouth on 10 April 1946, sailors fired the traditional court-martial gun and hoisted the trial flag, a Union Jack flown at the top of the mast.

Trevor Beet, who had taken command of the submarine after Lieutenant Butler had been wounded and after Lonsdale had left the boat to swim over to the German plane, stood trial first, with five naval officers in attendance. They charged him with negligently failing to prevent *Seal* from falling into the hands of the enemy. First came witnesses for the Prosecution, including Lt. Commander Terence Butler, First Officer, who had been seriously wounded, and Chief Petty Officer Warwick Higgins. Higgins told the Court that when the first German seaplane landed, he considered the situation "rather grim," as he thought the boat was sinking.

Q. "How did the Germans behave when they landed?"
A. "Well, as Germans, sir. They were rather excitable and flushed."
Q. "What did they do?"
A. "I forget the actual words, but they were frantically telling the

Captain to stop. … We still had the engines going. They were taxiing alongside as the boat was going ahead."

Q. "What else did they do?"

A. "They made frantic signs for the Captain to go over the side. He took no notice of this for the time being, and then the second aircraft or the observer pointed a Lewis gun … and made as if to fire and were frantically gesticulating for the Captain to go over the side. Lieutenant Beet then said 'I will go, Sir,' or 'Let me go, Sir.'"

Higgins declared that when Lonsdale had made it clear that he would be the one to leave *Seal*, Higgins assured him that he and Beet would take care of the sinking of the boat. "He left the ship confident that we should and would sink it, Sir."

After the second seaplane attacked the *Seal* and the German trawler had arrived, Higgins remembered that a "strange pair of legs" came down the conning tower ladder. At that point he turned to go forward and found Lieutenant Beet nearby. "Lieutenant Beet then said words to the effect 'Come on, let's open up forward and sink the ship.'" So Higgins and Beet walked forward and "were swinging off the flood valves when the German officer came into the fore end and took us back into the control room." When asked if the officer then assumed command, Higgins answered, "Yes, Sir. He had a revolver."

The prosecutor requested that Higgins tell more about the flood valves, and Higgins said that he personally had swung off on the D.S.E.A. flood valves.

Q. "Did you think it was necessary to swing off on valves in the fore ends when they could be controlled from the control room?"

A. "I admit it would have been far easier to have opened vents [vent valves in the control room], but there was a wounded First Lieutenant and the whole of the crew still inside the boat, Sir."

Higgins went on to tell the Court that the condition of the crew after surfacing had been "very, very bad" and that some of them had vomited and others needed help getting to their feet.

At the end of the questioning, the prosecutor said, "When you saw these strange pair of legs coming down the conning tower, what means were available to you for sinking the submarine?"

Higgins replied, "Under normal conditions, every chance, Sir." When asked by what means, he said, "Flooding by opening the vents, Sir."

Q. "Where are the vents in relation to the conning tower hatch?"

A. "Right opposite, Sir."

Q. "Would it have been possible to do it with the German coming down the conning tower hatch?"

A. "Yes, it would have been, Sir, but there is no saying what the German would have done."

Q. "What was your idea of going forward?"

A. "To get away from the German, Sir."

Next came short testimony from Chief Engine Room Artificer John Strait, who told the Court that he had believed that the *Seal* was sinking, because the boat was severely listing to starboard. Strait described the men's condition as "practically exhausted. It was an effort to do anything at all." That ended testimony by witnesses for the Prosecution (Captain R. F. Elkins); then ensued comments by the defending lawyer, Commander J. Cowell, "The Accused's Friend."

"The Prosecution's witnesses have given as clear a picture of the events in H.M.S. *Seal* as their brains, which were muddled at the time, and their memories will allow. ... The Accused is charged with negligently performing his duties. Defence will show that there was no negligence whatsoever ... and amongst others will call an expert technical witness to explain the development of air purification in British Submarines during the war and an expert medical witness to explain the effect on the crew when there is no air purification."

The Defence then called Lt. Trevor Beet, who described the mine explosion and struggles to get the *Seal* back to the surface. At the moment that Lonsdale left the submarine to swim to the German seaplane, Beet recalled telling him something like, "Don't worry, Sir, everything will be all right." After that, Beet had a dim recollection of what he did next. He knew that a second plane landed and that he sent the second coxswain over to it. "I still had a blinding headache, finding it very hard to solve any problem. My main worry was the safety of the crew. I was convinced the ship was sinking. ..." He hoped that the ship, which was listing heavily, would stay afloat until the wounded and the rest of the crew had been taken to a safe place, but he could not think how to do it. Then the German officer entered the control room and ordered Beet and the others to the bridge.

By now the German trawler had drawn alongside the boat and attached a towline to the bow, and Beet and the other officers were ordered to get into their motorboat. Upon further questioning, Beet declared that he was quite conscious of the fact that he was in charge of the *Seal* after Lonsdale left. He told the Court that he was convinced that the boat was sinking and that there was a depth charge in the bow set to explode over the Asdic gear. "Therefore, that was an additional worry, because if the ship sank quickly, this depth charge would go off with the men still struggling in the water above it."

Q. "Was that depth charge already [sic] to go off?"

A. "It was, Sir. It was set to go off ... so that when the ship sank, it would blow up the Asdic gear to stop it from being salvaged by the Germans."

Q. "At what depth would it have gone off?"

A. "At fifty feet, Sir."

Q. "How did you know that it was set?"

A. "Because I gave orders for it to be set, and it was reported to me that it had been set."

The prosecuting lawyer then asked Beet where the German officer went when he left the control room, and Beet said that he had walked forward and that he had gone with him. Beet thought the German was curious to see what the sub looked like.

Another witness, Captain Lionel Taylor, Fleet Engineer Officer on the staff of Admiral Submarines, testified that no provisions had been made on *Seal* for purifying or refreshing the air. When asked what improvements were made generally during the course of the war, he replied that it was not until February 1942 that Admiral Submarines had issued a general memorandum that all submarines were to carry shallow trays of soda lime for air purification. At the same time, new submarines would carry as many additional oxygen bottles as possible. It turned out that the soda lime trays were unsatisfactory. "The American and French experiments, pooled with our own developments, went ahead to a self-contained purifier and an oxygen candle, both of which are now in manufacture and shortly will be coming into general service use." No mention was made of the Germans' more successful methods to combat CO_2 on their submarines.[7]

The Accused's Friend called Dr George Brown, an expert medical witness, and asked him to describe the effects of high carbon dioxide and low oxygen on human beings. "Low oxygen causes a steady impairment of the mental facilities, leading eventually to unconsciousness and death," he replied. "It has a physical effect in causing deeper breathing, and renders any muscular work very difficult … because of the great increase in breathing which occurs. … The change in mental condition is greatly increased, confusion, difficulty to argue logically and to reason, loss of memory, unconsciousness and death."

He went on to say that he would expect that *Seal*'s crew would have suffered from severe carbon dioxide intoxication, breathlessness, and mental confusion; they also would have been likely to make silly mistakes. "There would be certain other but less important bodily symptoms such as headache, nausea, lassitude, and drowsiness." Upon returning to fresh air, the crew would have experienced immediate relief, then headache, nausea, vomiting, a feeling of cold and misery, and continued mental confusion, but the symptoms would vary from man to man.[8]

Several other witnesses testified, including Lonsdale and Captain G. B. H. Fawkes, of Max Horton's staff. Fawkes described the two signals that the Admiralty had sent to *Seal* and that had never reached her crew.

At 4:50 that afternoon the Accused's Friend summed up his case, then concluded that "The Accused is twice charged with negligence of duty, but this was no case of negligence. It he had been a fit man, it might be estimated that his judgment or his reasoning was at fault, but in the condition that he was in ... it was quite impossible for him to have acted in any other way." Lastly, Beet's defender asked that Beet be found "Not guilty" and requested that the jury give him an Honourable Acquittal. The Prosecution then protested that it was "one of the traditions of the Service that none of His Majesty's ships should fall into the hands of the enemy without the most strenuous and determined efforts being made to prevent it." Therefore, he submitted that the Accused never made these efforts.[9]

Shortly afterwards, the five officers made their decision, declared Beet honourably acquitted, and the President of the Court walked across the courtroom and smilingly handed Beet's sword back to him.[10]

The next morning Lonsdale's trial began, with the sword of the Accused lying horizontally on a table covered with red imitation felt. The defence attorney, Captain G. C. Phillips, entered a Not Guilty plea, then proceeded to ask Lonsdale 481 questions. Lonsdale testified that his crew had been trapped below the surface for twenty-two hours; that upon surfacing he had ordered the Confidential Books and Signal Publications thrown overboard; and he had ordered a cypher message sent to Flag Officer Horton describing the situation. He told the Court that he had attempted to reach the Swedish coast with his severely damaged boat by slowly travelling backwards.

Then the first German plane came in and attacked, wounding First Lieutenant Butler and another man.

Q. "Did you take any defensive action?"

A. "Not at this time, sir."

Q. "What guns did you have?"

A. "We had a four inch gun and two Lewis [machine] guns."

Q. "Was your four inch gun serviceable?"

A. "I did not consider it would be serviceable against aircraft ..."

Q. "Was this gun designed for anti-aircraft fire?

A. "No, Sir."

Questions continued as to Lonsdale's efforts to deter the second and third aeroplanes' attacks. Lonsdale responded by telling the Court that he had ordered up his two Lewis guns, but that both guns jammed after he tried to use them. With the boat sinking, starboard motor useless, and no way to defend himself, Lonsdale had at that point asked for a white tablecloth to be sent up to the bridge, and he waved it. The attacks then ceased.

When questioned about the secret equipment, Lonsdale said that all of it had been wrecked with the exception of the Asdic dome. "I thought the Asdic dome by itself would be of no use, as all the electric circuits had been demolished." By now, one of the German pilots was beckoning to the commander to come over to his plane, and Lonsdale focused his full attention on leaving the boat; he said that when he climbed into the plane, he felt that he had done the right thing. Asked why he undertook the swimming over to the plane, Lonsdale explained that he thought it would be difficult and hazardous, and that as captain it was his duty to do it.

Q. "Do you know if the Asdics were, in fact, smashed?"

A. "I have asked my crew since then if they were, and they have told me that this was done. I have also had a letter from a German officer to that effect."

Q. "How did this letter come into your possession?"

A. "Through Admiral (Submarines) and the Admiralty."

Q. "And is the letter available?"

A. "I have got it."

Q. "Will you read it to the Court?"

A. "May 6th, 1945

Commander R. P. Lonsdale

Dear Sir,

With great pleasure I deliver your pistol set to the Military Government of Hamburg and hope it will soon be forwarded to you.

When you had the misfortune to become P.O.W. I was i/c [in charge] of sifting all the stuff we took off your sub. I separated the pistol case at once, with the intention to return it as soon as circumstances would permit as it was your private property.

As a former sub. officer (1916–18) I and all my comrades fully realised what the loss of the *Seal* meant to you.

But it may console you that we found nothing we were eagerly searching for. Your gallant crew destroyed everything of secret nature and even your Asdic installation left no clue to us, as we found only untelling fragments.

With best wishes for good luck in future services I beg to remain, dear Sir,

Yours sincerely,

Wilhelm Ahlrichs

Formerly Lieutenant-Commander N.R."[11]

Q. "Have you ever met the German officer who wrote that letter?"

A. "No, Sir."

One of the last questions regarded the purpose of the depth charge. Lonsdale answered: "It was designed, Sir, to blow the Asdic Oscillator to smithereens if the ship sank in shallow water." Further, he explained that the depth charge was not designed to sink the boat. When the defence asked, "If you fired this depth charge while the submarine was on the surface by some method, what would have been the consequence?"

A. "The ship would have sunk – I would have imagined that the whole of the bow would have been blown off, Sir."

Q. "What would have happened to the crew?"

A. "They would have been left in the water – those that had not been killed by the explosion."

With this last question, the Defence finished his examination. The Prosecution had no questions for Lonsdale and asked for Trevor Beet.

Beet testified that he had been so sure that the *Seal* would sink that he was "horrified" when the Germans managed to tow her all the way to Denmark. "I spent the time absolutely glued to the scuttle [small opening with a hatch] when we were in the German boat, and I just could not understand it when I saw her getting appreciably worse and worse but refusing to sink." Then Beet said it had never occurred to him that any outside assistance would be needed to help sink the *Seal*.[12]

Captain George H. Fawkes, one of Max Horton's staff members, described what had occurred in regard to messages sent to and from *Seal*. He testified that his staff had received their first message that the boat was in trouble on 5 May 1940 and that the sub's stern was filled with water. Lonsdale gave his position, reported that confidential books had been destroyed; stated that there were no casualties; and that he was making for the Swedish coast.

When asked what action was taken after receipt of the signal, Fawkes replied that "it was realised that nothing could be done to help her from British sources. Accordingly, we got in touch with the Admiralty by telephone and asked them to make a signal to the Naval Attaché in Stockholm telling him of the situation and asking him to arrange all possible assistance to *Seal*. This signal was made by the Admiralty and also a signal was made from Vice Admiral (Submarines) to *Seal*." Witness then produced the signal and read it: "Your 0150 understood and agreed with. Best of luck. Well done." After that, the Admiralty sent their signal to the Stockholm naval attaché and a second message to *Seal*: "Safety of personnel should be your first consideration after destruction of the Asdics." *Seal* never received the last two messages.

At the end of his testimony, Fawkes stated that as far as he knew, the Germans had not used *Seal* operationally, and to the best of his knowledge, they never used her at all.[13]

Some interesting facts came from Commander William King, who in May 1940 was captain of the submarine *Snapper*. He stated that he had been at sea on the 4th and 5th of May in a location near Jutland Bank, off western Denmark.

Q. "What signal did you intercept from *Seal*?"

A. "A message which said that she was holed, the after compartment was flooded and that she was making for Goteborg."

Q. "What conclusions did you draw from that signal?"

A. "That the submarine was unable to dive; almost certainly unable to steer; and was no longer a fighting proposition."

Q. "Did you consider going to *Seal*'s assistance?"

A. "I did consider it, Sir, but owing to the distance between her position and ours and the weight of enemy anti-submarine patrols in the vicinity, I considered it was not possible." [He would have had to travel around the north-west coast of German-held Denmark.]

Regarding improvements that had been made during the war in anti-aircraft armament on submarines, Commander William King testified that the main gun armament was provided with time-fused (delayed burst) shells; and a 20-mm Oerlikon (anti-aircraft cannon) added; the Lewis (machine) guns replaced first by Bren guns, then the Vickers gas-operated. He said that the Lewis gun was continually liable to failure, mainly because the circular pans become damaged inside a submarine. "This caused me, personally, to return my Lewis gun and obtain a Bren gun in lieu."

Q. "Do you know for what purpose Lewis guns were originally designed, and when?"

A. "I believe as an Infantry weapon in 1911."[14]

Captain Lionel Taylor of Admiral Horton's staff, when asked what provision was made in *Seal* for purifying or refreshing the air, replied, "There were no provisions in *Seal* or in submarines generally at that time." Then came the question, "Will you tell the Court, briefly, what improvements were made in this respect to British submarines during the war?" Taylor repeated his testimony from Beet's trial that the subject had been discussed prior to the war, but that no general improvement was made until February 1942, when subs started carrying soda lime and lithium hydroxide, plus additional oxygen bottles from which oxygen could be circulated through the boat. Also, they had added dehumidifiers and air conditioning. "At the present time there is a self-contained oxygen producing candle which has commenced manufacture and is about to be issued for general submarine use."

Members of the jury, as navy men, could easily see that Rupert Lonsdale had made the best of a disastrous situation with a deck cannon useless against aircraft and two obsolete, unreliable machine guns. Moreover, he and his men had almost died of suffocation and had acted as rationally as they could, in spite of being severely debilitated both mentally and physically.

The next day, as members of *Seal*'s crew waited nervously outside, the jury of five naval captains deliberated for forty-five minutes, then made their decision. When Lonsdale and his men were called back into the courtroom, they saw Lonsdale's sword lying on the table with the hilt pointing towards them, indicating honourable acquittal. The jubilant crewmen hugged and congratulated their skipper, then proceeded to Lonsdale's quarters, where they drank a toast to their well-beloved leader and celebrated for many happy hours.[15]

After an initial reunion in 1946, seven *Seal* crew member got together in May 1988 for a two-day visit to Seal village, the town that had sent them many food parcels, clothing, and letters during their prison camp days. At a lunch provided by Seal Parish Council, the men passed around their old "tot" rum measure that they had used on their boat and that had been kept hidden from the Germans. The best fun was had when Happy Eckersall presented Taff Harper with a replica of the boat's "Lady Luck" statuette – this time draped in a little handkerchief to hide her nudity from Commander Lonsdale, now a priest of the Church of England.[16]

Notes

1. NA, ADM 156/283.
2. NA, ADM 199/1840, 90.
3. NA, ADM 156/283.
4. Ibid.
5. Harper interview, 3 February 2002.
6. Reynolds, "HMS *Seal*."
7. NA, ADM 156/271.
8. Ibid., 70.
9. Ibid., 76.
10. Warren and Benson, *Will Not We Fear*, 220.
11. NA, ADM 156/283.
12. Ibid.
13. Ibid.
14. Ibid.
15. Warren and Benson, *Will Not We Fear*, 225.
16. Taff Harper collection, *Navy News*, June 1988.

Bibliography

Books

Beierl, Florian M. *History of the Eagle's Nest*. Berchtesgaden: Verlag Plenk, 1998.

Bekker, Cajus. *The German Navy 1939–1945*. New York: The Dial Press, 1974.

Buckham, Robert M. *Forced March to Freedom*. Ontario: Canada's Wings, Inc., 1984.

Chancellor, Henry. *Colditz: The Definitive History*. New York: Perennial, An Imprint of HarperCollins Publishers, 2002.

Churchill, Winston S. *The Second World War: The Gathering Storm*. London: Penguin, 1962.

Churchill, Winston S. *Blood, Sweat, and Tears*. With preface and notes by Randolph S. Churchill, M.P. New York: G. P. Putnam's Sons, 1941.

Derry, T. K. *The Campaign in Norway*. London: Her Majesty's Stationery Office, 1952.

Encyclopedia Britannica, 1963 edition.

Frank, Wolfgang and Rogge, Bernhard. *The German Raider Atlantis*. New York: Ballantine, 1957.

Frischauer, Will and Jackson, Robert. *The Altmark Affair*. New York: The Macmillan Company, 1955.

Gimpel, Erich in collaboration with Will Berthold. *Spy for Germany*. London: Robert Hall Limited, 1957.

Giraud, Général Henri. *Mes Évasions*. Paris: Librarie Hachette, 1949.

Grunberger, Richard. *The 12-Year Reich: A Social History of Nazi Germany 1933–1945*. New York: Da Capo Press, 1995.

_____ *Jane's Fighting Ships 1941*. New York: Macmillan Company, 1942.

Jenkins, Roy. *Churchill: A Biography*. New York: Farrar, Straus and Giroux, 2001.

Kahn, David. *Seizing the Enigma: The Race to Break the German U-Boat Codes 1939–1943*. Boston: Houghton Mifflin Company, 1991.

Kaufmann, J. E. and H. W. *Hitler's Blitzkrieg Campaigns: The Invasion and Defense of Western Europe 1939–1940*. Pennsylvania: Combined Books, 1993.

Kersaudy, François. *Norway 1940*. New York: St. Martin's Press, 1991.

Kershaw, Ian. *Hitler 1936–1945: Nemesis*. New York: W. W. Norton & Company, 2000.

Lipscomb, Commander W. W., O. B. E., Royal Navy. *The British Submarine*. London: Adam and Charles Black, 1954.

Lloyd's Register of Shipping. London: Lloyd's Register of Shipping, 1940.

Manchester, William. *The Last Lion: William Spencer Churchill, Alone, 1932-1940*. Boston: Little, Brown and Company, 1988.

The Drama of the Graf Spee and The Battle of the River Plate: A Documentary Anthology 1914–1964. Compiled by Sir Eugen Millington-Drake. Foreword by Admiral of the Fleet Earl Mountbatten of Burma. London: Peter Davies, 1964.

Muggenthaler, August Karl. *German Raiders of World War II*. Englewood Cliffs, NJ: Prentice-Hall, Inc., 1977.

Nicholas, Lynn H. *The Rape of Europa*. New York: Vintage Books, a Division of Random House, 1995.

Reid, P. R. *Men of Colditz*. Philadelphia and New York: J. B. Lippincott Company, 1954.

Roskill, Capt. Stephen W. *Churchill and the Admirals*. New York: William Morrow and Company, Inc., 1978.

Roskill, Capt. Stephen W. *The War at Sea: Volume I, The Defensive*. London: Her Majesty's Stationery Office, 1957.

Rössler, Eberhard. *The U-boat: The Evolution and Technical History of German Submarines*. Annapolis: Naval Institute Press, 1989.

Sommerville, Donald. *World War II Day by Day*. New York: Barnes and Noble Books, 1989.

The Cabinet War Rooms. London: The Imperial War Museum, 2001.

Van der Vat, Dan. *The Atlantic Campaign: World War II's Great Struggle at Sea*. With research by Christine van der Vat. New York: Harper & Row, Publishers, 1988.

Warren, C. E. T. and Benson, James. *Will Not We Fear: The Story of Her Majesty's Submarine "Seal" and of Lieutenant Commander Rupert Lonsdale*. London: George G. Harrap & Co., Ltd., 1961.

Wiggan, Richard. *Hunt the Altmark*. London: Robert Hale, 1982.

Wiggins, Melanie. *U-Boat Adventures: Firsthand Accounts from World War II*. Annapolis: Naval Institute Press, 1999.

Articles, Published

Compton-Hall, Richard. "Century of the Silent Service." *Navy News*, Submarine Centenary Supplement (January 2001).

Hubatsch, Walter. "Tagebuch Jodl." *Die Welt als Geschichte*, Stuttgart, Heft 1/1952, Heft 1/1954.

"The Sea Devil." *Newsweek* (25 April 1966): 42, 43.

Articles, Unpublished

Truman, Ernie. "The Epic of the Seal." Royal Navy Submarine Museum.

Reynolds, Hugh (Mickey). "HMS Seal."

BIBLIOGRAPHY

Archival Sources
Bibliothek für Zeitgeschichte, Stuttgart
Hauptstaatsarchiv Stuttgart
National Archives, formerly Public Record Office (NA), London
National Archives and Records Administration (NARA), Washington, D. C.
Maritime Museum of the Atlantic, Halifax, Nova Scotia
Museum der Stadt Colditz
Militärarchiv, Freiburg
Portsmouth City Museum and Records Office, Portsmouth, England
Imperial War Museum, London
Royal Navy Submarine Museum, Gosport, England
U-Boot Archiv, Cuxhaven

Newspapers
Ballymena Guardian
Bournemouth Daily Echo
Daily Express (London)
Daily Herald (London)
Daily Mirror (London)
Daily Telegraph (London)
Navy News
New York Times
Sunday Chronicle (London)
The Portsmouth News
Yorkshire Post

Internet
"A Teacher's Guide to the Holocaust," available at *http://www.fcit.coedu.usf.
    edu/holocaust/resource/document/DOCSLA11.htm*
BBC News, "Lady Haw-Haw spared out of pity," available at *http://news.bbc.
    co.uk/2/hi/uknews/1016284.htm*
"BBC Past, Present and Future Written Archives," available at
    http://bbc.co/uk/thenandnow/history/1940sn.shtml
"Berchtesgaden," available at *http://warfoto.com/berchesg.htm*
"Harley Tuck's War Diary," available at *http://www.nmia.com/gwydion/
    WWIIS17b/powfin~1.htm*
"History of Lamsdorf," available at *http://www.uni.pole.pl/cmjw/ecmjwobie.
    html*
"Saale River Offensive: The Seizure of Halle," available at *http://
    www.104infdiv.org/saale.htm*
"Stalag VII A: Oral History," available at *http://www.moosburg.org/info/stalag/
    allaeng.html*
Yale University, "The Avalon Project at Yale Law School," available at *http://
    www.yale.edu/lawweb/avalon/lawofwar/geneva02.htm*

Index

8/13

Date Due
